The auto/biographical I

This book is dedicated to my Mum, Win Stanley,
entirely her own woman;
and in memory of Lilias Wise, 1926-1991.

The auto/biographical I
The theory and practice
of feminist auto/biography

Liz Stanley

Copyright © Liz Stanley 1992

Published by Manchester University Press
Oxford Road, Manchester M13 9PL, UK
and Room 400, 175 Fifth Avenue,
New York, NY 10010, USA

Distributed exclusively in the USA and Canada
by St. Martin's Press, Inc.,
175 Fifth Avenue, New York, NY 10010, USA

British Library Cataloguing-in-Publication Data
A catalogue record for this book is available from the British Library

Library of Congress Cataloging-in-Publication Data
Stanley, Liz, 1947–
  The auto/biographical I : the theory and practice of feminist
  auto/biography / Liz Stanley
    p. cm.
  Includes bibliographical references and indexes.
  ISBN 0 7190 2980 5
  1. English prose literature—Women authors—History and criticism—
Theory, etc. 2. American prose literature—Women authors—History
and criticism—Theory, etc. 3. Feminists—Great Britain—Biography—
History and criticism. 4. Feminists—United States—Biography—
History and criticism. 5. Women—Great Britain—Biography—History
and criticism. 6. Women—United States—Biography—History and
criticism. 7. Autobiography—Women authors. 8. Feminism—
Historiography. I. Title. II. Title: Autobiographical I.
PR788.W65S7 1992
820.9'49272—dc20   91-39708

ISBN 0 7190 4649 1 paperback

Paperback edition published 1995

Typeset in Joanna
by Koinonia Limited, Manchester
Printed in Great Britain
by Biddles Ltd, Guildford & King's Lynn

Contents

Preface and acknowledgements

This book has had an elephantine gestation period, although its precise moment of fertilisation was in December 1982 when Dale Spender asked me to write a brief essay about Olive Schreiner: Dale, you have an uncanny habit of turning up at the right time and in the right place. I've lived with Sue Wise for 18 years and I hope to do so for at least 180 more. She has also lived with my auto/biographical preoccupations with increasingly tetchy tolerance as hordes of the feminist dead have arrived to occupy all corners of our home; I confess here that another visitor is expected. David Morgan has been a colleague and friend for many years now and his insightfulness and generosity are much appreciated. The 'Writing Feminist Biography' conferences provided many fascinating moments and some lasting – albeit usually textually expressed – feminist friendships particularly through the admired work of Jo Alberti, Lucy Bland, Maggie Humm, Jo Stanley, and more than anyone Ann Morley. Grateful thanks to Chris Weedon for comments on Chapter 4; and especially to Treva Broughton, Celia Lury, David Morgan and 'an anonymous reader' for reading and commenting on the whole manuscript: it would have been a worse book without you. Rupert Ray and Edgar Gray Doe saw out one of its phases, Casper, Thomas Aquinas, Precious Mackenzie, Alfred Schutz, Tiny Stray, Jessye Norman and Mrs Whisky Rochester have seen in its final stages: furry thank yous all round. To sweet life and to memory: the most enjoyable pleasures I have. Treva Broughton's final remark stands as a comment on auto/biography, this book, life, the universe and everything: PHEW.

Introduction

On feminism, cultural politics and post/modern selves[1]

A reverie

Colette sits at the window of her upstairs apartment overlooking the gardens of the Palais Royal. She taps her teeth absently with one forefinger, eyes narrowed and concentrating. She looks at children playing, two women walking immersed in conversation, one of them weeping gently; she looks at them, but what she sees, ah what she sees.

Colette is a younger woman, that cat on her lap, both listening to a tale told by a stranger in a hotel; she is a child and Sido is relating what the spider in her bedroom has said; she is some age, no age, suffused with the smell and taste of a woodland spring and its icy touch, the sound of Paris, the smooth glistening of a lover's skin and its sexual smell, the beauty of hills and crisp dawn flowers. Which will it be then, while she can still hold the pen to craft those delicious words: an essay about food and cats and lovers, pleasures lightly called physical? a sketch of a moment from the golden seam of childhood? a story of the demi-monde? But yes, all of them, she would of course have all of them. She begins to write: 'I did not acquire my habitual mistrust of nonentities over a period of years...'.

Cultural politics and feminist sociology

Cultural politics refuses the conventional discipline boundaries that slice up contemporary academic life into bite-sized chunks. Its appeal is strong: it draws on ideas and analyses from a wide range of sources, including feminism, marxism, literary theory, psychoanalytic theory, history, and my own discipline of sociology, and uses them in radical and insightful ways; and, unlike other multidisciplinary endeavours, it does so while retaining a strong theoretical and analytic edge. In all this it echoes the prior voice of contemporary feminism, wherein my own academic and political work has been located.

Cultural politics is concerned above all to situate culture within a social and historical and thus a *political* context. This is far and away its greatest attraction, for by doing so it rejects treating ideas as merely idealism, merely ideology.[2] Cultural politics sees the material and ideological as symbiotically related, recognising that ideas have a material origin and that the ideological has importance through the expression of ideas in concrete material practices. With a few exceptions (e.g .Canadian sociologist Dorothy Smith (1987, 1990)), feminist social science remains in a timewarp in this regard, treating ideology as false consciousness and the work of those analysts concerned with taking its products seriously as naive idealism.

This book provides a feminist discussion of the material production of biography and autobiography as ideological accounts of 'lives' which in turn feed back into everyday understandings of how 'common lives' and 'extraordinary lives' can be recognised. There is a growing analytical discourse about autobiography, and very little that is comparable on biography, the editing of diaries and letters, or social science productions and uses of written lives. Yet largely the same epistemological, theoretical and technical issues arise, in relation to the ontological claims of each of these apparently distinct genres as do for autobiography. My aim in this book is to contribute to the groundwork of a feminist approach to auto/biography which rejects conventional generic distinctions and separations, instead showing how the same analytic apparatus is required for engaging with all forms of life writing, for the same questions and problematics demand critical inquiry. This is not to deny that there are differences between different forms of life writing, but it is to argue that these differences are not *generic*.

Auto/biography, a term I use to encompass all these ways of writing a life and also the ontological and epistemological links between them, is particularly suitable ground for a feminist cultural political analysis to be built on. Auto/biographies are among the most popular books sold today: advances to well-known writers of biography, particularly when they are writing about very well-known subjects (for instance, Michael Holroyd (1988, 1990, 1991) on Bernard Shaw), now reach astronomical levels. Both biography and autobiography lay claim to facticity, yet both are by nature artful enterprises which select, shape, and produce a very unnatural product, for no life is lived quite so much under a single spotlight as the conventional form of written auto/biographies suggests. Most auto/biography is also concerned with 'great lives', and these are almost invariably those of white middle and upper class men who have achieved success according to conventional – and thus highly political – standards. In addition, the 'auto/biographical canon' – that is, those biographies and autobiographies which are recognised as major pieces of writing and the critical and academic literature which promotes them as such – is currently being contested and revised, and a new canon is in the process of formation, and this itself is a highly political process. Finally, recent theoretical debates concerning 'the self', 'the subject' and her consciousness, and, relatedly, 'the author' and his presumed death, take particularly interesting shape when examined substantively in relation to lived and written lives: that is, in connection with the conjunction between auto/biography.

I call myself a feminist sociologist, by which I mean more than simply a feminist who teaches sociology. The term encapsulates a determination to re-make the discipline of sociology from the standpoint of feminism: no critique this, but a thoroughgoing top to bottom and inside out revolution. It involves a feminist praxis (Stanley, 1990a) in which 'theory' as conventionally seen (as 'abstract ideas abstractly related', as the dictionary defines) is rejected, as is the quite extraordinary elitism of scientific – 'scientistic' in Habermas's term – views of social *science*. No Leninist vanguard role for feminist sociology of this kind, but rather the recognition that everybody theorises about everyday life and produces analyses of it which range from the particularly crude to the particularly sophisticated – and that sophistication is not necessarily to be located among sociologists and academic fellow-travellers, feminist or otherwise.

To date most analytic interest in auto/biography has been located outside of the social sciences, particularly among literary critics interested in autobiography and its close if closet relationship to fictional forms of writing lives. There is now also the beginnings of interest in auto/biography in anthropology (for instance, Kessing, 1978, 1985, 1987; Young, 1983) and in sociology (and see here the journal *Life Stories/Recits de vie*, also Denzin, 1989), but by and large not among feminists in these disciplines. Given the large feminist reading audience for auto/biography, and the lively analytic and substantive interest in it from feminist literary studies, the absence of sustained interest from feminist social science needs explanation. This is particularly so given that the major epistemological issues of our time are raised in connection with the nature of 'selves', how to understand and how to study them under what kind of intellectual conditions and limitations.

From the publication in 1918–1920 of the volumes of William I. Thomas and Florian Znaniecki's *The Polish Peasant in Europe and America* (1918–1920) through to the Second World War, a biographical approach to sociology in which the analysis of social structures was located in an account of particular lives was a major possibility, although it coexisted with other more 'scientific' approaches (Plummer, 1983). The biographical approach enshrined two principles. The first was a rejection of psychologically-reductionist accounts of 'the individual', instead insisting that individual people are social and cultural products through and through. The second was the recognition that if structural analyses do not work at the level of particular lives then they do not work at all. Both principles inform my own approach to auto/biography and to other sociological work.

What prevented this approach from having the widespread impact expected of it was the Second World War and the accompanying changes in the nature of the state: a state which required and paid for consumable facts delivered wholesale by certified and guaranteed providers of the same: social scientists. Zigmaunt Bauman (1988) has suggested that the nature of the state in a postmodern world has changed yet again, from coercion to persuasion and seduction, and it no longer requires the services of its former agents. As a response, Bauman proposes that sociology should become a 'sociology of postmodernism' rather than a 'postmodernist sociology'; that is, its basic shape and nature should remain the same, but its investigative topic change somewhat. My conviction is that rather than providing 'facts' for their own sake, we should instead take leave of a realist sociological past, reject emulations of scientism and become a postmodern sociology, in spite of any loss of privilege and prestige.[3]

'Postmodernism' I use to refer to a theoretical stance, while I see 'postmodernity', claimed to be the condition of contemporary society, as consisting only in invocations of it. In my view 'it', *postmodernity*, does not exist outside of its invention by particular writers and their followers, then re-peddled second and third hand by others. This is not to say that there are not insightful ideas and analyses associated with theories of postmodernism; and I certainly align myself with these. It is, however, to suggest that the *social condition* which these ideas and analyses purport to be about either does not exist, or, more plausibly, does exist but is actually the hallmark of the despised modernism that writers on postmodernism so regularly denounce. This distinction between postmodernism as an intellectual stance, and postmodernity as a claimed condition of the social order, is crucial to the following argument.

There are a number of ideas closely associated with writing on postmodernism highly pertinent to an analysis of auto/biography. However, before discussing these I outline the notion of 'modern biography'.

Modern biography?

At a 1985 'Modern Biography' conference,[4] a goodly selection of the *crème de la creme* of British professional and academic biographers suggested that, while of course everyone now accepts that 'truth' about the totality of a life all depends on the viewpoint from which it is examined, the fundamental task of the biographer remains unchanged. Indeed, this task was seen as *unchangeable*: to assemble as far as possible 'the truth about subject X or Y'. More than this, ideas about biography associated with postmodernism were treated as a 'subtle ... (and) not-so-subtle denigration of biography' (Homburger and Charmley, 1988 p. ix), and the strictures about realist fallacies provided by the postmodernist critique dismissed: 'No historical biographer would be guilty of such naivety' (p. x). However, as such editorial protests are accompanied by claims that 'biography ... brings us closer to the reality of other people's lives' (p. ix), these should not perhaps be taken too seriously. Relatedly, with few exceptions (notably Skidelsky, 1988 and Glendinning, 1988b), classical modernist ideas about biography were stated rather than argued. I outline these ideas below and then begin the process of arguing back.

Now as much as in Boswell's Johnson or Froude's Carlyle, the modern biographer's task is marked out as an essentially social psychological one. The great, usually men but sometimes if infrequently women, have made a distinctive contribution to society such that 'the world' would have been different had they never been. The

biographer follows the linear trajectory of their subject's development by reconstructing, in as much detail as possible, their life from
cradle to grave, by locating their particular work and achievements
and their character within this mass of detail. Modern biography,
then, according to some of its most distinguished practitioners, sees
the central task of biography as the reconstruction on paper of the
essential fundamental person, from a myriad of contemporary
shifting and conflicting views of this event, that relationship, this
activity and that achievement. There are important caveats I want to
make to this view of the biographer's task.

The notion of the 'reconstruction' of a biographical subject is an
intellectual non-starter. It proposes we can somehow recover the past,
understand it as it was experienced and understood by the people
who actually lived it. Good history eschews such a belief, and so too
should biography. In contrast, within a feminist and cultural political
approach, questions like 'the past from whose viewpoint?', 'why this
viewpoint and no other?', and 'what would be the effect of working
from a contrary viewpoint?', should be asked. The past, like the present, is
the result of competing negotiated versions of what happened, why it
happened, with what consequence. Of course many biographers say
they recognise this. Nevertheless, they also see their version − the only
one fully represented in what they write − as privileged, a view that
is more truthful because it comes at the subject and their life with
more, and thus somehow less partial, evidence than the subject's
contemporaries or the subject themselves[5] did.

In short, biographers claim expertise. But there is another and
preferable way of evaluating their claims, in which biography is seen
as simply another plausible version of what happened and what it
meant. We should ask of biography the question 'who says?'. And
'who says' is someone who has produced one more interpretation
from among a range of possibilities, and who has produced it from
one particular angle rather than any other. In other words, 'the
biographer' is a socially-located person, one who is sexed, raced,
classed, aged, to mention no more, and is so every bit as much as an
autobiographer is. And once we accept that ideas are not unique but
socially produced even if individually expressed by members of
particular social, cultural and political milieux, then we can also
extrapolate this to the ideas and interpretations produced by the
biographer: any biographer's view is a socially located and necessarily
partial one.

Modern biography is founded upon a realist fallacy. The modern novel and modern biography had their origins in the same period of high Victorian positivism and both were fed from a staunchly realist stance. However, influential strands of fiction have moved away from realism, while the biography mainstream has moved increasingly towards it. The realist enterprise of reconstruction and expertise in biography depends on not only a foundationalist view of biographical research, but also a correspondence theory of the relationship between the written product of biographical research and the lives it investigates – that the text is precisely referential of the person. Similarly, it proposes that there is a coherent, essentially unchanging and unitary self which can be referentially captured by its methods.

The notion of 'greatness' or 'importance' is actually a historical, temporal and above all political product associated with particular persons but not others. It is no accident or coincidence that the 'great' and 'important' within modern biography are almost invariably people at the top of stratification systems based on sex, class, race, religion. In feminist and cultural political terms, however, the 'obscure' can be at least and are sometimes considerably more significant historically than the famous or infamous. The near-obsession of modern biography with the 'great' and 'in/famous' leads readers to misconstrue much of what passes for history: like generalising about icebergs from the bit that sticks up above water, which can be a very risky business.

Typically modern biographers advance or imply inflated claims about the importance of their subject's achievements; the most objectionable of these must be the claim for their uniqueness of contribution. This adds up to the presumption that only the conventionally important 'make a difference' to social life and the rest of humanity do not. Inscribed here are beliefs about 'ideas' as the product of a great mind and of this unique mind only. However, in feminist and cultural political terms, ideas are produced within a particular social milieu, for 'mind' is irrevocably a social product. The social networks within which the biographical subject located their activities and work need to be closely examined rather than being divorced from the social contexts within which they lived, or only one or two of their peers pulled out from the rest for special attention. In this alternate view 'ideas' are seen as the product of socially shared understandings reworked in different ways within particular cultural settings, although given a particular twist by the specificities of the life and work of a particular biographical subject.

Following the biographical subject in a linear and chronological way effectively trains a spotlight on them and them alone. The effect is that everyone else this person knew is thereby made to have only shadowy existence. Thus is the contemporary role of the biographical subject among their peers misrepresented, for we are shown them as a Gulliver among Lilliputians. The product of this approach, the resulting 'portrait' of the subject, is skewed away from a more complex portrayal of them as a friend among friends, a colleague among colleagues: instead they are cast as a giant among pygmies. In feminist and cultural political terms, people's lives and behaviours make considerably more sense when they are located through their participation in a range of overlapping social groups, rather than being portrayed as somehow different, marked out all along by the seeds of their later greatness.

Treating the production of biography in an epistemologically and theoretically more critical fashion requires recognising that the choice of subject is located within political processes in which some people's lives, but not others, are seen as interesting and/or important enough to be committed to biography. Authorial power is involved here not only in relation to who is deemed a 'fit subject' but also how their life and work is represented, including what sources are accepted as authoritative and treated as preferable to other contrary sources. Authorial power is involved in another way too: the biographer is an active agent in the biographical process, in the sense that she constructs the biographical subject rather than merely represents them 'as they really were'. The results have an individual stamp on them as much as a painting by Picasso or a novel by Henry James or piano music by Satie: Boswell's Johnson (1934), Richard Ellman's Oscar Wilde (1987), Froude's Carlyle (1882, 1884), Quentin Bell's Virginia Woolf (1972a, 1972b), Victoria Glendinning's Vita Sackville-West (1983), Michael Holroyd's Bernard Shaw (1988, 1990, 1991), Robert Skidelsky's Maynard Keynes (1980).

Locating the resulting biography as one competing version among others enables readers to make their own evaluation of whether and to what extent they find the result plausible or acceptable. To encourage this, biographers should not only make available to readers as much of the evidence, and of different kinds, that they work from as possible, but also an account of what facts, opinions and interpretations they find preferable and why: their 'intellectual biography' for this period of time. This approach guides my account of the life, friends and feminism of Emily Wilding Davison (Stanley, 1988b), a move in the direction of accountable feminist biography (and see Carolyn Steedman (1990) for a different route to the same end).

Treating notions of 'greatness' and 'uniqueness' as social constructions requires recognising that such people, like the rest of us, will have lived as an equal among equals. For example, John Maynard Keynes' economics may have seemed unique to his friends, Bloomsbury and otherwise, but by professional economists as an interesting but disputable synthesis of prevailing professional orthodoxies and heterodoxies. It is also important to move away from the circle of the great and famous, a largely self-perpetuating elite, and look for subjects who have *social* interest. Knowing the details of the lives of royalty or politicians or generals or film stars may tell us, often very competently, about members of particular elite groups, but for my money (and otherwise I wouldn't have edited her diaries) knowing about the working life of a Victorian servant like Hannah Cullwick (Stanley, 1984a) tells us about the working lives of the general mass of people – who may be neither kings nor politicians nor seen as 'important' in conventional terms, but who constitute precisely the vast majority of the population and who therefore have greater historical significance than the merely 'important'.

Seeing biographical subjects as to one degree or another sociable points up their connectedness with a multiplicity of other people throughout their lives. No person is an island complete of itself; and an approach to biography informed by feminist sociology and cultural politics should recognise that social networks are a crucial means of enabling us to get a purchase on other lives. For instance, looking at patterns of friendship through the to-ing and fro-ing of Elizabeth Gaskell's (1966) letters shows this supposed paragon of Victorian wifely servitude to have been closely connected with many of the most prominent British feminists of her day; and in tracing the feminist friendships of Olive Schreiner (Stanley, 1985a) I found that the social networks of these women gave a more complete picture of 'feminism' of the day than relying on membership of formal organisations alone.

Life presents us with complex views of 'the self': with competing estimations of character, motive, behaviour, intention. Biography

should recognise this, document and present these versions concerning its subjects rather than try to eradicate them through searching
for a seamless 'truth' about subjects and/or events in their lives. For
instance, biography tells us, variously, that Virginia Woolf was
entirely apolitical or was a quintessentially political writer; was
supported by Leonard Woolf or had her life ruined by him; was a
snob and an elitist or was a feminist and socialist of radical hue; was
completely asexual or was Vita Sackville-West's lover for some years.
Many, most, biographers play God, or the great leveller, and reduce
such complexity to one omnipotent view – 'the real Virginia Woolf'
– rather than accepting that all these competing truths and selves may
be true. What they do merely removes from the sight of *readers* some
of the most interesting material available to biographers. The implication of modern biography is that writers can cope with complexity, readers have to be protected from it.

What drives the 'purity of characterisation' approach, from Lytton
Strachey's *Eminent Victorians* (1918) to the latest professional biographical publication, is the motor of biographical realism. This takes
two main forms: recording in ever greater mass of detail – Holroyd
on Lytton Strachey (1968), Jill Liddington on Selina Cooper (1984),
Peter Ackroyd on Charles Dickens (1990); and the psychological
realism of a portrait of the inner life of a subject – Strachey on
Manning, Gordon and Nightingale (1918), Ellman on James Joyce
(1959/1982), Siegel on Karl Marx (1978). Both modes of biography are symbolised in the change from seeing Boswell as a scrupu-
lously objective recorder of the details of Samuel Johnson's life to
seeing him as an arch selector and interpreter: not representing, but
reconstructing according to his own authorial views and
understandings, the 'inner truth' of his subject.

Autobiographies, selves and postmodernisms

The autobiographical archetype is the *Bildungsroman*, the tale of the
progressive travelling of a life from troubled or stifled beginnings; in
which obstacles are overcome and the true self actualised or revealed;
and then the tale may, prototypically, end, or it may go on to
document yet further troubles turned to triumphs. A key present-day
example of the *Bildungsroman* autobiography much surely be Maya
Angelou's (1969, 1974, 1976, 1981, 1986) successive volumes of

autobiography, for troubles don't come much worse than to be a raped, mute, black working class girl in a racist and sexist society, and triumphs don't come much sweeter than to become a best-selling author and media star whose voice resounds internationally.

This dominant current in autobiography provides readers with exemplary lives. Also, by effect if not intent, it inscribes what 'a life' looks like, the form in which (written and spoken) tales of lives should be told and actual lives should be lived. These lives are linear, chronological, progressive, cumulative and individualist, and follow highly particular narrative conventions. The effect is truly ideological, because such ideas inform, even while they do not determine, readers' views about the frameworks within which we tell our own lives and expect to hear other people's. For Maya Angelou this effect is likely to be intentional: her artful creation of 'herself', in a re-working of the conventions of slave narratives, as the mythological black woman warrior, a contemporary Ni (Sistren, 1986) for other black women to admire and emulate, a eulogised symbolic life (Gilmore, 1978) par excellence.[6] But few Bildungsroman autobiographers are as artfully self-conscious as this.

However, the autobiographical form also encompasses very different currents, both referential of and acting as a challenge to this archetype. I mention two such currents here.

The first is the British flowering of autobiographies of 'ordinary lives', common lives, through the work of the Federation of Worker Writers and Community Publishers.[7] Some of the many I have enjoyed are Ron Barnes's Coronation Cups and Jam Jars (1976), the two volumes of Working Lives by A People's Autobiography of Hackney (1977a, 1977b), Just Lately I Realise: Stories From West Indian Lives (Gatehouse, 1985), and Doris Hall's Growing Up In Ditchling (1985). In some ways these are conventionally structured realist autobiographies – but with two crucial differences. These are not 'lives of the great', but common lives, typical lives – insofar as any lives are typical – of the mass of ordinary people but which are nonetheless extraordinarily interesting; and by being so they mount a considerable challenge to 'modern biography' orthodoxy about the conjunction of interest and 'importance'. Relatedly, these autobiographies are group projects: even those that centre on particular individuals do so in ways which stress the close interconnectedness of these lives and those of families, friends, enemies, employers and others.

This current in autobiography takes it as axiomatic that all lives are intrinsically interesting. It also embeds other equally subversive views: that to celebrate the elite few at the expense of the many, as the dominant form of auto/biography does, is classism writ large and confirmed by sexism and racism; and that, in spite of the academic hype surrounding an auto/biographical canon, telling the tale of a life is a skill we all possess, and this skill in speaking lives is translated into a written form by these working class authors.

The second current is the growth of autobiographies written by feminists, in particular those which experiment at the boundaries between different writing forms and with ideas about the relationship between the autobiographical self and others. I will briefly outline themes within two such autobiographies that have interested me greatly.[8]

Ann Oakley's (1984) challenge to boundaries in *Taking It Like A Woman* concerns those of fact and fiction. The 'author's note' that precedes the book laconically states 'Some of the characters in this book are real, and some aren't', leaving readers to make up our own minds which are which: the narrator herself, after all, could be a fictional representation of the author, and the unnamed lover a real man. Structurally, too, the book − with its 'scenes', 'chronologies' and commentaries of different kinds on people, events, emotions, ideas − continues weaving a hazy line between the conventions of fact and fiction.

Carolyn Steedman's *Landscape For A Good Woman* (1986) explores the relationship between daughters and parents, mothers in particular, although in a very different way. She is concerned with silences, with the inability as well as the unwillingness to 'speak' of those who live outside dominant and class-based discourses. She notes how easy it is for Ann Oakley, born into the articulate professional liberal middle class, to play with autobiographical convention − for the convention came into existence as an ideological account of such lives. And yet structurally her autobiography is at least as challenging: it dissolves apparent boundaries between the autobiographical self and others, including through the different structures of the book. It recovers and revalues common lives; and it explores the subtle gradations of difference that constitute class, as well as the gigantic differences made to working class daughter/mother relationships though the impact of education.

What these and other innovative feminist autobiographies add up to is a radical challenge to auto/biographical convention.[9] Conventional boundaries between different writing forms are explored, played with, crossed and recrossed. And a realist version of 'truth' as something single and unseamed is jettisoned in these autobiographies: perspective is all. Moreover, 'perspective' is highly complex: there is no easy invocation of 'subjectivity', but rather the exploration of the sometimes subtle and sometimes gross changes in perspective over time, including those that take place between the generations as well as within the life of a single autobiographer.

Linked with this is the way in which a 'self' is construed and explored as something much more than 'individual': unique in one sense, but also closely articulating with the lives of others, an articulation that can remain every bit as important after these others die, as Carolyn Steedman so convincingly shows. This in turn raises questions concerning the nature of 'authorship': a single hand writes, but the self who inscribes, who is, is herself emeshed with other lives which give hers the meaning it has. And it is not just 'the author' who takes on an ontologically shaky character in these autobiographies, for so too do 'selves' in general. That is, these autobiographical selves are both whole or struggling to become so and deeply and irresolvably fractured.

As these autobiographies recognise, auto/biographical authorship is even more complex than this, for written lives have an essentially intertextual character. That is, they claim referentiality (even if of a very complex kind) of 'the life' of the author, but our understanding of 'lives' and how they become 'written lives' is gained from written and pictorial auto/biographies – including fictional ones such as *David Copperfield*, *Jane Eyre* and *Anna Karenina* – and not only from life as it is lived. And more complex still, 'lives as they are lived' exist symbiotically with the written representation of lives: we expect our and other people's lives to have troughs and peaks, to have 'meaning', to have major and minor characters, heroes and villains, to be experienced as linear and progressive, and for chronology to provide the most important means of understanding them, all of which are characteristics of fiction.

A number of the characteristics I have discerned within innovative feminist autobiographies are also those assigned by various theorists to postmodernism. For these theorists postmodernist thinking is characterised by three ideas. First is a rejection of what is seen as the false referentiality of depictions of the modernist self, a rejection of its supposed essentialism 'within' and waiting to be actualised: the

Bildungsroman is its talisman and both enshrines and enforces its view of the self. Second is an equally severe rebuttal of modernist notions of authorship, the unique mind of the individual writer inscribing some quintessential inner truth. And third, by an insistence on intertextuality and a focus on language in use, particularly on the formation and perpetuation of discourses as sets of 'voices' speaking referentially to and about each other. This latter characteristic is one which, in relation to autobiography, points up the fact noted by quintessential modernist Gertrude Stein (1938), that 'auto/biography' and 'lives' do not each inhabit sealed units, but rather lives and fictional accounts of lives are intertextually related: everything is referential.

Architects of postmodernist theory such as Jean Lyotard (1984, 1989) or Jean Baudrillard (1979, 1988a, 1988b) have written nothing not written sooner and arguably better by Gertrude Stein. I make this claim because there are pertinent questions to be asked concerning the relationship between 'modernism' and 'modern biography'.

Postmodernist theory is predicated upon a critique of modernism. 'Modern biography' as I have described it encapsulates all of the problems critiqued by postmodernist theory – and more. However, there are good reasons to suppose that there is actually a gulf between the realism and referentiality of modern biography and a highly experimental and anti-foundationalist modernism. That is, the features colonised – I use the word precisely – by postmodernist theory are actually characteristics of modernist writing, women's writing particularly. Take the work of Colette: she of the fractured and non-referential self, she of the self made meaningful only by inter-connectedness with others, she of the life-long refusal of conventional boundaries between writing forms, she of the perpetual intertextual referencing of 'other' dimensions of her work/life. Take Gertrude Stein: whose autobiographical writing has no meaning apart from the intertextual referencing of life and art, whose work refuses conventional writing forms – the sentence, the paragraph – in favour of 'the voice', whose use of silence is resounding. Take Virginia Woolf: who nails feminist political colours to fictional masts, who speaks for common lives and common readers, who writes consciousness, who ties silken subversive threads around the necks of canons to the left and canons to the right of fiction, biography, autobiography, essays, reviews. Take Dorothy Richardson (1979), inscriber of a woman's sentence and a woman's voice, an

originator of 'stream of consciousness' fiction, a fictional biographer
of the inner lives of self-conscious subjects.

What I am proposing, indeed insisting, is that the characteristics
of postmodernism are actually those of *modernism*, ideas formed and
stated at the boundaries of literature and 'other' forms of writing in
the earlier part of the century (Scott, 1990). There is a chasm
between modernist ideas and those which define 'modern biography'. Modern biography is the realist impulse writ large; modernism is a fundamentally anti-realist impulse pillaged and colonised by
the imperialism of postmodernist theory.

'Tis the voice of the author, I heard her declare, 'I...'

Michel Foucault (1977), Roland Barthes (1977), and now deriva-
tively many others, have written of the 'death of the author'. The
argument here is that the conventional view of writing as the unique
product of a single unique mind is rather to be seen as a piece of
realist ideology which masks the social production of ideas; also this
ideology is dependent on equally facile presumptions about the
nature of 'the subject' as unique – an essentialist view which
underpins similarly essentialist views of 'the author'. So far so good:
unexceptional ideas long current in radical circles; but given,
paradoxically, a particular cache by being articulated by *Foucault*, by
Barthes – 'these authoritative authors, French intellectuals, speak the
death of the author: how marvellous'. A rich irony, for there is no
de-centering of the authorial subject here, readers should note. And
consider the life of 'the death of the author', its appearance within
most of the major and minor writings on postmodernism. Who are
these dead authors and what do they say? They are self-styled
theorists producing theory of an especially conventional elite kind.
They are white male authorities, patricians, a select number of
whom have become the latter-day prophets of postmodernspeak.
They themselves are apparently not there in their texts, there is only
'referential discourse' spoken by no one, by everyone. However, to
protest at exclusion is to be treated as a naive clinging to the
wreckage of bourgeois humanist referential essentialism – 'what,
you want to claim a self, to speak your oppression, to name
oppressors? really, how primitive, how naive'.

Consider what the denial of authorship actually *does*. It removes from existence as worth commenting upon, indeed as something which it is *authorised* to comment upon, the fact that this argument is actually articulated by a few white middle class male first world elite self-styled 'intellectuals'. A very convenient death – for them. At the very point when – due to the activities of anti-colonialism, the black movement, the women's movement, the gay movement – 'the author', the authoritative source of all that excludes, is named and has an accusatory finger pointed at him, the author at this very point conveniently dies. This is a suicide that is no suicide at all. This 'suicide' is alive and well and still calling the theoretical shots through its necrophilic relationship with both modernism and feminism. Merde!

What I am not saying: I am not saying that there is nothing in postmodernist ideas, that they should be dismissed or denied. Quite the contrary. The ideas are insightful, crucial to any egalitarian impulse within academic life. But they should not be hijacked by highly conventional and predominantly male theoreticians. And neither should these theorists be permitted to deny their dominant authorial presence in this activity. Consider the presence of the reader in these writings. Superficially readers are empowered – certainly we are told we are: in magisterial tones such as Foucault's, which brook no answering back, and also which provide no means for how this empowering is to occur, other than that it is.

In many supposedly radical books the reader is expected to assume, and maintain, a supine posture: prostrate before an authoritative voice speaking unassailable truths and arguments. The conventional power relations existing between authors and readers are among the last to be questioned and convincingly challenged. What readers require in order to do so is not hectoring from a still omnipotent although supposedly dead author, but rather the practical means of answering back. We already have these, I suggest in this book, within our critical reading practices; what is needed is to recognise and then codify these. In this book the voice of the reader is dominant. I wrote it as an inveterate reader of biography and autobiography and also of writings about them. The biographies I have written – on Hannah Cullwick, Olive Schreiner, Peter Sutcliffe, Emily Wilding Davison – each came into existence as a consequence of being a reader who wanted to answer back other writers who told me many things I knew I was unhappy about but which, as a reader, I was given few or no resources to deal with; and my own autobiography is completely and complexly intertwined with this biography. Readers of the composing chapters of this book will I hope find plenty of substance within its pages for argument and for travelling different intellectual routes to different conclusions from those I have reached.

As with feminism itself, from which it springs and without which it could not exist, this book and the ideas, arguments and descriptions it contains is located at the crossroads of Artemis: three roads. Down one, sameness and integration; down the second, difference; down the third – both. It is down this third road that I go in the rest of this book, arguing throughout that social life, lives, and the writing of lives, are all intertextually complex and that to every statement about them should be appended another beginning 'And also...'.

In the following chapter I pursue various arguments and ideas concerned with the relationship between biography and autobiography by looking at their supposedly referential character, a referentiality endorsed by the typical presence within them of photographs of their subject. These 'speaking likenesses' – there but mute, seen but not heard – are my topic.

Notes

1 An early version of this chapter was originally given at the University of Tampere, Finland, in March 1990; I am grateful to Liisa Rantilaiho, Leila Simonen and others present for their comments.
2 Here I am distinguishing between ideas, idealism, and ideology. 'Idealism' refers to a position which argues that ideas have innate existence rather than being generated in a material social context; few people identify themselves thus and the term is used mainly as a means of labelling and dismissing those analysts who are concerned with the social production and impact of ideas. 'Ideology' is often used to refer to ideas which exist at the level of ideas alone, which are not a product of material social life; again, it tends to be the same sets of people who interpret the term in this way. In contrast, I use 'ideology' to refer to sets of ideas often expressed within a discourse of competing voices and which have organisational or other material consequentiality within social life (an approach which is similar to that of Foucault and also of Dorothy Smith).
3 Of course sociology has always and continuously had an interest in the nature of 'the self' and its relationship to 'society', an interest foregrounded in the philosophy of Schutz, and the work of George Herbert Mead and symbolic interactionism. It is interesting to note that 'the self' has more recently become of interest to contemporary sociological theoreticians – for instance Anthony Giddens' (1991) discussion of the self within modernity, which raises many interesting questions and arguments but which, however, manages to devote an entire book to the question of ontology without any mention of *actual* lives.
4 This conference was held at the University of East Anglia in 1985; papers from it appear

in Homburger and Charmley (1988), although there are interesting differences between the conference and this published account of it, particularly that the conference gave a higher profile to a reconstructionist and realist view of biography.

5 A note on terminology and gender: Rather than writing of, for example, 'the subject her or himself', which unnecessarily clutters the page and reads awkwardly, I prefer to couple plural pronouns with singular nouns in spite of the 'ungrammatical' result: thus 'the subject themselves', 'the self ... they'.

6 Dolly McPherson's (1991) discussion of Angelou's autobiographical writing adopts a largely celebratory valedictory approach; there are feminist issues in Angelou's writing which deserve a tougher approach than this.

7 There are over thirty local Federation groups; their addresses, and lists of Federation publications, are available from: Federation of Worker Writers & Community Publishers, c/o Gatehouse Project, St Lukes, Sawley Road, Miles Platting, Manchester M10 3LY.

8 Another which I have found very stimulating is Kim Chernin's (1985) In My Mother's House, which is concerned with the interweaving of women's lives over successive generations, but also with the struggle the young have in understanding the old, given that they can never experience the events and circumstances that made the old what they are. Here there is no easy assumption of 'individuality' but rather a convincing demonstration of the positive and negative consequences of mother/daughter relationships.

9 I return to a discussion of this and related points in chapter nine.

2

Enter the author:
the auto/biographical I[1]

Auto/biography, photography and the common reader

Woman enters bookshop, browses along shelves. Stops, picks up and quickly puts down collection of essays on Hegel and feminism. Moves on, picks up and reads end of new feminist detective novel. Spots new biography of X, looks closely at front cover, reads blurb on back cover, flicks through a page or two, then goes to centre eight pages of photographs and scrutinises each with care and concentration.

This scenario will be familiar; perhaps most of the people who read this chapter will have behaved in a similar way, and probably fairly frequently, in our searches for 'a good read'. In our everyday reading lives we are accustomed to, we surrender to, the power of visual representation, photographs in particular, of auto/biographical subjects. But, ironically, one of the silences surrounding the production of auto/biography concerns the use of the 'speaking likeness' of X or Y in photographs of them, and the complex relationship that exists between these photographs and the text they are sandwiched between. There is now an extensive literature on photography: much is spoken and written of photography in the abstract and in general. But at the very point that photographs are at their most personal, their most concrete, their most speaking, and indeed are most surrounded by an ocean of words – within an auto/ biography – there is very little written about them.

This chapter is concerned with discussing the 'speaking' aspect of photographs of auto/biographic subjects. A 'voice' that speaks through representation in photographs is gendered as well as raced, classed; and 'seers' of these representations are also gendered, raced and classed beings. Photographs of auto/biographic subjects and our readings of them are importantly involved in constructing characters and biographies, lives-with-meaning.

For those of us who are or who have been sighted, the auto/ biographical I is a *seeing* I, a seeing *eye*. When someone we knew dies, we lament our inability to conjure up their image, their portrait, with clarity in our mind's eye as time passes. When we provide someone with the potted biography of a person known to us, we typically provide a physical description as an integral part of their biography, indeed of their character or personality. One indication of this symbiotic relationship between character and appearance lies in how we construct the biographies of various public figures about whom we have no first hand direct information about 'what they are like' at all, about whom we know only competing public mythologies. To take two examples:

It is difficult to escape the 'frothy nubile blonde' physical appearance of Marilyn Monroe in making assessments about 'what kind of a woman' she was (Steinem, 1986; McCann, 1988; Farran, 1990). The possibility that she might have calculatedly constructed herself as a marketable commodity by playing on heterosexual men's sexual susceptibilities as though they were so many fish on the end of a line does not come easily to most consumers and producers alike of Monroe biographies. And yet this character fits 'the facts' as well – or even better – than the stereotype of her as a 'dumb blonde'.

It is similarly difficult to escape the public images and character that accrue around Elvis Presley (Wise, 1990). Many of us have symbolically grown up with Elvis. There can be few Westerners of my generation who are not familiar with 'early', 'middle' and 'late' Elvis, irrespective of whether we ever saw ourselves as fans of the man and/or his music. Our familiarity comes from the sound of course, even if half-heard from other people's rooms, but also from visual representations on film and from posed and composed photographs displayed in public as well as private places. This linear chronological sequencing of visual biographic information has immense consequences for how we read 'a character' and events and their meaning within even such a public persona's life.

However, the linear sequencing of a biography does not operate in a forward mode only. From 'the end' – a death or some major rite of passage in a life – we can read images and other biographical information backwards through time, to impose 'real meaning, with hindsight': an account of 'what it all meant' that eluded us at the time but was supposedly 'really' always there. Thus the way that Elvis Presley looked on film and in photographs during in the weeks and days before his death (puffy, bloated, ugly, aged, decidedly off the ball) is 'read' in relation to the fact of his death as an irrefutible marker of the earlier physical and probably mental deterioration of the man. Elvis's death has been written – and over-written – as one presaged in his character or personality and actually 'always' discernible in certain outward markers; and this in turn is construed as a product of his reputably 'unhealthy' way of life. With hindsight, photographs of 'the young star' can be re-examined, literally but also in the mind's eye, for a sub-text that is seen always to have been there although only 'released' by later knowledge.[2] 'The fall' is seen to have been always present within 'the rise'.

There are examples of this 'dominance of the photographic image' to be found in my own biographical writing. Aspects of my work on the suffragette Emily Wilding Davison, and on the serial sexual murderer Peter Sutcliffe, are particularly relevant here.

Every schoolgirl knows that Emily Wilding Davison was the suffragette who supposedly threw herself under Edward VI's Derby horse for the vote in 1913. In a biography of Emily Davison (Stanley, 1988b[3]) I took issue with earlier interpretations of not only Emily Davison herself but also of the organisation and activities of the Edwardian suffrage movement. What I didn't comment on there is the extraordinary staying power of this 'she killed herself for the vote' representation of Emily Davison and its essentially visual basis. Both Emily Davison's funeral and the Derby incident itself were imprinted on what, for the sake of shorthand, can be referred to as 'the popular imagination' via photography and film. Most national and many local newspapers of the day carried pictures of the Derby incident and then later of Emily's London and Morpeth funeral corteges. All over the country 'moving film' was shown of both: indeed, within days of the funeral people in Morpeth queued to watch on film an event many had earlier been a part of in the streets of the town. And clips of the Derby film are still frequently shown as an evocation of the events of the Edwardian era.

It is a truism that the camera does not lie; it does not readily tell the truth either. Neither the camera nor the moving film show images that speak for themselves. In the case of the 1913 Derby incident, the film most often used (there are others from different angles) shows: horses galloping; then a woman rushing onto the racecourse among the horses; then the woman knocked down by the horses. But this film slowed down to a series of stills (and indeed published as such in June 1913 although rarely seen since then) provides a rather different view of the 'same' event: one bunch of horses gallop past Tattenham corner, then there is a break, then the King's horse Anmer; the woman moves onto the racecourse and stands waiting, something held in one hand; then she reaches up to the bridle of Anmer and immediately its speed pulls her body in front of the horse; then there is a tangle of the woman and the horse, in the air and then hitting the ground.

The first film can and has been read as 'intentional death', for it is said that nothing else could have been the result of such foolhardy impetuosity. The second 'same' but slowed-down film can be read, in contrast, as a deliberate and planned act — the placing of a suffragette flag on Anmer's bridle — and as a much slower, cooler act altogether: the woman here stands and waits, waits to carry out a particular act; this is certainly not 'the woman rushes headlong among the horses'.

An inquest reached a verdict of misadventure on Emily Davison's death. This verdict was based on a variety of evidence as to her 'state of mind' and political convictions, but also from strong circumstantial evidence. This came in the form of several items found in her bag in the form of a return ticket from central London to Epsom; her marked race card (do 'suicides' pick their racing fancies?); and, strongest of all, the helper's pass card that would have allowed Emily Davison to steward at a suffragette fair and bazaar in Kensington from 2 p.m. on that Wednesday afternoon (she had left London at about 12.30 p.m., the Derby was at 3 p.m., presumably she was expecting to be back in London by late afternoon or early evening). However, the power of the visual representation of a 'suicidal' or 'martyr' Emily Davison lives on, from the film via textual commentaries on what it is taken to show, from there to a small galaxy of history books, the majority of which repeat third-hand mythologies, and from there to 'what we all vaguely know' about Emily Davison. Its present-day life has been brought home to me in an unexpected way via the cover of my book about Emily Davison.

The cover is based on a photograph of an actual moment at the 1913 Derby, but one blown up many times and then presented in a collage of film dots and colours. This image was used because the book's message deconstructs it as the moment and the interpretation of those events, and instead locates it as one 'frame' among many prior and succeeding frames which tell of feminist organisation,

networks and political philosophies, and their complex
interweavings at national and local levels. However, almost the first
thing that was said to me publicly about the book was that the cover
confirmed the mythology of suicidal fanatical Emily and her 1913
death as the most important thing about her and her feminism. The
conclusion I draw is that the cover and its image 'work' only in the
context of the textual message it acts as a package for, and of which
the 'blurb' on the back cover acts as a foretaste. Without this textual
information on how to read the image on the front cover, 'what
everyone knows' about Emily strains people towards making a
directly contrasting reading to the one authorially intended.

Peter Sutcliffe is a very different case (Stanley, 1984b; Anony Ms,
1984). In the media-constructed guise of the serial sexual murderer
known as the 'Yorkshire Ripper', and through probably the biggest
media hype anywhere, a complete character and personality was
produced for this archetypal mythological being. The signifiers of
extraordinariness abounded: the 'Ripper' was powerful, crafty, never
made a mistake; came unseen from the dark, struck, and returned
into the unknown; was actually engaged in a duel with the police,
chancing his luck and liberty using women's bodies but with other
men in mind. And so on *ad nauseam*. The image that was constructed
by this word-mongering was of a veritable monster: stupendous, all-
powerful, a beast and absolutely not an ordinary man at all: Mr Hyde
rampant. That an ordinary man should have done these infamous
murderous acts was, literally it seems, unthinkable for many people.
When Peter Sutcliffe, that 'nondescript little man' as one newspaper
described him the day following his arrest, first appeared on the
scene the press was thrown into confusion.

The man that was serendipitously arrested was simply a man
among other men: married, with wider family and friends, a good
worker, someone who did not stand out of the crowd before his
arrest pushed him out of it. These signifiers of ordinariness were
remarked upon in the news media in the twenty-four hours or so
following Peter Sutcliffe's arrest before being submerged in a tidal
wave of 'beastliness' descriptors. The first photographs of Peter
Sutcliffe that were published (again, the day following his arrest)
confirmed this disjuncture between 'ordinary Peter Sutcliffe' and
'extraordinary Yorkshire Ripper': a bearded workman in a lorry; a
wedding photograph. But then newspapers and television, and later
books and reviews of these, worked hard at discovering the seeds of

the Yorkshire Ripper in even the earliest years of Peter Sutcliffe (cf Burn, 1984; Highsmith, 1984). What interests me here is the media reaction to the first published photographs of Sutcliffe, for this refutes the generalisation implicit in my remarks about the photographs of the 1913 Derby incident.

Photographic images are powerful. They are not, however, all-powerful. Photographs do not speak for themselves: they require interpretation and this interpretation may be mediated by words which surround, literally, particular photographs, or from 'texts' which readers of photographs import from their general knowledge. Also photographic and other literal or mimetic visual images are not the only sources of 'pictures'. Others can be built up in words themselves, as with 'pictures' of the appearance, character and personality of 'the Yorkshire Ripper'. These word-pictures can be and often are much more powerfully present in the mind's eye than the literal images provided by photographs and film. This is precisely the case with the Yorkshire Ripper. The 'ordinary Peter Sutcliffe' who appears in photographs and was invoked in the first media reactions following his arrest, was effectively obliterated by what has been taken as the 'more realistic' word-picture of the Ripper and his atrocities: a man who was a beast, a destroyer from out of the dark, a monster seen in our mind's eye and who stands between us and the merely literal photograph of a mere man. 'The facts' are truly complex.

It is useful to note in passing that Peter Sutcliffe's first 'serious' biographer (Burn, 1984) worked in precisely the 'reverse' mode of constructing 'a character' and 'a life' I have identified as operating following Elvis Presley's death. Here the beastliness of the man is sought – and found – in the child who was, in a causal sense, father to the beast. The origins of Sutcliffe's extraordinariness are traced back to – to what or whom? – to his mother, of course.[4] However, the approach taken by Brian Masters (1985), Dennis Nilsen's biographer, interestingly contrasts with this.

Nilsen was the serial sexual murderer of young men and hoarder of their dismembered, and dis-remembered and still nameless, remains. For Masters it is the absolute ordinariness of this man coupled with the devastating extraordinariness of his deeds that constitutes the central problem which should be addressed. Brian Masters seeks no easy causal solution in claims of Nilsen's *a priori* madness, or in mothers, or in monstrosity; and his biography stands as one of the best proto-sociological accounts of a serial murderer. It is also sexually politically naive, but contains enough detail for a feminist eye to catch these aspects and be able to construct a feminist account centering on (damaged) masculinities and their potential (in both senses) and often grisly consequences.

Feminist auto/biography and photography

Over the last few years, feminist analysis has become concerned with the artfulness of auto/biography. There have been different facets to this. One is to emphasise that those people 'important' enough to be subject to biography are infrequently women unless they are: infamous (Ruth Ellis, Eva Peron, Eva Braun, Ulrica Meinhoff), glamorous (Grace Kelly, Jackie Kennedy Onassis, Joan Collins), a 'star' (Maria Callas, Elizabeth Taylor, Marilyn Monroe, and any number of Hollywood movie 'stars'), and/or the wives of famous men (Jackie Kennedy Onassis, Cosima Wagner, Caitlin Thomas, Nancy Reagan). However, this is a base-line comment, essential but by no means the last feminist word on the topic. A second facet is the growth of a genre of feminist writing concerned with how fame has often destroyed, or exacerbated the destruction of, famous women: 'woman as star as victim', and of which Edith Piaf and Billie Holiday must be the twin-symbols (Archer & Simmonds, 1986; Steward & Garrard, 1984). A third facet is that British feminist publishing is currently being kept afloat and profitable on a sea composed not only of detective stories, but also tidal waves of biographies and autobiographies of famous women and rather less famous feminists.

   Of more direct interest to this discussion is a more recent facet of feminist commentary on auto/biography, one which has located the product – the auto/biography of X – within the processes of its production (see for example Rose, 1982; Farran et al, 1985; Stanley, 1988b, 1988c; Greer, 1989; Gender & History 1990; Steedman, 1990). In drawing attention to process, these feminist writers have been less concerned with the 'bias' of male auto/biography writers, or with the possibly different effects of fame on men and on women, than with how it is that 'a life' as it is lived in its length, complexities, contradictions, shifts and changes is reduced to 'the life of X' on paper and between covers. That is, this genre of feminist writing has

noted that *all* auto/biography writing is artful, not just that which is
ideologically unsound in feminist terms. Indeed, to make the point
more strongly: feminist and other 'right-on' auto/biography is as
artful as any other. However, there still prevails a virtual silence
about the role of the *visual* ('I saw her and she was like this'), and of
the photographic ('there she is') in this most recent feminist writing
on auto/biography. This statement is generally true; however, two
particularly interesting exceptions (and for others see Farran, 1990;
Steedman, 1990) concern the work of Annette Kuhn and Jo Spence.

Annette Kuhn is one of Britain's most distinguished feminist
writers on film and cinema – that is, the organisational apparatus by
which certain kinds of film are produced, directed, distributed and consumed. Her work has been of signal importance in the production of
feminist film studies, not least for the impact it has had on other
writers, commentators, and indeed on feminist film and video makers
(see for example Coward, 1984; Brunsdon, 1986; Lovell, 1980;
Moi, 1985). Given her concern with film and not photography, a
detailed discussion of Annette Kuhn's work would not be appropriate here. However, three linked factors within it are relevant.

The first is that the writing of an analytic appreciation of film as
precisely film and therefore *moving* involves some important and
largely unresolvable paradoxes, centering on the fact that to discuss
in detail requires the discussion of single frames or sequences of
single frames, that is, of *stills* from film. And so, for example, Annette
Kuhn discusses narrative structure and narrative discourse in Hollywood film of the 1940s and 50s via a discussion of a linear sequence
of narrative segments (her term) from *Mildred Pierce* (1945: directed
by Michael Curtiz and featuring Joan Crawford), and of the role of
close-ups, within-frame movements of a hero, and mobile framing
through the discussion of a series of stills from *The Big Sleep* (1946:
directed by Howard Hawks and featuring Humphrey Bogart and
Lauren Bacall). However, as Susan Sontag has noted in her essay
'Melancholy objects':

But the relation of a still photograph to a film is intrinsically misleading. To
quote from a movie is not the same as quoting from a book. Whereas the
reading time of a book is up to the reader, the viewing time of a film is set
by the filmmaker and the images are perceived only as fast or as slowly (?)
as the editing permits. Thus, a still, which allows one to linger over a single
moment as long as one likes, contradicts the very form of film ... which is
a process, a flow in time. (Sontag, 1977 p. 81)

Discussing film in detail raises an unresolvable contradiction, for by doing so what is discussed is transmuted: no longer film, but stills, segments, frames.

The second comment is that reading a still or a sequence of stills (just like the close reading of a written text) may yield interesting analytic points; however, it also inevitably produces a highly atypical reading. Film, like life and time, passes. We subject some parts of a film to close concentration, other parts we daydream our way through, other parts we barely pay attention to because we are willing it to move on to some expected or hoped-for event, denouement, climax, end. And of course exactly the same point can be made about detailed readings of written texts: in 'real life' no one reads them the way textual analysts of marxist, ethnomethodological and other schools do (see Chapter 7). By seeing (or reading) in close detail, we inevitably produce a fabricated seeing (or reading), not the kind of 'ordinary seeing' that the vast majority of, in turn and often in the 'same' viewing, ordinarily inattentive, sloppy, day-dreaming, concentrating, waiting, audiences do.

The third comment concerns the consequentiality – or rather lack of it – of these problematics. Annette Kuhn's prime concern does not seem to be with 'the film' in toto as a (usually) shared social experience. Instead it is with a set of psychoanalytically-derived theoretical ideas about 'woman' as the signifier within mainstream or dominant cinema, and with the filmic codes and conventions by which woman the signifier makes her appearances and how these are consumed by viewers. That is, her concern is with how filmic representations come to act as an 'ought'. Her detailed discussion of segments, stills and the like provides a route through to constructed ideologies about 'woman'. Rather than being concerned with seg-ments and stills as elements within the pattern of the overall experience of the film, Annette Kuhn uses these slices from its surface to allow her to make generalised statements about 'woman', that is, the sexually politically constructed 'woman' of dominant ideological discourse. She appears little interested in the experience of the film: how all its segments and stills hang together to produce 'a film' as a complete social experience. What she does is certainly analytically interesting and insightful, but it tells me surprisingly little about the films I watch and she comments on, however much it tells me about a particular genre of film studies.

Jo Spence is a feminist photographer rather than a film maker or commentator on film; and her writing (Spence, 1986; Spence & Holland, 1991) has been concerned with the conventions and codes which influence photographic representation; family photographs as constructed icons which show lies about family life; and feminist uses of photo therapy as a means of healing wounds in women's self-images and physical presences. Working out of similar feminisms, Annette Kuhn and Jo Spence have different subject-relationships with and to the representational forms they write about. Jo Spence is a photographer while Annette Kuhn is a consumer of film, albeit of a highly professionalised kind, rather than someone directly and professionally involved in its production. This gives rise to different concerns and the identification of different interests. For instance, Jo Spence's photographic autobiography is not only concerned with the portrayal of (or failure to portray) herself in 'family photographs', but also with the 'high street photography' codes, conventions and practices which produce particular kinds of stylisations of women, children, the family, for she herself has been a part of this high-street production process.

Jo Spence's critique has appealed to many women, myself included, because we too have a direct subject-relationship to such photographic stylisations. We have appeared in high street photographer's depictions of 'ourselves' as children, as brides, mothers; have been a subject – or object – of family snapshots. This may not be the double-edged involvement of Jo Spence herself, as a former professional photographer as well as subject/object of these and of family photographs, but it is nonetheless a direct involvement. The power and danger of photographic convention is that while everyone knows that neither family life nor children nor women are 'really' as they are represented, these representations act as an 'ought'. They act as a standard that everyone knows is false but worries whether and to what extent other people share this knowledge and belief. They also act as a standard that everyone thinks is or should be attractive and desirable and which they should aspire to or at least give the appearance (sometimes literally) of doing so.

For Jo Spence there are two main ways out of the damage caused by false expectation and representation, such massive failures on women's part to come up to scratch, to match up to image (supposedly a truer reality of womanhood than actually being a woman). The first is through the set of practices which Rosy Martin and Jo Spence call 'photo therapy':

we all have sets of personalised archetypal images in memory, images which are surrounded by vast chains of connotations and buried memories. In photo therapy we can dredge them up, reconstruct them, even reinvent them, so that they can work in our interests, rather than remaining the mythologies of others who have told us about the 'self' which appears to be visible in various photographs ... Through the medium of visual reframing we can begin to understand that images we hold of ourselves are often the embodiment of particular traumas, fears, losses, hopes and desires. (Spence, 1986 p. 172)

From what follows, it is clear that the 'others' who have told us about the 'self' in photographs are frequently adults to the self that was a child, adults usually if not exclusively parents; and the reframing that needs to take place is consequently seen to be a reinvention and reconstruction of the then-child through the photo therapy of the now-adult.

Photo therapy is psychoanalytically informed. For those like myself who disagree that 'the child is mother to the woman' in quite this way, its personal usefulness is limited – however, this is not to dispute that for many people it may yield great benefits and provide much help on the route to psychic healing. Connectedly, photo therapy is premised on the notion that the route into changing the present is by changing the past, changing one's perception of childhood in particular. Again, I find this personally unhelpful, preferring to change the present by (trying to) change the present. In addition, photo therapy is premised on a view of childhood as an inevitably scarring experience – and indeed of much of adulthood as similarly damaging to physical and psychic well-being. Of course childhood is often literally so, for the abuse of children is common-place; but what is being written of here are existential crises, not behavioural ones. Again, for those who do not understand childhood in these terms, its usefulness is limited. Moreover, this approach avoids considering to what extent such existential crises are *post hoc* constructions: childhood as it is recollected and reconstructed from adulthood, not as it was necessarily literally experienced at the time.

The second way out of photographic mis-representation identified by Jo Spence is one in which the camera is reappropriated by women, by feminists, and used to make visible previously invisible aspects of everyday life which photographic convention has refused to see (the trivial, everyday, repetitious), or to see what has previously been seen but now in new and politicised ways. This is perhaps the aspect of Jo Spence's 'reframing' of the self that has had the most appeal for many women, at least in part because it connects directly with their everyday experiences in a way that photo therapy may not. Certainly her photographs of mundane everyday life excite powerful reactions, Lastly, paradoxically enough there is for many readers a sub-text: Jo Spence's aid in the reframing of their selves has come importantly from the example of her 'life', her known autobiography and in particular how she has dealt with cancer in her life – and has written and spoken about this in moving and empowering terms. How very disconcerting it must be for Jo Spence the inverter of family photographic iconography to experience becoming a feminist icon in her own person.

Of iconography, truth and lies

For Jo Spence 'family life' photographs are false icons, and hence the need for their subversion through the assemblage of a photographic anti-convention. The dominant convention permits only one 'side' of people to be represented in photography – both a stereotype and anyway removed from everyday life. While rejecting an essentialist view of 'self', her argument is that by photographing what has previously been 'unseen' by the photographic eye, and also by photographically deconstructing the dominant conventions, many more 'sides' of people's selves will gain representational form and the sum total of these will provide a more complete 'picture' of the subject.

My response is 'maybe, maybe not'. I don't accept that conventional iconography holds nothing of value or of direct use, and that it tells nothing but lies. I also think that lies, 'false representations', can be at least as complexly interesting and useful as 'truth' to the inquiring analytic feminist. In addition, there is a distinct possibility that new conventions may arise from photographic reconstructionism that may become just as much of a straightjacket. My concern here is particularly with the linked topics of truth and lies.

At the front of her book Jo Spence places in 'poetic' form a passage from Adrienne Rich's *On Lies, Secrets and Silence*:

In speaking of lies,
we come inevitably
to the subject of truth.
There is nothing simple
or easy about this idea.
There is no 'the truth!'
'a truth' –
truth is not one thing
or even a system.
It is an increasing
complexity.
The pattern of the carpet
is the surface.
When we look closely
or when we become weavers,
we learn of the tiny multiple threads
unseen in the overall
pattern, the knots on the
underside of the carpet.   (Rich, 1979, p. 187)

Jo Spence's search is not for 'the truth' or even 'a truth', but rather for the increasing complexity of many truths, and for a non-referential and complex notion of the 'self'. Toppling photographic convention from its constructed place as 'truth', she wishes to construct a myriad of counter-truths.

My interest, in contradistinction, is with lying, and with what feminists can do with lies: with conventions and stereotypes, with mythologies false and otherwise. The basis of my interest can be illustrated by transposing 'truths' and 'lies' in Adrienne Rich's words, so that they read 'In speaking of truths,/ we come inevitably/ to the subject of lying./ There is nothing simple/ or easy about this idea./ There is no "the lie!" / "a lie" -/ It is an increasing/ complexity.'

To stretch this 'carpet' metaphor further: Jo Spence is concerned with the *pattern* of the carpet in her search for the greater complexity of multiple truths, so she wants to examine more of its upper surface. My concern is with the system of threads and knots *beneath* that is the equally patterned lie. The crux of my interest is whether and to what extent photographic iconography can be explored by feminists, given the highly particular subject-relationship we have to our own family or other iconography. My fascination is with the 'surface' of the photograph and the way that its 'slice of time preserved' quality opens up for us time itself.

'The gaze'

John Berger's *Ways of Seeing* (1972) was published in conjunction
with a television series about the 'visual eye' in painting. Not only
has the book aged well, but also much of its contents speak as
relevantly to advertising, television and photography as they do to
painting. Two of its arguments especially are as pertinent now as
when first published.

The first concerns John Berger's discussion of 'the image' as a
product located within a particular set of relations of production,
distribution and exchange. Here as with other kinds of product
within industrial capitalism, consumers buy a visual representational
product produced for a market. Thus producers – artists, designers,
photographers and so forth – operate in a context in which
'creativity' and 'artistry' are closely linked, if not entirely subjugated,
to 'what will sell'. Of course Berger is discussing a particular kind of
representational image, 'the painting', and the production of many
paintings are not, at least in the narrow sense just described, tied to
the operations of a market. Nevertheless his wider argument still
stands, for painting and other art produced for sheer pleasure as well
as directly for sale, and also as family photographs and personal
snapshots, are all consumables which take more and less acceptable
forms, and their 'acceptability' is closely linked to dominant photographic, artistic and related conventions.

A second still highly pertinent idea concerns what Berger says
about 'the nude', although his argument can be applied equally
usefully to other representational uses of women's bodies and faces.
Nudes in paintings were, until relatively recently, produced for very
particular consumers: often for one man who directly commissioned
them from the artist and who 'consumed' the result in a private place
such as a study, which was taboo to women in his family but open
to a select group of other males.[5]

The conventions of 'the nude' in painting apply, by and large, to
nudes in photography. And Berger asks the apparently simple
question of how such images are 'seen' by women. Designed for a
man, to be looked at by a male audience, Berger says that women
have two options. One is to look through male eyes at such an
image: we have to see it 'as a man'; and here we have no *subject*
relationship to the image at all but rather 'it' has an object
relationship to us, for the woman whose representation constitutes

the image becomes an object for us as much as for the implicitly heterosexual male intended audience. The other option for women is to see ourselves as 'the woman in the picture'; and here we have a direct subject-relation to the image, but in having it we thereby render ourselves object, in the same way and by the same means as the image is an object to the male heterosexual audience.

Berger's argument is illuminating, for it makes one self-conscious about 'the gaze' one gives to representations of women and its sexual political basis. However, I would argue strongly that the options are now demonstrably greater than when this was first written. For one thing, 'men' are not all the same, and certainly gay men have a very different kind of relationship to images of 'desirable' women; for another, at least some heterosexual men themselves look on such representations of female bodies and faces with sexual political scruples: they refuse 'the gaze'. The image does not determine one highly particular 'sexual' reading, then.

However, the major change since Berger wrote this concerns the renaissance of feminism, which provides women with a radically different option, a third seeing I, which enables us to deconstruct the object/subject relations of dominant representations of women. But not only this; it also enables us to 'see differently', to have a different 'gaze', to look, not through the eyes of 'the man', but through our own feminist women's eyes (Gamman and Marshment, 1988). Consider any well-known 'glamour' photograph of Marilyn Monroe. To accept John Berger's argument is to say either that we 'consume' Marilyn Monroe as a man does (assumed to be heterosexual, reputedly does), as a sexual object in relation to us as a consuming subject, or that we locate ourselves as the woman in the picture and become an object for the male sexual gaze as an ur-Marilyn. Feminism provides other possibilities: we stand and look from outside of this particular thought-system, neither the woman who is a sexual political object nor the man who is a sexual political subject, but ourselves, on the one hand a refusing female subject and on the other an analytically inquiring feminist subject.

Feminism, then, takes John Berger's ideas some steps further. We can deconstruct 'the man' to different kinds of men with different 'gazes'. And we can conceive of a woman as a knowing subject and not merely as an object of a male gaze or as a kind of mutant male eye. However, this 'feminist gaze' requires analytic means, not just feminist intent.

Erving Goffman has also been concerned with analysing the assemblage of representational ideas about 'woman' as a gendered object in the essays and photographs in Gender Advertisements (1976). Here he focusses not through advertisements to general abstract ideas about nature, culture and so forth (as Judith Williamson (1978) does in her work on advertising and Annette Kuhn in hers on film) but actually on the advertisements themselves, on their 'surface', their compositional form. In doing so he makes use of one basic theoretical understanding and one basic analytic tool.

Goffman theorises 'gender' as the construction of 'peak performances' rather than as a quality of actual persons or routine everyday behaviours. This does not deny the importance of gender, nor its central organising presence in the ways people assemble character, carry out conversations, manipulate power in certain interactional settings, and so on; rather, it proposes that gender's very power and importance lies in its actual interactional atypicality. Advertisements embody gender at one of its most extreme, most stereotypical, most atypical forms, as blatantly unrealistic descriptions of women and men, girls and boys. Their social role is as an 'ought'; and in order to counteract this 'ought' we need to understand just how a piece of advertising is assembled, how it 'works' because people put their knowledge of the blatant propaganda of them on one side.

The basic analytic means used by Goffman is an inventory approach to the single 'frame' that is the press advertisement, in particular by examining what he calls the 'demeanour' (the use of bodies and gazes together with a wide variety of 'props' which include clothes, make-up, furnishings and other artifacts) of participants. What interests me is not so much the inventory approach itself (although when used to suggest a less deterministic approach to 'readings' of advertisements than Goffman himself provides, it can take us a long way in unpacking these), as the notion that a piece of magazine advertising, in particular its photographic components, can be seen as single frames. The idea of 'the frame' also encompasses the idea of prior and subsequent frames as well as that which composes 'the advertisement' itself; and what thus becomes available to us is the possibility of examining 'strips' of linked frames only one of which need be an advertisement, a photograph, a painting, itself.

I am using the notion of 'frame' here less in the photographic or painting sense (the frame which holds the specific picture) and more in the sense of four (or less or more) sides which can hold –

Figure 1. Alexander Gardner, portrait of Lewis Payne, 1865

whatever is placed within the frame. Like the mind, this 'frame' is a potential and not an actual space. The other sense in which I am using the notion of a 'frame' is as a 'moment'; that is, not as an actual moment in 'real time' but as an infinite moment in the mind's being.

Virginia Woolf's 'moments of being' (1976) are those constructed out of the relationship between present and past self, in which she assembles just enough of the present to act as a platform, just enough of the past to act as another, on which to locate that elusive being, her 'self'. The substance of these platforms is provided by the 'moments of being', those luminous moments, whether actual moments, memories, half-memories, of people, of sights, of smells and tastes, feelings and thoughts, that remain in the mind and memory, now floating, now half-submerged, now grasped at least in shadowy form on paper. These 'moments' and their 'platforms' of 'now', the present, and 'then', the past, enable the mind's eye to do things with time. And let us not forget that these delicately threaded 'moments' once 'brought to mind' can implode into our consciousness with all the force and devastation/creation of an emergent inner galaxy. Let us not forget the cataclysm caused by the surfacing in Woolf's mind of the continual sexual abuse she had suffered, and her astonishing capture of this in powerful autobiographical writing, nor the effects on her of awareness of Freud's denial of the reality of such pain (DeSalvo, 1989).

Photography and the elegaic mode

People who write about photographs very quickly slip into what Susan Sontag has called an 'elegaic' mode (1977, p. 16). Time is a slippery will o'the wisp: now you have it, now it's gone. Photographs conjure up time in a very direct way, for time and its passing is of their very essence: if photographs are icons, they are indubitably icons to time. As Sontag argues:

All photographs are momento mori. To take a photograph is to participate in another person's (or thing's) mortality, vulnerability, mutability. Precisely by slicing out this moment and freezing it, all photographs testify to time's relentless melt, (Sontag, 1977 p. 15)

She suggests that in photographs people are symbolically possessed, violated, and that photographs act as 'a sublimated murder — a

Figure 2. Paul Nadar, Savorgnan de Brazza, 1882 (© DACS 1992)

soft murder' (Sontag, 1977 pp. 14-15); and this 'murder' is one
which is embedded in 'a privileged moment, a slice of time one can
look at again and again' (Sontag, 1977 p. 16). Dead moments
indeed. Susan Sontag's On Photography is nearly all quotation, and I
could continue picking out more infuriating, inspiring, contradictory and illuminating passages in its composite essays. But instead I
want to pursue the question of time a little further.

The photograph of Lewis Payne was taken by Alexander Gardner
in 1865 and included in Roland Barthes's book on photographs
Camera Lucida (1980). For me it speaks of this 'slice of time' quality in
photographs like no other. The photograph was taken not long
before Payne's execution by hanging.[6] Its caption in Barthes's book is
'He is dead and he is going to die' (p. 95) and for me as for Barthes
what it so powerfully brings to mind is 'that which has been' but
also 'that which will be'. On this, Barthes says:

> he is going to die. I read at the same time: This will be and this has been; I observe
> with horror an anterior future of which death is the stake. By giving me the
> absolute past of the pose ... the photograph tells me death in the future ...
> This punctum, more or less buried beneath the abundance and the disparity of
> contemporary photographs, is visibly legible in historical photographs:
> there is always a defeat of Time in them. (Barthes, 1980, p. 96)

This is the quality of photographs which exercises Susan Sontag so
deeply: again and again she returns to it in On Photography. Photographs contain what is most mysterious and unassimilable of all –
'time itself. What renders a photograph surreal is its irrefutible
pathos as a message from time past'; photographs contain a 'privileged moment, a slice of time one can look at again and again'
(Sontag, 1977, p. 16). However, Sontag's time is a one-way process
only: we look back on time past, its dead moments. In contrast,
Barthesian time is a flux and a two-way flow: we look back to 'then'
and from 'then' we look forward, to death. What Barthes's work, in
Camera Lucida in particular (but also in Image – Music – Text (1977) and
in Roland Barthes by Roland Barthes (1975b)) begins to suggest is that the
photograph can become a tardis, a Dr Who time-machine that
enables us to go a-travelling. Barthesian time is most definitely worth
pursuing.

Camera Lucida tells us just what Barthes thinks of my discipline of
sociology: not much. He identifies and defines the 'studium' of the
photograph, its 'study', as what a 'polite interest' would take in. The
studium, says Barthes, is a kind of contract between creators/operators

Figure 3. G. W. Wilson, Queen Victoria, 1863

and consumers, a contract derived from shared cultural understandings which provides 'ethnological knowledge' (Barthes, 1980,
p. 28). Barthes specifies study of studium as the realm of sociology.

However, the photograph's other and for him more important
and consequential aspect is its punctum, that which 'pricks', which
punctuates, which penetrates (a sexually politically unfortunate
choice of words in either original or translation or both: or perhaps
it derives from the Lacanian psychoanalytic phallusism which has
influenced Barthes here and elsewhere). Barthes says that the punctum
is uncoded, quite unlike the studium which is all code, all cultural
reference. The punctum is a detail which fills the entire picture, which
suffuses everything else about it. Barthes eloquently describes the
resounding difference between them in relation to Nadar's 1882
photograph of Savorgnan de Brazza:

The studium is ultimately always coded, the punctum is not (I trust I am not
using these words abusively). Nadar, in his time (1882), photographed
Savorgnan de Brazza between two young blacks dressed as black sailors; one
of the two boys, oddly, has rested his hand on Brazza's thigh; this
incongruous gesture is bound to arrest my gaze, to constitute a punctum. And
yet it is not one, for I immediately code the posture, whether I want to or
not, as 'aberrant' (for me, the punctum is the other boy's crossed arms).
(Barthes, 1980, p.51)

The uncoded punctum needs to be examined more closely. I do so
first in relation to Barthes's discussion of the punctum of another
photograph, Wilson's photograph of Queen Victoria taken in 1863
(1980, p. 56).

About this photograph Barthes says:

Here is Queen Victoria photographed in 1863 by George W. Wilson; she is
on horseback, her skirt is suitably draping the entire animal (this is the
historical interest, the studium); but besides her, attracting my eyes, a kilted
groom holds the horse's bridle: this is the punctum; for even if I do not know
just what the social status of this Scotsman may be (servant? equerry?), I can
see his function clearly: to supervise the horse's behaviour: what if the
horse suddenly began to rear? What would happen to the queen's skirt, i.e.
to her majesty? The punctum fantastically 'brings out' the Victorian nature
(what else can one call it?) of the photograph, it endows this photograph
with a blind field. (Barthes, 1980, p. 57)

But Barthes was a Frenchman, with a Frenchman's knowledge of
English history and not that of a British reader. The groom is of
course John Brown; and the British reader immediately codes what

Barthes could not. Certainly *lese majeste* may be visible in this photograph, but of a different kind from that perceived by Barthes: was
John Brown Queen Victoria's lover? did he replace Albert in her life?
and so on. We code what Barthes uncodes, as 'aberrant (of a heterosexual variety)'; so let us return to that other earlier 'aberration'
Barthes detects in Nadar's photograph.

Barthes and Berger share a common standpoint: that of what can
be called 'the dominant ideology'. For all their radicalism on one level,
they remain white, male, middle class, to all intents and purposes heterosexual (I have no *textual* means of knowing whether either or both
are or not, outside of what they have written and I have read). Their
minds leap to see the world through dominant ideological eyes at the
same time that they struggle to draw their distance. Earlier I argued
that feminism has opened up, for women, another possibility. Our
'gaze' does not have to be that of a man, or that of the woman who
is object, for we can become seeing feminist subjects. Now nearly
twenty years of a lesbian and gay male political sensibility has most
certainly done the same thing for 'out' lesbians and gay men.

Looking at Nadar's picture, I do not see 'aberration' (or at least
not the one that Barthes sees) even on Barthes's 'whether I want to or
not' terms. I do not see it as a heterosexual person does (presumed to
accept dominant ideological assessments of heterosexualty and homosexuality); another 'gaze' is possible for me. I look at it as a
lesbian feminist subject, just as gay men will look at it through their
own subject eyes. Of course none of us can avoid knowing that
same-sex sexual and loving relationships are usually coded as
deviant, as aberrant in Barthes's terms. But this is not the same as
looking at it so, coding it so. I look at it seeing three men between
whom there may be sexual relationships and knowing that for some
people this will be seen as deviant, aberrant, but not accepting this
myself. Twenty years of practice at looking at the world through my
own eyes is consequential for how I see and what I see. Like other
long-term 'out' gay women and men, my relationship to conventional definitions of 'normality' and 'deviance' is a complex many
layered one and I will not have it reduced to a one-dimensional
heterosexual male gaze. Nonetheless, I *do* see aberration. The 'aberration' I see here is that of *colonialism* and its barbarisms expressed by
sexual political means. And Barthes writing about 'blacks' and not
'black people', and 'boys' and not 'black men', is included and
implicated in this mundane racism.

Death by empathy

Returning to Barthes' notion of the *punctum* as 'that which is uncoded': as discussion of the Queen Victoria photograph demonstrates, 'uncode' is liable to be 'cultural ignorance', a mere lack of knowledge of what the code might be. But of course 'ignorance' is itself a code, and indeed it is also — like Kant's unknown unknowable thing-in-itself — a contradiction in terms. By saying 'I do not know', something is known; by saying that the thing-in-itself is unknown and unknowable we render it knowable and indeed know something about it. And from sociology another objection to 'uncode': *nothing lies outside of culture*, outside of the realm of the social; and the knower, the seer, the thinker, the writer, is always a social subject, the product of culture. However, here Barthes slips away from culture and its social life into — into what?

The plug-hole in culture for Barthes is the unconscious: through the unconscious we slip from the social into something Other. However, the unconscious, like other psychoanalytic concepts, is an invention and not a discovery; no proof of its existence is possible; and it and its fellows are inventions to which I have many intellectual and political objections. I am a *social* scientist and as such insist on the primacy of the social, cultural, material.

Barthes's original plan was to have written an essay on his family photographs, one that would have followed more deeply the surface story in the first part of *Roland Barthes on Roland Barthes*. His mother had died; a photograph of her that has mythic proportions in the text of *Camera Lucida* makes its (*unseen*) appearance only on page 62, half way through the book; it is this absent photograph that is the progenitor of *Camera Lucida* like its original was of the author. Much is said of this photograph, taken in 1898 when Barthes's mother was five; but Barthes figuratively cannot face its actual image, and so will not let his readers literally face it either.

Instead he, and we, face a series of magnificently *public* photographs: Wilson, Gardner, Nadar and others. As Barthes notes, he has no special relationship to these photographs: he was not their 'originator', the person who actually held the camera and posed the 'shot'; equally, he does not have another 'special relationship', that of the person who develops, prints, touches, retouches. In relation to these photographs, as with those discussed by Sontag, both he and we are 'the public', our gaze is that of Outsider, stranger.

Barthes uses these 'public' photographs to begin to open up time; he uses that which he cannot face, the photograph of his mother, to open up time to death. For Barthes, what all these photographs contain is time and its passing, leading inexorably to death, to the end; Gardner's portrait of Payne simply shows this more starkly than the others. But there is a wilful absence here, a death denied.

More than Lewis Payne, into whose seeing eyes we look and who so steadfastly looks at us, it is Barthes's mother of whom he should have said, 'she is dead and she is going to die'. It is her eyes that should have met ours, ours and his. But he could not, certainly he did not. Instead, and most paradoxically in this of all books, there are words alone. In front of the mother stands the son: it is his own death that Barthes avoids confronting. In looking at Lewis Payne we confront, if we have imaginations and any degree of empathy, death by hanging, pain, almost unimaginable pain, the end of his life; but also *our own deaths*: death by empathy. However, if Barthes had had more courage here, had brought himself out of his private pain into the public realm of the text, he might have seen something other than death: life.

Time does indeed pass. We do indeed all die. However, there is more to time than this, as shown by photographs we have a particular kind of subject relationship to and can construct both their prior and subsequent 'moments'. This can be shown by discussing some actual photographs.

Consider again the photograph of Lewis Payne. I can locate this photograph in moving time by whit of imagination and intellect: for its prior 'moment' I conjure up political reasons and a consequent killing, then the detention and trial of Lewis Payne and his co-conspirators; for its subsequent 'moment' I conjure up a beating thudding bounding heart, the rush of blood and panic, being taken, a hood, a noose, and then, then something my mind and feelings shy away from, return to only in unguarded moments of thought. I have seen photographs of the Lincoln assassins being hanged; from frame to frame I have followed the twists and turns and kicks of those men, although in an experience from which my feeling mind slides.

As my conjurings make clear, these are not actual moments, actual slices of real time, but are rather constructions made up of thoughts, feelings and assessments which coalesce in a particular form when I think about this photograph and no other, when I think about this photograph now and at no other time. And nor are any of these 'moments' actually mine, for I am 'in them' only as Stanislavsky (a reputedly poor actor) is in any of the acting roles he describes: not actually the policeman, the judge, the husband, but playing one. Here I play at being in the role of Lewis Payne, inside but only to a degree, actually always on the outside looking in. And then of course here there is time in its role of death: Lewis Payne is dead and he is going to die. However, there are other photographs, other 'moments', other kinds of time.

The photographs I consider now are 'personal' photographs, photographs that the seer has a direct subject relation to, and indeed often in as well. The 'moments' the seer can construct as prior and subsequent to these photographs enable more analytic purchase on them and on 'the self' as a socially located construct, rather than a psychoanalytic reduction; and this social location is often, indeed typically, one produced by the social consumption of photographs, for they are often looked at in different kinds of groups and during occasions when other people contribute to knowledge of both the occasion of the photograph and also the biographies of those in it and those associated with it. In taking further this notion of the photographic 'moment', I discuss some photographs I have a direct subject-relation to.

Dr Liz and the tardis

Consider the child in the photograph by Long of Portsmouth. On the back is the statement 'Lizbeth Ann Stanley aged 2 years and 3 months' in my father's handwriting. This photographed child has all the hall-marks of 1940s and 1950s high street dominant cultural convention that one could hope to find: so clean, so posed, so careful. The photograph is a monument to 'the child' as she ought to be. The child is me – or so she is said to be, so I am told. But I do not know her. My memory cannot reach this child: she sits alone looking out and I look back into her eyes and see and feel nothing. No prior 'moment' exists here for me except through imagination and intellect: neither memory nor feeling reach back this far into the only 'the past' that is indubitably mine, except that here I have no such possession, no 'mine' exists here.

Should we leave it at this? turn our minds away having merely

Figure 4.
Author seated in frock

Figure 5. Author with football

named the convention? Surely not, for this is to miss opportunities for a richer feminist analysis, one which advances beyond knee-jerk dismissal.

Consider this second child, the footballing girl, also me. Here, like Athene from the head of Zeus, I, a conscious subject, spring into life. Here I am four in Johnny Davies's grandparents' back garden. Here memory reaches, and reaches beyond. In the 'moment' of this photograph is collected a perpetual transformation of clothes – what I was supposed to wear and what I wanted to wear. It also encompasses all the forbidden activities: streams and newts and dirt and forbidden building sites and, more concretely, scrumping apples, for in this child's shirt there is literally stolen fruit. And beyond the photograph, in its subsequent 'moment', lies a round of battles over what kind of a child I was to be, mine or my parents'; a round of partial losses and later gains. And there is more here, for I can connect this child to the 'me' I know now.

Both of these moments collect in what is of course not literal memory, in the sense of recollection which has a direct and unproblematic link with past 'facts'; it is rather a post hoc construction of the past based on the understandings, assessments, conclusions and conjectures of 'now'. 'Now' is a kind of prism through which both 'moments', and also the pivot of the photograph to which they connect, are refracted.

In this photograph the child who was me stands, foot on ball, hair scraped back in a pony-tail, silver bracelets still on her wrist two years on from the first photograph of the stranger-child to whom I stand outside. She is encompassed in time, this second child, surrounded by it; for she still lives in and through me. This photograph does not end in death – or at least not yet, for I still live, kick, write. And when it does it will be death for some other seeing eye than mine, for my own death is one death I will never gaze back on from any subsequent moment. In this sense 'my' death will never belong to me, only to those who live after and remember. In this second photograph 'I' am set free from the cage of unself-consciousness I was in in the first; as I write these words I am still free, for, unlike the photographs of human flies in amber lingered over by Barthes, here I have movement and thought; and living memory aided by these small pieces of sliced time enables me to chart in various ways the route between 'then' and 'now', and I delight to do so.

As far as I can remember (construct, refract 'then' through 'now'), much (how much is 'much' I wonder?) of my childhood was spent in small rebellions, dark tempers, hot angers. Beneath the surface of convention an angry only barely conforming girl is coiled, waiting. A third photograph of myself. This one I call 'rebellion', for its irony is that the polite cursory gaze of an outsider at its punctum reveals only convention and conformity.

Here is yet another model clean and feminine girl. And yet there are clues. There is the upturned mouth in what is not a smile, the eyes looking out but with no hint of laughter. The beret sits; certainly the moment before it must have been placed just so, the moment after and off it would have come, a prop to be used in that one particular second captured here. This child speaks to me, mutely calls me and only me; I want to answer 'time passes' and 'things will be different'. I want to be a ridiculous knight errant to the rescue of my young damsel past; but she cannot hear, see, she only is in a perpetual present, and my heart aches for this captured child.

Susan Sontag talks about photographs as invitations to deduction. This may be so for those photographs we are strangers to except by imagination and intellect (consider: there are no photographs at all in Sontag's book). Those photographs that grab us by the memory, that stir our own emotion recollected in something like tranquillity, need and deserve more attention to what lies *inside* them for seeing eyes: induction. Such 'seeing eyes' have their sight enabled first and foremost by the direct subject-relation of the seer as a participant, an insider; then, secondly and connectedly, by the fact that the memory of participants and insiders can locate the moment of the photograph, its small slice of time, to other moments and other times. Instead of sliding through the surface into generalisation, as Susan Sontag does, or through the surface into the unconscious as Roland Barthes does, we are better served by using it to open up *conscious particularities.*

Susan Sontag also talks about photographs as 'attempts to contact or lay claim to *another* identity' (Sontag, 1977, p. 16, my emphasis), an assessment that could be made only by someone writing and thinking about basically anonymous public photographs. A more interesting task is to use iconographic photographs from our own constructed pasts to enable us the better to lay claim to our *own* identities. I intend this not as the capturing of any essentialism of course, but rather as one means among others of understanding

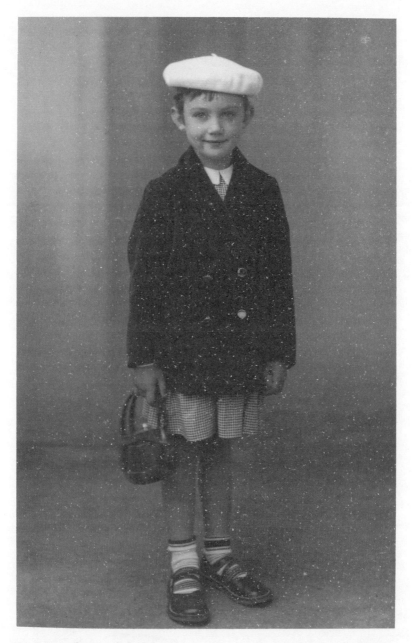

Figure 6. Author with beret

Figure 7. The auto/biographer's desk

something of the social and thus political sources of 'who I am', in the sense of 'how I understand and construct myself' in the here and now.

I may seem to have travelled a long way from the use of photographs in auto/biography. However, I am actually only a short step from where I started: what is confusing is the intrusion of time. Memory is the key here, that slither of constructed *post hoc* understanding that apparently acts as a shaft of light reaching from now back into 'the past'. But I take it as axiomatic that it does not and cannot actually 'reach back into the past'; and my interest in this constructionist view of memory is one which is directed towards a better understanding of the parameters of 'here and now', because 'here and now' has little meaning unless it encapsulates some understanding of a 'there and then'. More simply and succinctly: the appeal of photographs such as these is that they provide us with a history made visible (seemingly so), an almost tangible autobiography. Representation may not be all, but it is certainly something.

A romantic end

I pursue this point by means of a romance. Consider the last photograph here, which I call 'the auto/biographer's desk'.

A romance is 'a story', a tale; not 'facts', not 'the truth'; in some senses 'a lie'. As I noted earlier, lies and lying are immensely complex, at least as complex as truth – indeed the one is often mistaken for the other. And lies work in precisely the same way that truth does: both are socially accomplished using the same means, both *artfully* put together and put across, except that the one is (presumed to be) less self-consciously artful than the other.

Another paradox: a lie can often hold more truth than the truth. This photograph of the auto/biographer's desk is precisely a lie, for it is a construction for the moment of the photograph. My desk has never looked quite like this, its collection of things has been assembled for the particular purpose of telling this artful truth or this artful lie – whichever you the reader prefer – about myself as an auto/biographer. Much like a sample survey, it sets up an unreal reality, an intellectual framework within which to collect together a number of artifacts which, taken together, add up to 'a thesis'.

However, I do have this desk in this room; these bookshelves are to that side; and at least some of these items are usually and typically resident on my desk. Realism intrudes, then. Indeed the room is as it is, the desk is the one it is, its artefacts are those that I have chosen and placed in order in *everyday life* to create a pleasing fiction, a romance about the auto/biographer's desk which daily surrounds me as I work. The 'lie' of the photograph embodies a 'truth' which is itself 'a lie' but a lie made truth. Precious little realism, but a good deal of enjoyment in a kind of joke on myself and my own seriously romantic sensibilities about auto/biography writing. I take the piss out of myself, but in a loving way.

The 'moment' before this photograph is a complex one, full of sights and sounds and smells and tastes. It is actually Christmas Day, December 25 1986. I have recently returned from a pre-Christmas visit to my mother with family photographs, a sock present in the first photograph of me at 2 years and 3 months, a hairbrush and mirror from the same time. I am indulging in Sontag's 'imaginary possession of a past that is unreal' (1977, p. 9). Imagining the unreal: remembering the real: imagining the un/real.

The surface of this photograph is filled, auto/biographically speaking. The open notebook is my diary in which I am writing of the visit to my mother; on its blank left page is a lock of my two year old curiously blonde hair; above it to the left is the album from which the photograph of the footballing four year old me lives. To the top of the album are photographs of Hannah Cullwick, whose diaries I edited and published. In front of these is Ruth First and Ann Scott's biography of Olive Schreiner, about which I have written. To the right of the book there is a photograph of my mother, resplendent as Greta Garbo or quietly noble as Celia Johnson. Then above this the larger photograph of my father, extraordinarily aged only 17 and looking like a mafia hit-man: baby-face Joe. Then there are books, each speaking to 'a slice of time' in my life.

Romances have an innocence, however artful their composition, for they contain no foreknowledge. With benefit of hindsight, from a subsequent 'moment' to that of the photograph, I can see this innocent lack of knowledge. What came after was my father's death, that of my lover's father and those of two friends, then my mother's devastating stroke. The photograph holds, but does not reveal to any outsider, pain, death and loss. However, the seeing eye that perceives this is still 'I', still mine, and anyway this succeeding 'moment' holds more than pain alone. The seeing I is currently alive and kicking.

These deaths and those biographical ones I have written about –
Hannah Cullwick, Olive Schreiner, Emily Davison – are encompassed
in this frame; but each of these people also has life of a kind, through
me. It is said that this is what parents want children for, to achieve
this special kind of immortality. If this is so, then I am the child of
the childless Emily Davison and Hannah Cullwick and of Olive
Schreiner, the grieving mother of a still-born daughter, more truly
than of any 'real' parents.

Only when the seeing eye that gazes on the photograph has this
particular subject-relation to and with the image therein can the
'death and again death' quality that Roland Barthes sees as the essence of
all photographic moments be, if not banished, then at least put in its
rightful place as a part of life. John Donne's poem says '... Death/ Be
not proud... Death,/ Thou shalt die'. Death does indeed 'die' in this
photograph, at least as an absolute end. Death becomes a mere
qualification to life within this photographic frame; it takes on a 'but
also' quality, as individual lives and deaths meld into the flow and
become part of other future, now present-day, now past, lives.

The seeing eye is always a living eye, a living I. When the seeing
eye gazes on photographs with which it has a direct subject-relation,
its gaze infuses the photograph and everything therein with life, even
if only of a kind. Of course this is not to banish death, but it does put
a perspective on it quite absent from Barthes's elegiac lament on
death's all-power and absolute infusion of all photographic representation. The central lie of *Camera Lucida* is fascinatingly knotted, multi-
coloured, invitingly patterned; it is a lie worth examining, unpick-
ing, re-knotting, more than most truths are. But it remains a lie,
composed to stand between Barthes and a mother and a self he could
not face, and, like a pied piper, he seduces readers away from facing
it as well. We must become willing to let death in the door, have its
place at the table, in front of the camera, look it in the eye, for only
by doing so can we diminish it by seeing it as it is. To recoil, to try
to banish its actuality by banishing its photographic presence in
photographs of past times, to refuse to confront living *and* dying
people, is understandable given Barthes's then-recent loss of his
mother. Understandable and unforgivable, the intellectual short-
change presented in rainbow colours.

Once we reject death as an absolute end to personal time, then
gaining an analytic purchase on photographs enables us to become
time-travellers. Sontag moves from 'now' to 'then' in a one-way

A. H. Lawrence

movement. Barthes moves from 'now' to 'then' and then forward
into death, in a two way process but one with an absolute end. Once
death is shifted from the position he assigns it, becoming simply a
falter between the heartbeats of one person and others, a stage
within the long stretching line of common lives, then we can
encompass death within our lives, move both to it and from it.

The photograph 'the romance of the auto/biographer's desk' is a
tardis; when I enter the photograph I can move through time, move
through a variety of times indeed. Herein is Hannah Cullwick in the
1870s, Olive Schreiner in the 1890s, my father and mother in the
1920s and 1930s, myself in the 1940s, as well as myself in person
but not in presence in the 1980s. These 'times' I create in my time-
travel are not 'real time' of course, but then neither are actual times
past real to us either.

It is not only biography that is a construct: so too is autobiography. Autobiography is at least as much the imaginary possession of a
past that is unreal as any photograph, and the 'self' it creates is at
least as 'unreal' in the Sontagian sense as the image in a photograph.
How ironic it is that Colette, that most self-conscious of artful auto/
biographers, should have been 'accused' of tampering with her past,
of creating contradictory realities that confuse and annoy commentators and biographers intent on tracking down 'the truth'. How
pleasing it is that she should have written, from her upstairs
arthritic's prison that became a tardis for her free movement in time,
that her past was the coinage of all her writing − 'fiction' and 'fact'
− and that it was hers to spend as she chose. In the last analysis (the
only one worth making?), the *autobiography* 'the life of Colette' was
the conscious product, the artifact, of the *biographer* Colette's art, her
fiction. Or, another way to see it, her *fiction* was the product of her
life and thus of *fact*. Or, yet another way, the *biography* 'the life of
Colette' (by various biographers) was actually the artful product of
her as an active *autobiographer*. Or, she lived and remembered and
wrote.

Exit the autobiographer, myself as a fictive textual construction
even if not a fictional one.

Notes

1 An early version of this paper was given at a 'Writing Feminist Biography' conference in Manchester in 1988; it later appeared in *Studies in Sexual Politics* no. 26/27. I am grateful to Maggie Humm and to Jo Spence for comments on this earlier version.
2 And even more so with James Dean of course.
3 This work for this book was was carried out with that most exemplary of researchers Ann Morley; Ann, however, preferred to work on the research part of this joint endeavour and not its writing aspect.
4 And see here the discussion in Stanley, 1984b.
5 See for example Munby's diary entry for 17 March 1866 (Hudson, 1972, pp. 219-20) for an example concerning written rather than visual texts.
6 Barthes says this was for the attempted assassination of American Secretary of State W. Steward, while other books say for his part in the assassination of Abraham Lincoln. Whichever, the man was indeed hanged.

Part I: On auto/biography

Introduction

The two chapters in the Introduction have set out the various interlinked topics and themes to be addressed in the rest of this book. The chapters which compose Part 1 pick up and explore these, focussing in particular on autobiography, although necessarily also dealing with its intertextuality with fiction and with biography.

In Chapter 3 a number of fictional accounts of autobiographical research processes of different kinds are discussed in some detail, as well as the role of fictions, or 'fictive devices', in written and spoken accounts of lives. Fictional accounts of the production of written lives explore many dimensions of this process which convention requires should be omitted from published lives, and so these can give readers insights which autobiography denies them. The origins of both autobiography and the novel are intertwined, and Chapter 3 is concerned with a number of variants of this intertextuality.

Chapter 4 looks at feminist theoretical accounts of the autobiographical enterprise and relatedly at the constitution within these of a feminist canon of 'good' autobiographies written by women. Key arguments of such canonical writing, greatly influenced by postmodernist ideas, propose anti-essentialist ideas of 'the self' and anti-representational views of writing, resulting in the analytic excision of 'bio', or 'life', from 'autography'. In contradistinction, Chapter 4 proposes that by focussing on 'bio', the narrative of the life itself, autobiographers' own sense of the ontological complexities of self is revealed, whereas canonical writing treats such an awareness as an analytic privilege only.

The intertextuality of autobiography encompasses biography as well as fiction. Chapter 5 suggests that within biography this intertextuality is denied by excising the active and contingent presence of the biographer, thus preserving the de facto positivist claims of biography as constituting a kind of science producing 'the truth' about its subjects. Conventionally biography enshrines an essentially closed text to which readers have a 'take it or leave it' relationship only. Accounts of biographic processes, however, encourage active readership by making available for scrutiny aspects of the 'intellectual autobiography' of biographers – how and why they reach conclusions - or lack of them – about their subjects; and Chapter 5 provides a detailed example of this.

3

Fictions and lives

Fiction and autobiography

The complex intertextuality of fiction and autobiography is as old as the novel: *Robinsoe Crusoe, Clarissa, Sir Charles Grandison, Tristram Shandy, Pamela*, and later *Jane Eyre, Oliver Twist* and *David Copperfield*, come readily to mind. Less well known perhaps is just how often those women who were early contributors to the novel did so through writing fictional autobiographies. One of the best must surely be Frances Sheridan's gripping, witty and often hilarious *Memoirs of Miss Sidney Biddulph* (1761/1987). This was preceded by Sarah Fielding's *The Governess* (1749), and Eliza Heywood's *The History of Miss Betsy Thoughtless* (1751) was a great influence on Fanny Burney's *Evelina* (1778), which itself influenced a later generation of women writers.

What such a mixture of genres permitted, indeed encouraged, was a focus on the unfolding of one particular life, one particular self. For writers such as Frances Sheridan, this new form enabled a focus of attention not on any self, but a *female self* and one who thereby became a woman of importance, of study, of interest, as did the seemingly ordinary facts of her life. The growth of the novel went hand in hand with the claiming and identification of a *referential* self for women as key actors in the drama of social life.

It is instructive to note that it was the *novel* and not autobiographical writing that initially enabled women to make directly referential claims for the female self, for made through fiction these could be presented as less seditious, and less seductive for women readers, than seems actually to have been the case as witnessed by women's contemporary letters, journals and diaries, and journalistic writing. Women's published autobiographies of the eighteenth century, like those of the seventeenth century (Graham *et al*, 1989), continued to find other sources of legitimacy and authority. Then later the actor Fanny Kemble's diaries (1835, 1863) became an important nineteenth century influence in increasing the acceptability of a more immediately referential style of women's autobiographical writing, in part because of her fame and social acceptability, in part through the interest in the very public breakup of her marriage, but also because of their testimony against slavery.

The intertextuality of different genres and particularly the intertextuality of fiction and autobiography are as important now as they have ever been. Indeed arguably more so, for in the last decade of close analytic attention to the poetics of autobiography there has been ample recognition of the role played by fictions within the apparent facts of autobiography, of the genre's *creation* rather than representation of self. I discuss the feminist contribution to this in Chapter 4, while outlining an extension of such a theory to other forms of life writing in Chapter 5. However, in this chapter I explore the connections between fiction and autobiography by looking at themes within a number of fictional accounts of the process of producing autobiography.[1] I discuss how Julian Barnes's *Flaubert's Parrot* (1984), through the use of metaphor and a particular kind of narrative structure, encourages readers to treat biography and autobiography as intertwined, and how Maxine Hong Kingston promotes dissolution of the boundaries between reality and mythology, between self and other, in *The Woman Warrior* (1977). I then look at the contrasting treatments of feminist biography provided by Alison Lurie's *The Truth About Lorin Jones* (1988) and by Jan Clausen's *The Prosperine Papers* (1988); and then move on to discuss Rosemary Lively's *Moon Tiger* (1987), which offers a particularly stunning perspective on the relationship between history and auto/biography. However, I begin with a more general consideration of some strands of the complex and fascinating relationship between fictions and the writing of lives.

The autobiographical pact and the autobiographical canon

Philippe Lejeune (1975, 1977, 1989) proposes the existence of an 'autobiographical pact' tacitly held between, and governing the relationship of, an autobiographer and their readers. This 'pact' is said to have originated with Jean-Jacques Rousseau's *Confessions* (1782/1953) and is one in which the autobiographer confessionally writes, with his hand on his heart, 'the truth, the whole truth, and nothing but the truth' about his life and self. Thus the reader is assured they are reading an essentially referential account of the autobiographer's life, one which represents as truthfully as possible that life on paper, for there is a complete synonymity between the protagonist, the writer, and the person whose name appears on the title page.[2] It is on these grounds that Lejeune bars Colette, whom many consider France's greatest writer of autobiography, from the autobiographical canon. Hers are writings which artfully mix fact and if not entirely fiction then a great many 'fictive devices' of various kinds, and they are writings which openly play with the conventional boundaries between the writing genres of auto/biography and fiction. Indeed, there are few women who are admitted to the canon as specified by male writers on autobiography: substantially the same relentless progression of the names of 'great male autobiographers' is invoked in whatever account one turns to.

There are good reasons for the excision of women autobiographers from the canon: a good many of them are dangerously ironic in their treatment of the genre, and they explicitly and artfully play with the conventions of genres, for part of the project which underpins their autobiographies is to recognise the necessary role that 'fiction', in the form of non-referential accounts of the self, has in autobiographical writing.[3] Of course there is more going on here than simple exclusion: like any other hegemonic structure, the power of the canon lies not in its existence as a fixed body of texts but rather its operations as a process which can absorb and neutralise opposition and challenge. Equally, the critic is not all-powerful, and successful challenges to the canon can be mounted by both writers and readers of a particular genre.

The writer of auto/biography has, at the 'moment' of writing, an active and coherent 'self' that the text invokes, constructs and drives towards. Nevertheless there is also textual recognition that 'the past' is indeed past and thus essentially unrecoverable – that, in Barthes' (1975) terms, 'the self who writes' no more has direct and unproblematic access to 'the self who was', than does the reader; and anyway 'the autobiographical past' is actually peopled by a succession of selves as the writer grows, develops, and changes. Such a view of autobiographical writing, for instance, is explicit in Mary McCarthy's *Memories of a Catholic Girlhood* (1957). Here memories are invoked and lovingly described in close convincing detail – and are then shown to be faulty and based on a mixture of fictions and fact. McCarthy, for instance, remembers being punished for stealing her brother's tin butterfly, actually removed by the uncle who punished

her for her supposed transgression. However, she later discovers that
the uncle's transgression was a wishful fiction retrospectively constructed. McCarthy suggests that only comparatively rarely are lives
deliberately fictionalised: rather they are the product of memory
with all its faults and tricks. When it comes to the past, memory
actually witholds the key, for we inevitably remember selectively.
Memory's lane is a narrow, twisting and discontinuous route back
through the broad plains of the past, leading to a self that by
definition we can never remember but only construct through the
limited and partial evidence available to us – half-hints of memory,
photographs, memorabilia, other people's remembrances. Autobiography and biography are as one here.

But there is more to the fictionalising of the auto/biographical
past and present than this. Because memory inevitably has limits, the
self we construct is necessarily partial; memory ties together events,
persons and feelings actually linked only in such accounts and not in
life as it was lived; it equally necessarily relies upon fictive devices in
producing any and every account of the self it is concerned with.
Also we assume, those of us involved in the production and
consumption of such accounts, that people do indeed have 'a self'
that can be invoked and described in autobiographical (written and
spoken) accounts. We may accept that this self is a 'Western' notion
rightly disputed by anthropologists as less than fully meaningful in
other cultures, but how many see it as a cultural imposition by the
literate intelligensia which has worked its way into the speaking and
thinking practices of the non-literate non-intelligensia? Yet it is
surely so, and here it is instructive to contemplate my Mother's
remark,[4] made in her late seventies and with all relatives and friends
of her generation now dead, that she no longer exists, no longer has
a life. In addition, if memory is necessarily limited, and fictive
devices are always necessary in producing accounts of our selves,
then all selves invoked in spoken and written autobiographies are by
definition non-referential even though the ideology of the genre is a
realist one. And lastly, the apparently referential and unique selves
that auto/biographical accounts invoke are actually invocations of a
cultural representation of what selves should be: these are shared
ideas, conventions, about a cultural form: not descriptions of actual
lives but interpretations within the convention.

Everybody's autobiography

At the height of the modernist movement, indeed at its epicentre in Paris in the early decades of this century, Gertrude Stein was busy dismantling the still-emergent auto/biographical form described in Chapter 1 as 'modern'. The arguments treated as the cutting edge of a 1980s and 1990s postmodernist position were staples of Gertrude Stein's writings and particularly of The Autobiography of Alice B. Toklas (1933) and Everybody's Autobiography (1938).

The Autobiography of Alice B. Toklas is written as a straight (pun intended) autobiography by Toklas, although centrally featuring Stein, until near its end when it is 'revealed' that its author is Stein herself; the reader then figuratively re-reads the book as actually Stein's biography. Its publication made Stein open enemies among erstwhile friends because it fictionalised ruthlessly aspects of their characters and behaviours, leaving them vociferously to protest that these things weren't true (Hobhouse, 1975). What none of them commented on was that equally it fictionalised and mythologised the behaviour and character of Gertrude Stein as a genius, and portrayed genius as the source of her wayward, eccentric, egocentric and difficult character. Indeed, this book should be seen as a key means of constructing Steinian mythology, not merely reflecting it.

Everybody's Autobiography moves Stein's larger deconstructionist endeavours several stages on. On one level this book is concerned with the impact on Stein's life of the lionising in America and elsewhere that followed the enormous popular success of Alice B.... It is also, and I would say primarily, concerned with two closely intertwined understandings: that fictions are a major source for understanding and producing the facts of our lives and our selves; and that constructions of selves are so culturally embedded that even the study of apparently atypical autobiographies (of 'geniuses' like Stein in particular) in fact opens a route to everybody's autobiography: we all share knowledge of the conventions of typical selfhood and its accoutrement, and also of typical departures from convention; and one self is linked, by convention, to all others.

These ideas deny the masculinist perception of autobiography – centrally present in writing about the autobiographical canon if not so clearly or so often in many autobiographies written by men – as the unfolding or development of a coherent, mature and completely actualised unique self. No wonder Colette has to be driven out, the lid to the canon (rather like that to the ark of the covenant) slammed shut. No wonder that among those few women's autobiographies admitted to canonical status (although still subsidiary within it) are those of Maya Angelou, for these preserve the 'pact' by being constructed and presented in apparently the same representational form as those autobiographies of male members of the canonical club. There are no doubts here, no discovered tricks of memory, but a clear narrative complete with the thoughts and detailed conversations of many years before (although alternatively Angelou's work can be seen as an ironic plundering of the canon for political purposes, along with other black spiritual, slave and blues autobiographies).

Yet writing of the shared 'masculinist perceptions' of autobiography is to do many male autobiographers an injustice, to reduce complexities to a type. Consider F. Scott Fitzgerald's 'The crack-up' (1936), in which the autobiographer has no self, is a hollow man indeed whose psychological survival is dependent on the deliberate construction of a public self based on characteristics and behaviours drawn from admired male friends which literally masked an inner absence, a nothing. The alternative, however, is that this is a mask for a denied self, a self which can consequently be seen not as responsible for itself because it does not exist.

And yet the point remains that those critics who invoke and maintain the existence of an autobiographical canon do construct it in referential and representational ways and see fictionality as the complete antithesis of autobiography. However, many interesting autobiographies and theoretical discussions of autobiography are to be found in quasi-fictional or actually fictional form. Consider again Mary McCarthy's Memories…, some of which was originally published as fiction although not all of this was submitted by her to journals as such. McCarthy rescues this writing and re-presents it as accounts of acts within an autobiographical corpus; but at the same time deconstructs it to show readers not only the role of non-remembrance, the tricks of memory even when written in the most determinedly factual manner, but also and perhaps more interestingly the ways in which 'memory' and 'fiction' fuse – or rather how fictions may actually hold more truth about the past than a factual account (for the uncle was persecutory, filled with ill-will, wanted to do injustice, whether he 'really' hid the tin butterfly or not).

This symbiotic relationship of memory and fiction is challengingly explored by Colette and by Gertrude Stein. Often a reading of

Colette's work implies a stereotype of her as 'the woman novelist' who cannot invent character because of her lack of inventive powers and so who has to use real people and events as the basis of her writing. Gertrude Stein's work is frequently presented as wilfully mystificatory; either empty phrasemongering or resoundingly encoded to hide her lesbianism. A feminist re-reading of both against a backdrop of deconstructionist ideas about selves and fictions, however, proposes a different view of their writing as actually showing the complexities of 'different' genres.

The work of both women traverses the conventional boundaries of genres, thus its classification is difficult to achieve: Is Colette a novelist introducing fictions into her biographical and autobiographical work, or an autobiographer introducing real life into all her fictional compositions, or someone whose work elides both of these interpretations? Is Gertrude Stein a philosopher unable to cope with the discipline of formal philosophy and who therefore writes the same ideas in apparently fictional form? Or is she a ruthless autobiographer interested in ideas and fictions only so long as these can be made to cohere around her relentless exploration of her own ego: or perhaps a deconstructionist analytically taking apart the notion of 'genres', 'style', 'form' and 'self'? The work of both writers frequently traverses the conventional limits of existing genres. However, their rejection of the artificial in terms of genre boundaries by no means excludes or rejects artifice as a characteristic of its content.

The artifices whose ramifications Colette and Stein, in their different ways, are concerned with, stem from their recognitions that 'fiction' cannot actually be separated from fact, both in autobiography, and in lives as they are lived:

And identity is funny being yourself is funny as you are never yourself to yourself except as you remember yourself and then of course you do not believe yourself.... it could not be yourself because you cannot remember right and if you do remember right it does not sound right and of course it does not sound right because it is not right.... It is funny about novels and the way novels now cannot be written. They cannot be written because actually all the things that are being said about any one is what is remembered about that one or decided about that one. And since there is so much publicity so many characters are being created every minute of the day that nobody is really interested in personality enough to dream about personalities.... But now well now how can you dream about a personality when it is always being created for you by publicity, how can you believe what you make up when publicity makes them up to be so much realer than you can dream. (Stein, 1938 p. 53)

Both Colette and Stein treat 'self' as a fabrication, something pieced together over time, and past versions of which are worked and re-worked from the vantage point of whatever 'the present' such re/working is done from. There are radical differences between the 'Gertrude Stein' of *Alice B...* and of *Everbody's Autobiography*: in the former the author is omnipotent; in the latter Stein undercuts her authorial presence and authority, writing in a way that positions the reader within the text, moving the text and the story forward. 'Colette' is an ironic and seemingly peripheral presence within her overtly autobiographical writing, best seen for example (Colette, 1922) through the others she creates and especially through her depictions of her mother Sido, Sido's house, Sido's garden, and Sido's magical effect on her family and others. Yet this virtual silencing of self and the recreation of a Sido-filled childhood Eden stands between Colette and a betrayal of her mother, her surrendering of self to Henri de Juvenal, Sido's dislike and mistrust of him, and Colette's absence from Sido's last illness and death; while through and in the text Colette encapsulates the time before her fall, excises her betrayal of love. The autobiographical self in each woman's writing is a *writer* above all else; however, the circle between writer and autobiographer is sealed because of the implication throughout that writers – in any and every genre from philosophy to fiction – are also and necessarily dealers in autobiography: life is, after all, all any of us has.

'The past' is a very large place and stretches from the beginning of time to the instant before the moment at which you read this. 'Fiction' often has a very real and tangible presence in our lives, both for readers and also in an even more pertinent and undeniable way for writers. Such an intermingling of memory, autobiography, fiction, and the facts of everyday life, is interestingly explored from a feminist vantage point in Frankie Finn's novel *Out On The Plain* (1984), which shows 'reality' as a very shaky ontological experience indeed when we explore the boundaries between these supposedly different realms of experience. Within its pages a reader of the novel-in-progress by the author first takes over the task of writing and then becomes a character in the text ('out on the plain'); characters dispute their characterisation and dialogue; another reader rejects 'the end' and compels the novelist to continue.

Fictions have an immense draw for writers of autobiography – as autobiography does for writers of fiction of course. This is because fictions often enable more of 'truth' about a life to be written than a strictly 'factual' account, and this is particularly true of 'deviant' lives, such as those of lesbian women whose 'real' histories are sometimes impossibly difficult to investigate.[5] However, fictions also pose a threat to the autobiographical form: convention, in the work of those who write about the autobiographical canon and the precepts it is founded upon, specifies that autobiography is a factual account that enshrines a 'pact' between author and reader of truth-telling and the recreation of a life in written form. The draw but also the threat of fiction for autobiography is one well worth exploring further. I do so by looking at some fictional denials of the relationship; and I then look at fictional acceptances and explorations of it by five very different writers of novels.

In the arc-light of Schindler

In 1982 Thomas Keneally's Schindler's Ark was published, a fictionalised account of the real-life activities of Oscar Schindler in rescuing German and other Jews from Nazis and helping them escape to other countries. Schindler's Ark won the Booker Prize of that year, but in the context of a controversy which suggested that Keneally had done little more than to redescribe under a 'fictional' label the details of an account already published and known in factual form. The response was that the fictionalising was all-important and that Keneally's had been done outstandingly well. Slightly earlier, D. M. Thomas's The White Hotel (1981) was published; it too, among other matters, deals with the 1939-1945 war and the holocaust; and it includes a long sequence from its main protagonist, Lisa, drawn from published non-fictional sources. Thomas's novel was also highly praised; and it too occasioned a controversy about its use of unacknowledged non-fictional sources presented as fiction; and it was similarly successfully defended. Consider: Dr X or Dr Y in a sociology or an anthropology department publishes an ethnographic account of an urban western factory or a rural eastern village to a respectful and indeed rapturous academic reception, Later, reviewers point out that nearly all the included materials are factionalised versions of obscure 1950s novels. The response is that the factionalising is outstandingly well done and within a short time X or Y becomes a professor in their discipline. Well no. What is sauce for novelist geese is definitely not sauce for academic ones, for X or Y would be censured by professional colleagues for blatant and unethical plagiarism.

But techniques like these are not the only means novelists have for exploring the relationship between autobiography and fiction, and they are certainly not the most artful, inventive or sophisticated. I now move on to discuss a group of novels, each of which explicitly explores the fiction/autobiography conjunction in complex and interesting ways: Julian Barnes's Flaubert's Parrot (1984) and Maxine Hong Kingston's The Woman Warrior (1977), and then in more detail Alison Lurie's The Truth About Lorin Jones (1988), Jan Clausen's The Prosperine Papers (1988), and Rosemary Lively's Moon Tiger (1987). My particular concerns are with how each depicts the relationship between the narrator and both the subject and the reader; with their ideas concerning the autobiographical 'truth' about the subject; with how narrator and subject are dealt with as 'selves'; how time is dealt with, and how 'the past' is treated – what is suggested about how we can/should/might understand it; and finally with what 'biography' is seen to be, and its implications for 'autobiography'.

Who is the parrot?

Flaubert's Parrot is about a narrator, a recently widowed general practitioner, who is an amateur would-be biographer of Gustave Flaubert. It deals with his travels in France in search of Flaubertian memorabilia, his lengthy statements to a stranger on a channel ferry, his encounter with another biographer who later finds some long-missing Flaubert letters and then destroys them; and it also contains a sub-plot about his wife's suicide and her persistent sexual encounters with other men.

On one level that is. On another level, it deals throughout with the quirkiness, obsessive curiosity, concern with trivia, of a biographer; it respectfully parodies and also illuminates Sartre's certainly quirky and obsessively curious biography of Flaubert (1971). Its pinpointing of the oddities of the biographical quest was treated by some reviewers as indicating the particular and peculiar character of the doctor as a man, not as a biographer, and this is seen as a factor in his wife's infidelities and then suicide. However, these traits are actually the product of the relationship between any biographer and their 'subject', for circumstances drive the obsessiveness. The doctor's quest is to catch the elusive essence of Flaubert, which always eludes him, for every time he draws close he finds it gone: the parrot he finds is not the parrot of the book's title and Flaubert's life, but a random parrot from a museum store of dozens; Flaubert's house is gone, replaced by a railway yard; his letters were first found but then denied the narrator by being destroyed.

Biography is like marriage or any other longstanding intimate relationship. The parallels between the elusiveness of the essential Flaubert and the elusiveness of the doctor's wife are unmistakable. Both are actually unknowable, uncommitted to the narrator although central to his life, because other people are actually, essentially, unknowable to us, for we can never achieve a complete symbiosis with anyone else. Each self, like the doctor, is alone. Finding out about Flaubert is a metaphor for the doctor's other biographical investigation concerning his wife: and vice versa. Almost possessing Flaubert's letters, and thus knowing Flaubert's passion for Julie Herbert through his eyes and voice, is a metaphor for the narrator almost but not quite discovering and understanding the existential source of his wife's self-alienation and thus her anonymous adulteries and ultimately her suicide.

For the reader, this is heard in the voice of the doctor who is a direct and centrally present narrator. He speaks to us, we see things as he does howsoever we may then draw our distance. We listen to him – perhaps we are the stranger on the ferry; we are there and involved. He also makes it apparent on a number of occasions that he is witholding information about himself – so we are always also at a distance from him, separate, detached.

'The truth' about Flaubert/his wife is sought, but never found. This particular reader thought the doctor/narrator never wanted it to be finally found and possessed: better mystery, the journey, hope, than the banality of arrival. The complexity and elusiveness of what we call truth is signalled in a number of ways: the word-games that Flaubert plays, his shifts of character indicated by his animal guises; the word games indulged in by the doctor – the Flaubertian alphabet/dictionary he composes and which is presented in the text, for instance, but also his starts and shifts in talking to the stranger. Here too 'the self' is existentially alone, never finally meeting any other, subject to change by producing 'faces', now the bear, now the camel, the tiger or whale, in our relations with others. There is most certainly no representational view of the self in Flaubert's Parrot. The doctor is half-heard, half-seen in the dark on board ship, but these glimpses are fabrications of his, always covered with evasion, elision, excision. The parrot is a metaphor for the self: it could be the one, is actually one of many, could be and probably is any one of these others: a decentred self in metaphorical flight.

Because of the analogy between Flaubert and the doctor's wife, but also between the doctor and Flaubert, time shifts and buckles in complex ways. The doctor's Flaubertian biographical quest takes place in the actual present, but also in the documentary past which contains a time which still 'is' in the contemporary sources he is concerned with. The doctor's other biographical quest, for the meaning of his wife's life and death, is the sub-text that his search for Flaubert illuminates – and clouds; and this too shifts between present-time conjecturings and the conjuring up of past times which have been lived through and still possess an 'is' and not 'was' quality in the doctor's mind. These time-shifts parallel shifts between biography and autobiography, fact and fiction, in the world of the text. Here biography and autobiography, it becomes apparent, are indissolvably linked. The biography of Flaubert is pursued, explored and understood out of the autobiographical experiences of the narrator; the search for the Flaubertian presence and past is the search for the wife's presence and past but also the doctor's own elusive self as well: 'he' can exist only through these others, and, as 'they' do not exist except through him, 'he' as an essential self does not exist either.

Every girl her own

Maxine Hong Kingston's The Woman Warrior (1977) has won acclaim as a novel, as has her China Men (1981). It is often discussed as unproblematically autobiographical in both mainstream and feminist discussions of autobiographical writing (for example Eakin, 1985; Friedman, 1988). However, my discussion treats it as fiction, albeit fiction that is autobiographical. It tells the tale – is a 'talk-story' in its terms – of a Chinese girl growing up in America and thus among ghosts: grey spectres, not real people like the Chinese. Ghosts have a greater reality within its pages than white America: the ghost of the narrator's mother Brave Orchid's past as a doctor and healer; the ghosts of family history in China and especially the horrific death and bitter ghost of the aunt who was No Name Woman, (avenged by being named thus by the girl narrator); the ghosts of Chinese mythology re-worked and re-presented by Brave Orchid; the central presence of the triumphant and respected mythological woman warrior Fa Mu Lan, who the girl narrator becomes, entering this reality to dispute and transform her own.

Readers tend to assume a synonymity between the girl narrator and the young Maxine Hong Kingston, for the voice that speaks in the text is that of a narrator who is the writer of the tale. This voice is an immensely personal and personable one, admitting her readers into unknown times, places, people both mythical and real; we share her problems in discerning what is real, often rejecting reality as implausible, preferring the truths of myths and legends. It is also a voice with silences, for rather like Maya Angelou's rape and betrayal-produced refusal to speak, so the betrayals and intrusions of American society produce a similar refusal and muteness for the girl narrator. Yet as soon as readers know this, share the silence, so we also have foreknowledge that the future holds a triumphant kind of speaking in a different and authoritative voice: that of the author, whose realities we participate in on her terms.

The subject and the narrator are one person in The Woman Warrior, but they constitute a single self who fragments, becomes whole, dissolves and takes on the chosen identity of the bold, brave and triumphant woman warrior herself. The wheel turns another circle here: Brave Orchid in her own way, before the ghosts ate her soul, was a woman warrior, a shaman-healer, a successful battler with dirt and disease but also with ugly and malevolent ghosts such as the sitting ghost Boulder; and even after coming to America she successfully, albeit by telling it slantwise to avoid bringing ill-fortune on them both, sows the seeds of rebellion in her daughter.

The talk-story of The Woman Warrior takes place in present time, but a very particular and actually past present time: specific periods in the narrator's childhood. However, this time is cross-cut by lengthy removals into family and ethnic mythologies: the fate of No Name Woman, the exploits of Brave Orchid, the narrator's own exploits as Fa Mu Lan. But how to tell 'reality' and 'myth' apart here, for the archetypal heroic or victimised mythical Chinese women are also the women of her own family. Her own aunt is the No Name Woman used to frighten girl children into submission, her own mother is the woman healer and teacher, her own self is Fa Mu Lan: fictions and facts meld, as do America and China in the person of the narrator. There are also interesting complexities in distinguishing 'time' in the sense of chronology. The book has a timelessness about it: there is change and development but only within particular periods of childhood or out of time within mythological periods, and anyway these two times are interleaved.

The book leaves particularly female readers with much to think about regarding the position of women and girls in patriarchal societies such as the China the narrator/author invokes. There is the utterly ambiguous response of the mother to her daughter: know your place and stay in it, but escape if you're brave enough. There is the Chinese woman as victim, crushed, for all Chinese women are no name women who do not count; but privations make for rebellion and daring: a Fa Mu Lan lurks inside every girl and woman's heart, and a Brave Orchid is there who will not be constrained by circumstance to return to the place she had once escaped from. It also leaves us thinking that this is about China, and Chinese America, of the past, but also about all societies now. We see through the eyes and words of the girl narrator; we live in her reality. The parallels are unmistakable: this is all our lives.

The truth about ... ?

The Truth About Lorin Jones by Alison Lurie (1988) concerns the life and times of Polly Alter, an art historian turned biographer of dead female painter Lorin Jones, whose work is being re-valued (in both senses). Polly is a feminist whose once-hesitant political convictions are encouraged to take a stronger turn by feminist friends, particularly the marxist lesbian feminist historian Jeanne. Her marriage breaks up; and she discovers Lorin Jones and biography, and has an unsuccessful and disappointing affair with Jeanne. Jeanne tries to persuade Polly to reject her teenage son Stevie as well as her ex-husband and all other men. In Polly's interviews of the friends, colleagues, husbands and lovers of Lorin Jones, provided in the text through transcriptions of some of them, she hectors her interviewees and imposes her reality on theirs, for she wants only one truth: that Lorin Jones was a put-upon feminist hero put down by the male and masculinist art circuit circles she moved in. She starts an affair, passionately wonderful, with a jobbing builder met at one of the houses Lorin had lived in. Later she discovers both that Mac the builder was Lorin's last lover, a poet, and that Lorin had feet of clay and actually many of the men in her life, particularly Mac, had been highly supportive of her. She decides to move to Florida with her son to live with Mac, thinking about having another baby.

The main characters in Alison Lurie's book embody political

positions: Jeanne is the feminist, ergo also (all bad things) lesbian, marxist, man-hating; Polly is the brain-washed woman who only needs a good man and his sex to come to her senses; Mac is the wronged man blamed by feminists for women's own inadequacies. *The Truth About Lorin Jones* has been described as humerous and ironic. I see it rather as a morality tale preaching a warning against feminism and its man-hating simplicities. Its biographical aspects are instrumentally present only − the issues Polly faces as a biographer are products of her own approach, not those innate within the biographical enterprise itself, and their solutions require only a different attitude of mind. However, the means by which this morality tale is told are worth looking at, for its discrediting of lesbian/feminism is accomplished by interesting features of narrative style and structure.

The voice that speaks in the text is detached, omnipotent; it is a voice in the third person which comments on Polly rather than one which represents matters from her viewpoint. However, this voice is by no means the only one that speaks within it. Its detached narrative is cross-cut with transcripts of the interviews that Polly carries out; the reader 'hears' the hectoring and insensitive voice of Polly − a model of how not to interview, overriding the voices of those she interviews. But, interestingly, we hear her voice in *absentia*, through the responses to her of interviewees; her own speech is not transcribed but is actively inferred by the reader − we are thus made to discover her insensitivities and simplicities for ourselves.

The transcribed interviews, then, more than confirm the unsympathetic view of Polly as a feminist biographer. And that it is Polly's *feminism* which is at issue is made clear over and over: Polly's name is 'Alter', and in her unreformed pre-Mac state she also stands for the role of feminism in misunderstanding, manipulating, precisely altering from its slanted simplistic viewpoint what is actually complexly true. Polly cannot, until her relationship with Mac, even see, let alone handle, the truth about Lorin Jones. It is for this reason that she loses control of interview situations, reacts in the way she does, for the complexities of the 'real biography' of Lorin cannot fit in with the feminist approach Polly, through Jeanne, has adopted.

'Polly used to like men', the book begins (p. 1); Jeanne does not. Jeanne was raped and abused as a child; and this, the implication clearly is, has produced her manhating and lesbianism. Lorin too had a similar experience in childhood; Lorin too had damaged relationships with men. What Polly experiences as Jeanne's frustratingly passive and inorgasmic style of love-making is produced by the fact that she is a woman: this is how women without a man/penis are. Polly later willingly and gratefully surrenders to Mac, not least because he takes charge of sexual proceedings and her body. This surrender brings Polly back into the fold in more ways than one. Realisation breaks upon Polly. She fantasises of the glories of Mac's penis, his complexities as nurturant as well as controlling. She rejects the false self that has been constructed through Jeanne's influence; if she continued, 'She would become an angry, depressed lesbian feminist or a selfish successful career woman. And Lorin Jones would be established in the public mind as an innocent victim or as a neurotic, unfaithful, ungrateful genius; but it would all be lies' (p. 290). Angry or selfish are the only possibilities presented within feminism. But her fantasies then take her to Florida with Mac and her son; Polly is smiling and 'It was the real story that she was typing, the whole truth about Lorin Jones, with all the contradictions left in' (p. 291). Feminist biography is a false story, one which removes contradictions thus leaving effectively lies.

The descriptions, characters and roles assigned to Jeanne and to Mac, Polly's bad and good angels, are worth comparing. Jeanne is soft, rounded, never confrontational nor open nor honest, always evasive, refusing to say what she really means or wants. She tries to manipulate Polly's son Stevie out of his home – a growing male, he is *verboten* on Jeanne's territory – but shields this in lies and half-truths, manipulating Polly as well as Stevie. Jeanne is sexually passive, her love-making as rounded, smooth and unpeaked as she is herself; there are no climaxes here, only unfulfilled arousal. Jeanne stands for feminism: women damaged by atypical men and unrealistically hating the rest, women only half-actualised because of their separation from men. Jeanne is supposed to be a historian, but no signs of her intellect or profession appear anywhere in the book: she merely reads magazines, smokes endlessly, bakes, eats chocolate, and manipulates Polly. Mac is handsome and muscular; a poet and a manual tradesman, and we see him at work. He is active and in charge, passionate but also gentle, thoughtful and loving. He is open about his feelings, initially hides his identity but only to avoid Polly's rejection and guard his privacy. Mac is a fulfilled, actualised, sorted out human being: irresistible, Polly's happy end, and with a rosy penis to boot. But Mac is more than this. As well as representing

normal, ordinary but glamorous and commanding men, Mac was
Lorin's child, a younger lover, a toy boy who ended by supporting
and looking after his lover/mother. Polly has spent her life wanting
an involved loving father rather than the one she had – another
betrayal leading to a damaged feminism. Mac is some twenty years
older than Polly, a scholar/manual worker who is lover/father to
heal the wounds in her life.

The structure of the narrative is important in several ways to the
accomplishment of Polly's ultimate rejection of feminism and its way
of treating lives and biography. For instance, Polly becomes a part of
'the biography' of Lorin Jones. She identifies closely with Lorin, at
times imagines herself to be Lorin or to be possessed by her spirit or
ghost. She then 'becomes' her alter ego Lorin even more thoroughly
through her relationship with Mac, for Polly has the relationship
with him that Lorin was incapable of. By entering the relationship
with Mac through her identifications with Lorin, Polly becomes an
involved and committed presence in the biography she is composing.

The traditional happy ending to the book, Polly's unity with a
good man/rosy penis/new baby, is a move back to a version of Polly
before she was altered by Jeanne/feminism. Polly used to like men
and now does so again: and consequently feminism's distortions are
displaced, replaced. In addition, Polly finds the 'real truth' about
Lorin Jones, not the corruptions of truth enforced by lesbian feminist
(terms which the text treats as effectively synonymous) biography.
The 'real truth' biography of Lorin is inseparable from Polly's vision
of her new life with Mac and Stevie in Key West (and perhaps this is
also 'real (i.e. heterosexual) America' as opposed to the effeteness of
New York as represented by Jeanne and the art dealer Jacky,
homosexual, manipulative, camp and bitchy).

Finally and perhaps most importantly, there is Polly's symbolic
absorption into the past. Her own actual past contained the imposed
(from Jeanne/lesbian feminism) rejection of husband Jim. By the
end of the book and through Mac, Polly enters a time in which, to
paraphrase Betty Friedan (1963), there is no 'problem without a
name'. The problem of men has once more become the problem of
women, a product of women's misrepresentation, maliciousness and
manipulativeness.

The relationship between past and present, biography and autobiography, fact and fiction, centres on the message that the truth about
Lorin Jones can be recovered outside of the misrepresentations of

feminism. This truth may be contradictory, but it is nonetheless the truth. A representational view of biography and the self who is its object is implied by the rebuttal of feminism and its misrepresentations. Moreover the structure of the book excises 'the past' in another and crucial sense, for the book's contents are located in an ever-present: Polly, those people she knows or meets, those she interviews, all these voices speak in the present. There are no 'documents' of the past here other than brief references to Lorin's paintings; the key materials with which biographers work are absent. Moreover, these voices are the source of the competing and contradictory interpretations of Lorin Jones: it is clear that it is *interpretation* which is the source of contradiction and misrepresentation; but, beyond these, 'the past', with Lorin at its centre, is actually there in a graspable truthful form. Polly finally gains access to this, through Mac but also because her eyes have finally been opened to the ways in which misrepresentations and distortions occur. Paradoxically for a book that was described as encapsulating complexities about biography as well as for its wittiness about feminism, it in fact promotes a largely realist representational view of biography (of the truthful rather than the feminist kind).

Three cheers for Rose Bright and the past

The Prosperine Papers (Clausen, 1988) deals with the quest by feminist academic Dale McNab, initially to encourage her grandmother Rose Bright Schlaghoffer to put on paper a selection of her family stories and memories, and later to find out about and gain access to the papers of Prosperine Munkers, Grandma's loved friend and prototype lesbian feminist as well as socialist activist and journalist. Dale intends to publish a book about Prosperine, which would be partly a biography but also and importantly contain some of the published pieces Prosperine had written as well as material from her letters. Dale has to persuade Rose to let her have access to these, and does so while working in a half-hearted way on Rose's own writing. More and more Dale comes to see Prosperine as a right-on foremother, and one who will help her gain academic tenure and publishing success: tenure is denied Dale and her job comes to an end because of departmental prejudice against her as a feminist and a lesbian.

Grandma Rose and the rest of Dale's family live in Minnesota; Dale, her lover Linda who is a literary agent, and Linda's daughter Fiona, live in Manhattan. Dale arrives in Minnesota from a night of academic conference passion with a right-on black feminist. Her later confession of this is followed by Linda's affair with a younger woman, an author, Val. Dale descends into drunken self-pity and destructiveness in her personal life as the relationship with Linda ends. Her retreat to Minnesota to write becomes not only an escape but a means of healing herself; it also fuels her plans regarding Prosperine. However, during her absence and breakdown Grandma Rose has died and Dale finds she had deliberately destroyed her personal papers by and about Prosperine.

Increasingly books are being written for an explicitly feminist audience (Cranny-Francis, 1990). Jan Clausen takes for granted that her readers will know about the complexities of feminism, identify with it, and find lesbian relationships an ordinary and in themselves unremarkable fact of life; while Alison Lurie's book was written for an explicitly non-feminist audience, which is expected neither to know about nor to identify themselves as feminist or pro-feminist, and to find lesbian relationships peculiar. There is no inquiry here into what made Dale what she is, nor is it an issue. Dale is the narrator of this story and also (or is she?) its main protagonist; thus the reader sees and hears everything from Dale's viewpoint. The interspersing of her narrative by letters from Properine to Rose and extracts from Prosperine's other writings confirms her as a biographer going about her business. Only slowly do we recognise the specificity and partiality of Dale's viewpoint, that this is not quite what she has led us to believe; but by this stage readers have identified with Dale so much that we are fully complicit in her fall.

Her 'fall' as I have phrased it is two-fold. Gradually readers find out that Dale is an alcoholic, that she has consistently been drinking to excess and lying (including to the reader) about this, and that drink is the source of many of her problems – the troubles with Linda, tenure and her job among them. This process of finding out is subtly done, so that only on re-reading does the reader see just how many references to drink, to drunkenness, to lack of control in drinking, the text is spiked with from the outset. We are also made aware by the end of the book that Dale's desire to recover Prosperine and gain tenure has led to a moral fall, in which she abandons Gradma Rose's writing activities and uses her to get access to Prosperine's letters and other papers.

Dale's intent is to plunder the past to bring back a right-on feminist hero who will make her reputation and fortune in the

future. Her motives for doing so are, almost, acceptable: Prosperine
Munkers is a fascinating woman who lived out during the first two
decades of the century many of the sexual political and other
dilemmas that face contemporary feminism and socialism. But
Prosperine, as Grandma Rose makes clear, belongs to the past; our
present understandings of love, friendship, lesbianism, feminism, are
precisely those of the present and cannot be applied to Rose and
Prosperine without misrepresenting them, without being ahistorical
and ageist and riding roughshod over how they articulated their lives
and feelings.

'The subject' in this book is a split subject. Initially Dale is centred
and the reader is led to identify with her; later we find that the self
Dale has presented to readers is not her actual self. Then Rose takes
centre stage and the reader explores her present in the retirement
home and her past as a powerful although home-based matriarch,
and also an author because of the telling of richly evocative stories.
Rose is then displaced by the discovery of Prosperine and the search
for her through her own words. When Rose dies, having re-exerted
her authority over her own and Prosperine's past by denying Dale
the textual ability to impose her meanings on their lives, she enables
the past to re-possess itself by being and remaining precisely *past*,
finally unrecoverable. Readers increasingly construct their own biography of Dale and her activities, reach a rather different estimation of
her and what she does, and produce a moral judgement about Dale's
biographical intentions that reasserts feminist ethics over her lack of
scruples.

The 'real truth' about Prosperine is what draws Dale on, makes
her want to reclaim Prosperine for contemporary lesbian feminism.
But this 'real truth' comes out of Dale's moral as well as alcoholic
haze; and we are made aware of this through things additional to the
growing awareness of her drink problem. There are a series of minor
betrayals: she ignores the suposedly mundane past of Rose for the
heroic one of Prosperine; she consistently fails to suggest to Rose that
her papers should be properly archived while all the time implying
she will do this at some point; she steals a photograph of Prosperine
from an archive in one of the towns Prosperine has worked and been
politically active in. Together these signify her larger untrustworthiness, regarding drink, her relationship with Linda, Rose, and also
herself. She is a hollow woman.

At least two rather different views about 'the self' are present in

The Prosperine Papers. There is the realist project that Dale engages upon, to recover the true Prosperine, the baby dyke and all-round right-on feminist. Prosperine is to be reclaimed for present-day lesbian feminism, to be enshrined as herstory – and that this realist aspect of feminist biography is misguided is made clear as readers unpack the layers of misrepresentation Dale has provided. Then there is the anti-realist project that the book inscribes. The complicated contradictions that are Dale are unravelled, and thus the elusiveness of reaching any truth about her. And if there is no way of establishing the truth about Dale, then what chance of doing so for Prosperine, removed in time and in many other ways from contemporary comprehension? By the end of the book Dale has to learn to surrender her ego/self: the 'emptying' from Minnesota of the history of Prosperine and Rose enables Dale to retreat there annually, to leave behind the complexities, difficulties and self-filled life she leads elsewhere.

Time is an elusive presence in *The Prosperine Papers*. A single present-time narrative voice is maintained, that of Dale; but this is interspersed within another, although for us actually past, present-time: the time in which Prosperine was alive, active, thinking and writing. The voice that cross-cuts Dale's is that of Prosperine: a free, independent, loving and thinking presence confronting her life and its puzzles as best she can. Her struggles are incomparably greater than Dale's – no wonder her appeal. The past and its relationship to the present is signified in this 'dialogue'. There is the past as interpreted by the present in the form of Dale; but there is also tantalising and fascinating snippets of 'the past' in the form of Prosperine and her letters; and this past was then, at the time of writing, a present with its own concerns and modes of comprehension – and incomprehension, as witnessed by Prosperine's struggles to understand and name her emotions and desires for other women.

Biography and autobiography truly mingle here. Dale is trying to piece together a biography, Prosperine is trying to piece together an autobiography in which her self can be named. Dale is avoiding an autobiography and any kind of naming of her self, yet the reader is piecing together a biography for her. Dale is falling in love with Prosperine as an idealised lesbian feminist anti-racist socialist, but Dale is also *coveting*, as a possession,[6] Prosperine in a very instrumental way, wanting Prosperine for what she can do for her. This itself has a number of layers, providing a major publication, a tenured academic job, fame if not fortune in the eyes of other feminists. But it also gives Dale some kind of integrated coherent sense of herself, her history, where she has come from in terms of understanding and naming the loving of other women. Dale, it becomes apparent, has few inner resources such that she can accomplish this in her own time and through her own lesbian feminist connections. What she covets is a ready-made heritage but such greed for a past, it becomes clear, results in a betrayal of those women who lived before us. Dale's project of biographical reclamation is to claim these women as though they were us in fancy dress; but their struggles were theirs, not ours, their understandings their own and not failed versions of ours.

Was she was somebody?

Rosemary Lively's Moon Tiger (1987) is neither about feminist auto/biography nor is it by a feminist writing about auto/biography in novel form. It is however one of the most complex and erudite discussions of the epistemology of history and historiography and the place of individual biography within this that I have come across. Its plot is apparently simple: Claudia Hampton, a former highly successful writer of popular history, is dying from cancer in a nursing home; medical and nursing staff come and go about their business; she receives some visitors: her daughter Lisa, her sister-in-law Sylvia, a former lover Jasper, and Laszlo, a young Hungarian man she had befriended. As she dies thoughts of the past run through her mind. Other than that on the last page of the book Claudia dies, nothing of any significance happens. And yet everything happens: not just one life but many, from the beginning of time to the present; and through this major questions concerning the relationship between biography and social structure, between the individual and the many, between the past and the present, between the self and others, are teased out. Claudia does indeed write the history of the world, as she had said she would as the book and her dying began. More than this, Claudia is concerned also with the relationship between history and historiography, between the past and writing about it; and thus of course between her own thoughts and the actual past these are predicated upon.

The narrative structure of this book consists mainly of inner monologues, descriptions and reflections by Claudia on the personal but also the impersonal past: her life but also its stock in trade which was the lives of past others and how to write about them. These are interspersed by brief intrusions, in the form of an outside detached narrative from the present in which she is dying: doctors and nurses come and go about their business, the present is crucial and immediate for those locked within it and yet it intrudes on the past only minimally. Readers experience the past in the mind of a present-day consciousness, which is all the reality it now has. And because the past exists only through those representations which the mind constructs in the form of written and visual images, time exists in Claudia's mind out of chronological order. Time here is structured by the interconnections of the mind at work. And Claudia's mind is working very hard indeed, and these connections are highly logical ones in terms of the flows and ebbs of her thoughts, not thoughts ruptured to preserve temporal sequencing. The essential unity of things within the consciousness of the historian-author is explored in Claudia's attempts to investigate and understand historical events and persons: and, as a mirror of this, so too the reader tries to investigate and understand this particular past and this particular person who is Claudia.

The self here, Claudia's self, is a product of time, is in time, and is also a consciousness that does things with time. As she notes, unless she is in everything then she is in nothing. But this Claudia is her own woman, largely unknown to her daughter and even to Jasper. Claudia is guarded, secret, private; while another Claudia exists and has inner life. There is also the possibility of other Claudias, in particular the outer woman who might have lived had Tom, her lover met in wartime Egypt, not been killed. This Claudia died with Tom, or rather she was displaced and lived and grew older as the public Claudia did so. Tom too continues a life after his death. Claudia preserves a view of Tom; and yet when, as a consequence of an article and picture about Claudia in a newspaper, Tom's sister sends Claudia his diary written just before his death, she is made startlingly aware that this 'real' Tom is now a stranger, not hers any longer, for her Tom has moved on as she has moved on.

There is no 'narrator' as such in *Moon Tiger*. Readers are in Claudia's mind: rather than she having a voice which speaks to us, we inhabit her thoughts. It is obvious that 'the subject' of this fictional biography is Claudia; but for all her uniqueness, quirkiness, her education and erudition, Claudia is also everywoman. The reader is Claudia because we see and experience with her. We may identify with Dale, but we do not read as though we *are* Dale whereas we do with Claudia. I for one disliked Claudia, an arrogant ambitious male-

identified woman who has no female friends or colleagues nor even
any ordinary memories nor, seemingly, ordinary experiences. But
this made little difference to my interest in her, respect for her,
willingness to accept that this was indeed how Claudia experienced
things and to find this absolutely compelling reading.

'The self' is presented in Moon Tiger in non-realist terms, as
changing, complex, contradictory, never quite at home with itself,
never quite what it wanted or intended to be. Claudia's once
incestuous relationship with brother Gordon is presented as an
ontological puzzle for Claudia: Gordon is always other to her, yet
always the same; and where she leaves off and he begins remains an
issue, although one which changes as both grow older and then
Gordon dies. Tom becomes a part of her, a part of her self, and this
unity is encouraged because of the absence of an actual Tom.
However, the arrival of his diary also re-occasions Tom's presence as
an other, separate from her. There is no 'truth' held out here about
any of these people or relationships; they may be one thing or they
may be another, but they are just as likely to be both.

Claudia's ruminations on the relationship between history – that
is, the past – and writing about the past – that is, historiography –
also throw into sharp relief her ideas about the relationship between
self and others and particularly between the historian/writer, biography and autobiography. As she lies dying Claudia plans a history of
the world:

A history of the world, yes. And in the process, my own... Let me
contemplate myself within my context: everything and nothing. The history
of the world as selected by Claudia: fact and fiction, myth and evidence,
images and documents. (p. 1)

And as readers of Claudia's work have come to expect, in this there
will be no single narrative form, but rather 'life and colour... the screams
and rhetoric' (p. 2), because for Claudia what moves her to
investigate the past and its relationship to the present is the half-echo
of its sound, hint of its smells and tastes, almost feel of its emotions.
It is this that still anchors her to Tom and their love affair: even many
years on something unexpected will evoke the heat of Egypt, the
smell of Moon Tiger warding off insects, the feel of love and passion
and despair, so that she is both there and irrevocably parted from it.

Chronology irritates Claudia, for inside her head 'there is no
sequence, everything happens at once' (p. 2), and the Palaeolithic

period is only 'one shake of a kaleidoscope' away from the Victorian. She intends her written history to contain many voices, or perhaps it will be produced as a film – silent, impressionistic and dreaming. Her history is the product of what is inside her head, both public knowledge and private creation, in a process in which other lives are slotted into her own. As she notes, 'truth' is tied to the testimony of print, to words on a page. Moments in our own lives of enormous significance vanish as though they had never been; while many fictions not only endure but have complete reality. For Claudia, the substance of history as a professional activity is standing different versions of the past against each other and arguing out the pros and cons of each. Her commitment to versions is signalled also in the book's structure, for at a number of key points different versions of the same event – Claudia and Gordon squabbling over fossils on a cliff and Claudia falling, Claudia not wanting to have sex with Jasper at a conference in France – are provided. The reader is not only told about 'shakes of the kaleidoscope' but *experiences* them as we read.

The product of history, on the other hand, is immortality: 'I am the life hereafter. I, Claudia. Squinting backwards; recording and assessing' (p. 30). For as long as the present remembers the past, seeks to understand it and its links with the present, then the past continues to exist. Tom and then much later and in a different way Gordon continue to have life in her after their deaths. But that this is life of a different kind is made clear with the appearance of Tom's diary forty years after his death: this Tom is very different from Claudia's Tom; and Claudia's Claudia in the present is a very different woman from the one who was in love with and was loved by Tom. Claudia comes to think of herself then as 'she', not 'me'. And similarly with the writing of history, for 'I cannot shed my skin and put on yours, cannot strip my mind of its knowledge and its prejudices... I am as imprisoned by my time as you were by yours... Even so I get a *frisson* from contemplating you' (p. 31). Perspective is all, as her views about the history of Cortez and the Aztecs (pp. 153-65) emphasise. 'I Claudia'. *Moon Tiger* pays its dues gracefully, by such subtle acknowledgement of Robert Graves' *I, Claudius*, also a novel/autobiography about a historian who is both in the thick of things and removed, detached by cast of mind as much as his physical afflictions. Both Claudius and Claudia are mirrors of their times, but as active and minded interpreters – they make their selves, but not in conditions of their own choosing.

Alternative Claudias, the possibility of things being different than they are, quietly appear in the interstices of the book, leaving readers to think, including thinking about ourselves. And there are alternative histories too: Claudia 'intrudes' into the historical past in a Massachusetts tourist attraction which recreates the settlement of the Pilgrims in 1627, warning a puzzled 'pilgrim' of the 'future' dangers of using imported labour and pointing out historical inaccuracies of speech. Gordon can contemplate alternatives in personal history only; while, apart from him and Tom, Claudia's greatest emotional allegiances are to the many of humanity that people the past, the Aztec masses in one passage, endless lines of soldiers in the desert in another. Claudia understands that childhood is a past to which we no longer have access and tries to enter the secret inner world of her young daughter Lisa, who fends her off and keeps her privacy. Later Claudia is as completely wrong about the grown-up Lisa, as unable to move beyond the surface of appearance. But then Claudia is as secret, as separate and as removed from the surface appearance of herself, as is Lisa: all her deepest emotional responses are guarded and private. The odd confusion of private and public selves is mirrored in the relationship between past and present. Claudia uses Egypt as a metaphor to explain this, for she experiences Egypt as a continuous temporal phenomenon in which its kilted pharaonic population spills out into the twentieth century – 'Past and present do not so much co-exist in the Nile valley as cease to have any meaning' (p. 80).

Readings

What appear above are readings, particular readings, of the novels discussed. Other readers may well read and interpret characterisation, events and so forth differently. 'Reading' is a contingent activity deeply rooted in our autobiographies and the tools, means and knowledges these provide. One simple example is that I, a lesbian feminist, read Alison Lurie's novel through the knowledge I have about women and men like Jeanne, Jacky and Polly; whereas a reader who is neither is likely to read and understand the book and these characters very differently. I cannot separate how I read from my understanding of myself as someone who also writes histories of lives as well as reads them. Moreover, my reading is of the text, the book, the words on the page; it says nothing, nor should be taken to imply anything, about the intentionality of the authors of these books, for intentionality cannot be read from the text at all and anyway is an irrelevancy: what matters, and what is immediately accessible, is the book itself.

These books share an interest in the intersection of lives and fictions, but also in the complexities of the relationship between the past and the present and how this should be represented. They explore these matters often very differently, although with a perhaps surprising degree of overlap in the structural means they use to do so.

A variety of 'voices' speak in these novels, involved, representing particular and partial points of view. Readers experience through Claudia's mind, see and understand as Dale McNab does, are spoken to directly by the doctor, are told talk-story by the girl narrator of The Woman Warrior. But even Lorin Jones, with its detached third person narrative, also contains the voices of Polly's interviewees and through these, and the active reading of the reader, the voice of Polly herself.

Notions of auto/biographical 'truth' in any simple sense are eschewed in these novels. The past – and how it was understood by participants for whom it was their present – is re-claimed from Dale through Grandma Rose 'doing her duty' by burning Prosperine's papers; those of the present cannot understand the past and its people in anything other than their own essentially alien terms. Claudia Hampton is clear throughout that what the historian writes is her interpretation pieced together from the comprehensions of the present-day. In Flaubert's Parrot 'truth' about Flaubert and the doctor's wife is pursued but always eludes the biographer-narrator. And in The Woman Warrior more truth lies in myths and legends than in narrative descriptive accounts of the protagonist's everyday life. Again, The Truth About Lorin Jones comes closest to presenting a representational view of biography, with its emphasis on 'the truth' about the past lying behind the layers of interpretation, but nonetheless this book too sees interpretation as the material that the biographer has to deal with and come to terms with.

'The self' is depicted in complex non-representational terms in all of these novels. The self is fractured, changing, alterable and frequently an object as well as a puzzle to the subject whose self it is; and just who and what the biographical self consists in all depends on who is doing the seeking and what their viewpoint is. This is shown perhaps most clearly in *The Truth About Lorin Jones*, where a succession of people recreate entirely believable but actually different Lorin Joneses, each one of which at the time of telling Polly finds – as readers do – entirely plausible. It is also shown in the girl narrator being the woman warrior Fa Mu Lan as well as her everyday self, in the successive unpacking of new understandings of the character and behaviour of Dale, in the lies and evasions of the doctor, in Claudia's explorations of the links between her self and others such as Gordon and Tom and her acceptance of alternative pasts in which 'she', her past self, becomes an other to her present self.

Past and present are shown to exist in a complex relationship in which recreation and recovery are impossible. 'The past' is a plausible creation, a mythology created out of scraps and traces and partial interpretations – those from the past as well as those of the historian-auto/biographer. However, this does not mean that the past and its mythologies aren't 'real', for certainly what passes for everyday reality can similarly be understood as a chimaera, ghosts who may be powerful and intrusive but who, finally, do not give life and thought its meaning. In a literal way *The Woman Warrior* depicts the power but also the insubstantiality of 'ghosts', white America and everyday life, as compared with the realities of myth and legend; while the reality for the reader of what is inside Claudia's mind and consciousness, as compared with the 'real' but irrelevant intrusions of doctors and nurses, shows this equally clearly and powerfully. This view that the present, in the form of the mind of the historian-biographer, is what creates and gives life to the past, as Claudia's ruminations emphasise, has enormous epistemological consequentiality: the past is not 'there' to know; knowledge about it is the product of particular minds creating a symbolic account supported by scraps of evidence. However, it also has equally important ontological significance, for it raises questions concerning not only the relationship between the writer of histories and those many who peopled these pasts, but also the relationship between the writer as a self and 'the other'. Ultimately, as shown by the stories of Claudia in one way, the doctor in pursuit of Flaubert, his wife and his own past life in another, and Polly Alter in yet another, we can never breach the boundaries that exist between ourselves and other people no matter how extensive the knowledge we may piece together about them. And to the extent that each of these protagonists is in search of themselves as much as another person, this also suggests that the boundaries within each self may be as great as those between one self and another.

Paradoxically readers experience none of these producers of lives as *writers*. The only one of these novels which centrally positions the act, and the art, of writing lives is *Moon Tiger* – but Claudia is the one protagonist who *cannot* write. Each of the other protagonists of these novels grapples with the complexities of the relationship between truth and lies, between reality and mythology, between reality and ideology, between past and present, between self and other; but each of them does so outside of a consideration of how this process will be affected by the exigencies of textual production. Only Claudia is aware that the act of writing is not only a central part of the process of writing lives and histories but is also *transformative* in its own right of the relationship between truth, lies, past, present, reality, ideology, self and other.

Many of the issues raised here in relation to fictional interpretations of auto/biography have been discussed in a more formal way in feminist literary theoretical engagements with women's autobiographical writings. In the following chapter I look at this feminist engagement with autobiography, again doing so as a common reader of both autobiography and of literary accounts of it.

Notes

1 There are other fictional accounts of auto/biography I have not discussed here, such as A. S. Byatt's *Possession* (1990), which, even though it was published as I was completing this chapter, I have not included because, whatever its virtues as a novel, in my view it does not add anything substantial to the accounts of auto/biography provided by those novels already included, by Barnes, Kingston, Lurie, Clausen and Lively.

2 It is interesting to note that eighteenth century women's fictional accounts of lives work the opposite way: by showing women in fiction to have lives and selves, their actual lives could be read as referential of these fictional claims.

3 This is neither to argue that all women's autobiographies are ironic and 'fictive' in this way nor that no men's autobiographies are. It is rather to suggest that when women do write such ironic and playful autobiographies, their challenges to the boundaries between fact and fiction are seen as much more seditious and damning than those of male biographers.

4 In a project entitled 'Our Mother's Voices' I and a number of other working class by birth feminist sociologists focussed on our mothers' pasts and the intertwining of these with our own and with the dead-weight of academic work on class (Stanley, 1985b). I tape-recorded my mother on a number of occasions from 1984 to 1989 concerning 'her' autobiography, which was in fact the history not only of her family/friends but also of the complexities of working class Portsmouth in the inter-war period, producing some fifty hours of talk. Her remarks about the social basis of 'individual' lives has

recently become especially ironic, for as I discuss in the last chapter, a massive stroke in 1990 has left my Mother physically alive but severely brain-damaged and without language.

5 And see here Isobel Miller's *Patience and Sarah* (1969) and Caia March's *The Hide and Seek Files* (1988) as well as my later discussion of Jan Clausen's *The Prosperine Papers* (1988), and contrast with the discussion in Chapter 8.

6 And see here A. S. Byatt's *Possession* (1990) for a rather different view of possession as the motor force of biography and the role of feminism within this.

The presumptive feminist: reinscribing 'bio' in autography[1]

A feminist autobiographical canon?

Since 1980 an influential group of American feminist edited collections concerned with the theory and practice of women's autobiography have been published: Estelle Jelinek's *Women's Autobiography: Essays in Criticism* (1980), Domna Stanton's *The Female Autograph: Theory and Practice of Autobiography* (1984), Shari Benstock's *The Private Self: Theory and Practice of Women's Autobiographical Writings* (1988a), and Bella Brodzki and Celeste Schenck's *Life/Lines: Theorizing Women's Autobiography* (1988) (and see also Heilbrun 1988a, 1988b; Jelinek 1986; Personal Narratives Group 1989a). Each of these collections was produced within a literary criticism/literary theory framework and, with the partial exception of Jelinek's, are marked editorially by the theoretical preoccupations of feminism but also of male theorists of the autobiographical canon (Pascal, Lejeune, Gusdorf and Olney among them), the male theorists of postmodernism such as Derrida and de Man, and Lacanian approaches to language and the psyche. These theoretical influences cut across the intentions of many of the contributors and sometimes the editors themselves – for example, most of Benstock's contributors ignore her psychoanalytic approach to theorising the female self and instead opt for a historical and cultural approach, while Benstock herself promotes a view of specifically women's autobiographies *and* also deconstructs gender as rather genre – a textual construction rather than a material given. Clearly the combination of these different theoretical influences unsettles, challenges, many of the assumptions and understandings that feminists bring to a concern with autobiography, and is therefore worth closer scrutiny.

The editorial stances adopted in these collections have implications for readers of, and not just writers about, autobiography. By questioning the relationship between the textual and the referential self, they thereby come at 'difference' and its relationship to the

category 'women' in ways that parallel Denise Riley's (1988)
stimulating discussion. The writing of history and the writing of the
history of a life raise similar puzzles and problematics; and in the
second section of the chapter I discuss Riley's work in relation to the
diaries of Hannah Cullwick.

Feminist autobiographical theory tends to castigate referentiality
in writing autobiography. In discussing women's autobiographies
which make highly referential claims, I argue that these autobiographers are at least as aware of the ontological shakiness of the self as
any contemporary deconstructionist theorist. Indeed, the only way
fully to explore such ontological puzzles and their epistemological
consequences is to confront in an appreciative way not only the
textual making of selves – their 'graphing' of the 'auto' – but also
what these texts say about the living, growing I and its life – that is,
their inscription of the 'bio' of each author. However, the editorial
stance in these collections varies from completely rejecting any
notion of referentiality, to being embarrassed by it, to making
watertight referential claims, while my concern is rather with
analytically exploring how such claims are made using what textual
means and with what effects for the reader. This analytic approach
necessitates taking the 'bio', the narrative of the life, seriously rather
than, as within these collections, theorising only 'auto' and 'graph'.
My concern throughout the chapter is with the role of these editorial
preoccupations in the constitution of a feminist autobiographical
canon and how common readers are positioned within it.

A feminist autobiographical canon is in the process of formation.
Paradoxically in view of its proponents' sometimes harsh criticism of
the guardians of the often explicitly male autobiographical canon, it
has many of the same modes of operation and standards of critical
judgement, and produces a similarly small, select and largely agreed
upon group of 'good autobiographies' written predominantly by
women who are deemed to be 'good writers'. At least in part this
process of canon formation can be observed by tracing the arguments of feminist theoretical writing about autobiography – but only
in part, for its constitution also derives from teaching, graduate
supervision, conference presentation and more informal collegial
talk. Out of a growing plenitude I am concerned with only a small
number of writings, the collections referred to earlier (and for
different feminist approaches see also *Women's Studies International Forum*
1987 10:1 special issue; *Gender & History* 1989 2:1 special issue).

These have been highly influential in academic feminist circles in Britain, Europe and Australasia as well as North America, and not only within the framework of feminist literary criticism and theory. They now form a set of almost required references for any academic, feminist or not, seeking to demonstrate their familiarity with the accepted literature on the topic of autobiography.

Frameworks can be useful; canonical writing – and writing about canonical writing – can stultify even while it does not prohibit free thought. Orthodoxies, including feminist orthodoxy, should incite rebellion, iconoclasm; I look for a rebellion of the active reader, a common reader who disputes academic insistence upon how texts 'ought' to be read and interpreted, instead trusting their own interpretive powers in the face of theoretical vanguards.

Women's Autobiography (Jelinek, 1980) formed the first major academic feminist theorising of autobiographical writing. Its editorial approach emphasises the existence and importance of women's autobiographies in the face of a refusal to 'see' them on the part of many writers about autobiography, and also draws crucial connections between autobiography and other more provisional forms of life writing. Its prime task, then, was that of all contemporary academic feminism: to insist upon the re-evaluation of women's lives and experiences as important and worthy of serious study.

In going about this, Jelinek's editorial stance is not only appreciative of women's autobiographies but valorises these as located within a women's world of the private and thus distinct from male autobiographies, located within the public world: it proposes the existence of a *separate female tradition* of autobiography. This approach sees women's writing in realist terms, reading off the condition and experiences of the writer's and other women's lives from their autobiographical textual representation (this approach is continued in Jelinek's more recent work (1986); and see also Mason, 1980/ 1988; Friedman, 1988).

The theoretical stance of Domna Stanton's *The Female Autograph* (1984) is very different, its agenda located firmly within a deconstructionist rejection of any 'facile presumption of referentiality' (de Man's phrase) in autobiographical writing, and an insistence that instead feminism should explore the 'graphing' of the 'auto', that is, the creation of a textual self:

the excision of *bio* from *autobiography* is designed to bracket the traditional emphasis on the narration of 'a life', and that notion's facile presumption of referentiality. (Stanton, 1984 p. vii)

This is not merely a change of emphasis from the life to writing
about the life – it is rather the excision of the life, a concern with
writing to the exclusion of the text's narrative referentiality. Stanton
argues for the replacement of autobiography with 'autography', later
called 'autogynography' (Germaine Bree's (1976) term). Auto-
graphic writing constitutes the female subject – graphing the auto is
presented as an act of rebellion and, literally, self-assertion; and it is
positioned in opposition to writing by 'the author' of both autobiography and those who write about it, authors who hold a phallic
pen transmitted from canonical father to son. Stanton's evidence is
damning enough: the exclusion of women's autobiographies from
most critical discussion of the genre.

She highlights the intertextuality of autobiography – 'every autobiography assumes and reworks literary conventions for writing and
reading' (p. 9) – and also the oscillation of writers on autobiography
between seeing it as the re-creation of the past (its claims to facticity)
and as the creation of a textual representation of the past (its
ficticity). However, in her view this 'turn to textuality' does not
resolve problems concerning the identity of the subject or its
referential status: the referential ghost of the autobiographical subject
haunts postmodernist-influenced deconstructionist views of the
genre (and consider here the defection of Alain Robbe-Grillet, arch
postmodernist, whose autobiography Le Miroir qui revient (1984), states
that everything he wrote in fiction is actually referential of his life).
To consider 'the subject' more closely, Stanton turns to feminist
writings on autobiography.

These are predominantly concerned with the difference of wom-
en's autobiographical writings from men. Considering, rightly in my
view, that such contentions should be the goal and not the assumption of feminist autobiographical work, Stanton outlines a number of
claimed differences. The first of these is that men's narratives are
linear, chronological and coherent whereas women's are discontinuous, digressive, fragmented: and yet, as she notes, there are women's
narratives which are 'male', and anyway these 'female' qualities are
those seen as integral to definitions of the (male) genre. Secondly,
female writings are associated with the personal, the intimate,
whereas male writings are concerned with public achievements: and
yet, as she suggests, the confessional mode of Rousseau is seen as the
origin of modern autobiography, and besides many women's autobiographies inscribe the apparently confessional to hide other aspects

of their selves. Finally, women's autobiographical narratives are seen as emphasising the relationship of self to others: and yet, as she argues, this manifestation of difference might be seen as a strategic conforming to propriety rather than indicative of 'real' difference.

Stanton's approach to difference is different. She sees auto-gynographic writing as marked by conflicts between public and private and personal and professional; she also suggests its funda-mental difference, which produces conflict and a divided self, is the act of writing itself (p. 13). The symbolic order, she suggests, equates writing and the author with a phallic pen and thus positions the female author as a contradiction in terms. The argument then proposes that:

autogynography... had a global and essential therapeutic purpose: to constitute the female subject. In a phallocentric system... the *graphing* of the *auto* was an act of self-assertion that denied and reversed women's status. (Stanton, 1984 p. 14)

This is truly the excision of 'bio', the removal of the subject's life from writing, because for Stanton autobiographical writing is the source and origin of changes in women's status, rather than being a product − albeit in dialectical relationship with − of other kinds of change. This is the primacy of the textual, not of the social and material world within which it is located. It is rather a Baudrillardian world created and maintained through texts and commentary on texts − an intertextual reality composed by representation only. This view excludes recognition that most autobiography is not produced through 'graph' at all but through *talk*, through spoken versions of self and other, in which biography and autobiography are closely intertwined; it also perversely refuses to see the relationship of verbal and written auto/biographical texts to the materiality of social life.

I am proposing here that social life is by definition theorised by those who live it − there is no pre-theoretical notion of experience being implied or intended here − and also that for much of the time what social life consists of is the construction, presentation and negotiation of accounts or versions − everyday verbal 'texts', rather than behavioural events themselves. Social life is, then, theorised through and through and is concerned with textual representation. However, ordinary social life and interaction takes it as axiomatic that these accounts or versions are contingent upon real events: births and deaths, shopping and childcare, loving and hating, work and holidays, rapes and assaults, elections and wars, and all the other material events that are lived (and died) by people. What those feminist theorists influenced by postmodernist and deconstructionist thinking seem decidedly in danger of forgetting or even denying is that this ordinary and extraordinary material world exists and is prime – not the world of texts.

The editorial approaches of Jelinek and of Stanton are at opposite ends of a spectrum. Both are concerned with 'making visible' in feminist terms, but the aim of the former is appreciative, indeed valoristic, of women's autobiographical selves, identities and experiences, while that of the latter is deconstructionist and rejects strongly such referentiality to the point of banishing 'life' from its concern with self and writing. The collections edited by Shari Benstock (1988a) and by Bella Brodzki and Celeste Schenck (1988) occupy different parts of a middle ground between the valoristic and the excisory.

Benstock uses the language of autobiographical convention – 'private', 'self', 'theory', 'practice', 'a collection' – to structure the contents of her collection, but then editorially challenges such convention. No, the autobiographical self of women isn't actually private; no, theory and practice shouldn't be treated as distinct in feminist work; no, not so much a unified collection, more a set of voices, a polyphony of readings of autobiographies which often overlap but also contradict, digress. Nevertheless, the structure of the book stands intact and it is difficult not to conclude that the editor's mind if not her heart feels more comfortable with even a moribund convention than with jettisoning it for something that more closely fits the collection's proclaimed iconoclasm.

In common with Stanton, Benstock defines the focus of attention as 'a theory of selfhood that is always under examination in analyses of autobiographical writings, whether or not this analysis overtly raises questions as to how selfhood ... is defined' (p. 1). In other words, even if this is not what analyses of autobiographical writings actually *do*, this is how such writings should be *read*. Read by, I would suggest, a reader assumed to be a literary critic, indeed an academic literary theorist, for Benstock's argument is that theorising women's autobiography, including writing about such autobiographical writing, makes both kinds of writing legitimate presences within 'the academy' (p. 2). Claims for the academic legitimacy of women's autobiographical writing, and of writing about this writing, is a key editorial concern. In keeping with this, Benstock, like Stanton, critically discusses guardians of the male autobiographical canon such as James Olney (1980) and Georges Gusdorf (1980), although in a more conciliatory and indeed complimentary fashion than Stanton's enjoyably swingeing remarks about their determined masculinisms.

Benstock understands the self in largely Lacanian terms, the initiating of self and language within the mirror stage of Lacanian theory being paralleled by the invention of self within the written language of autobiography. Autobiography, she suggests, prepares a meeting of self and writing – in the terms I have used earlier, a meeting between the referential I and the textual I – that is always deferred because such writing actually reveals gaps, not only between the self and the social, but more significantly between the presumption of self-knowledge that initiates autobiography and its end in the creation of a fiction.

But of course this is to consider the matter from the viewpoint of that highly particular reader the feminist literary theorist. I doubt that Harriet Martineau (1877/1983), Helen Keller (1905/1954), Ann Frank (1947), the Sistren Collective (1986) or Claribel Alegria (1983) as autobiographers were concerned with such a gap, and nor do I think that as a common reader of their autobiographies I was concerned with or aware of it either. The narrative carries the reader of these autobiographies forwards into the life, rather than into suspending trust and a narrative reading in favour of a theoretical and anti-referential one. The 'gaps' Benstocks writes of may well be there: but they require reading against the grain of the ways that these autobiographical accounts are written, the narrative conventions they work within, for their narrative pace leaps over, ignores or otherwise silences such questions in the reader's mind.

Certainly there are other women's autobiographies that are not written in this way, and do not require reading against the grain to discern problematics regarding the self and its constitution. However, my point is that Benstock's approach specifies a principle for reading which requires all autobiographies to be treated as sources for investigating textual 'gaps', in effect ignoring the very different ways they are written, the entirely different projects constructed by their authors within them. She is concerned with one highly specific kind of autobiography – 'good autobiography' – only.[2] This is not to suggest that Benstock's approach is less than interesting and defensible. It is however to speak to one of its silences, a silence that resounds through her text when it is re-read 'from below' by that common reader who is so thoroughly removed from its pages.

And there are other silencings in Benstock's argument. One of her most illuminating arguments uses the Lacanian 'mirror stage' as a metaphor for reading Virginia Woolf's 'A sketch of the past' (Woolf 1978b), in which the text inscribes both a developing self and its enforced fractures and silences. Here Woolf certainly sought self-knowledge, using her writing to dredge to the surface half-memories, echoes, glimpses, of her childhood and later sexual abuse (as discussed in detail by Louise DeSalvo, 1989). One wonders what Virginia Woolf, a redoubtable dealer with critics, would have made of a rejection of the referentiality of her account (for such it is, however 'fictive' her approach to its telling) as 'facile'. If Louise DeSalvo is right, a similar response when she met Freud, the fraudulent denier of abused children's misery (Masson 1984), produced the depression that resulted in Woolf killing herself. But this is argued by DeSalvo as a (likely) reaction to a perceived response by Freudian theoretical understanding to Woolf's self, whereas it needs to be kept firmly in mind that there is no complete synonymity between 'a text' and 'the life of the writer'. To read Woolf's work in a realist fashion as truly revelatory of her life is problematic in the extreme, not least because Woolf's entire writing career was concerned with the demolition of 'Mr Bennett and Mr Hardy', those doughty champions of textual realism.

In saying this I am not denying the presence of sexual abuse in Woolf's childhood and later, nor denying that she wrote about this real experience outside of fiction; I am instead emphasising that realist readings of Woolf's and other autobiographical writings have to bracket away – indeed more strongly to deny – the fictive elements necessarily employed in producing these written accounts of the histories of lives. As Stanton suggests, it is all too easy (I find it virtually impossible) not both to embrace anti-realist principles but then also slip into quasi-realist readings of autobiographical writings; and at the end of the chapter I return to this power and pull of the narrative flow of autobiography.

Benstock's view of 'the self' is different from Stanton's, more closely derived from Lacanian ideas, and her treatment of male theorists of autobiography more respectful. However, in her approach too the emphasis is on the writing of a self, although here the life is bracketed away rather than excised from auto(bio)graphy. But in sharp contrast with both Stanton and Benstock, Brodzki and Schenck's declared aim in *Life/Lines* (1988, pp.1-2) is to reclaim the female subject even while foregrounding the problematic nature of 'the self'.[3] Relatedly, Brodzki and Schenck recognise that these twin tasks are precisely those of feminist scholarship in general; and thus they implicitly open up 'the autobiographical' as a common feminist interest shared and reclaimed across all discipline boundaries and differences.

Rejecting the critical stance that autobiography is a mirror held up to reflect a self and a life, Brodzki and Schenck also problematise the 'masculine' autobiographical approach which conflates an actually highly particular self (one with a specific gender, race, sexual orientation, class, education and so forth) with general humanity, and which assumes both that 'the reader' will share exactly these assumed-to-be-universal attributes with the author and that the author's life is exemplary of the development of all selves. In contrast, Brodzki and Schenck's approach adopts feminist, psycho-analytic and deconstructionist ideas to focus on a dispersed displaced female subjectivity while still arguing that the importance of 'the life itself' should not be elided. In arguing this they criticise Stanton's view which, by excising the 'bio', thereby excises the crucial differences that 'life' reveals between women on grounds of class, race and sexual orientation.

'Women' as a generalisation is both invoked, as in Brodzki and Schenck's sub-title to their book, and rejected in proposing that the contents of their collection 'make it impossible to generalise about female experience' (p. 14). Here they display precisely the dilemma of all feminist deconstructions of the category 'women' – they both preserve the edifice, for without it their book could not exist as a 'theory and practice of *women*'s autobiography', *and* they say that the ground must be removed from under it.

Stanton is a more acute observer here, for she is the only one of these editors to recognise the fundamental nature of this contradiction. However, Stanton, like Benstock, effectively ignores the fact that her *practice* is of women's autobiography even though her *theory* challenges the validity of the practice and also of the experiences of women that led them to write autobiographically as precisely women and not as unsexed persons. And what none of these editors broach is that denying validity to the referential specificity of women's lives as distinctly female means that the bottom drops out of autobiographical accounts by Zora Neale Hurston, Maxine Hong

Kingston, Maya Angelou, Alice James, Colette, Mary McCarthy, Audre Lorde, Virginia Woolf and others. These names, paradoxically, are foremost within the developing feminist autobiographical canon, albeit alongside 'unwomanly' female autobiographers such as Simone de Beauvoir and Gertrude Stein.

Brodzki and Schenck share the insistence that the diversity of approaches within their collections results from principle, not compulsion or chance. However, with yet one more invocation of this formula suspicion grows that the underlying differences of theoretical opinion and understanding thereby escape serious scrutiny and discussion – a point I return to.

While there is common ground between my approach and those of Jelinek, Stanton, Benstock, and Brodzki and Schenck (and particularly the latter), there are also differences and disagreements. These collections are successively referential of each other – they entail a high degree of intertextuality. Following Ann Jefferson's (1990) terminology, this is productive of a metanarrative in which successive editorial texts act as commentaries on those that came before; however, a metanarrative is also present here in the stronger sense of a structure of shared ideas that overlap their various differences. My reservations cohere around this metanarrative.

The first such reservation concerns the polyphony of these collections. Their embodiment of many voices is editorially enshrined. However, a reader cannot but become aware that these collections contain explosive differences of understanding and approach to fundamental matters such as the nature of 'the self', how and in what ways autobiography should be understood, and how the relationship between a life and a written account of it should be theorised. These differences form the real excision from these collections, for 'the life' cannot actually be excised by the individual contributors and indeed most do not want to. The editorial approaches are celebratory of difference between women and between analytic approaches to women's autobiography writing, but nowhere discuss what this difference consists of, nor what the consequences might be in terms of a feminist theory of autobiography. One consequence is that the dominant voice is the voice of the editor/s (which my discussion here echoes), leaving those contributors who disagree in a textually subordinate position. The substance of their disagreement is nowhere taken seriously, nowhere recognised as having a valid basis even though the editors might think differently.[4] Polyphony is the wrong word really, for these voices are not of co-equals; the result is more like an opera composed of a few protagonists and a chorus composed of ertswhile protagonists from several other operas. The *subordination of contrary voices* is then the first theme in this feminist canonical metanarrative.

The second is that the breaking of definitional boundaries is seen as an important feature of each collection, rejecting the fixation with making fine definitional distinctions between memoirs, autobiographies, diaries, journals and collections of letters. This is certainly helpful, for it enables similar reading principles to be adopted regarding what are actually highly similar forms within a single genre of writing lives. However, two boundaries remain seemingly inviolate; one between biography and autobiography, and the other between the written auto/biography and the autobiography of the reader.

In the following chapter I shall argue that biography and autobiography cannot sensibly be treated as distinct, and that the development of a poetics or theory of autobiography needs to be extended to its sisters-under-the-skin form of biography. I shall not foreshadow this argument here except to say that feminist biographers are notable by their absence from these collections, and yet their perspective would bring to the interpretation of autobiographies a rich source of knowledge – but this of course would be of the life as well as of the work of autobiographers, the life that these editors determinedly excise or bracket. Biography creates serious troubles for auto(bio)graphy as it is positioned in these editorial stances.

The other intact boundary is similarly crucial to a feminist theory of autobiography, for, whether the majority of these editors are willing to recognise it or not, readers read autobiographies because in a myriad of ways these have reverberations for how we understand our own lives, experiences and times. And by a 'myriad of ways' I include that some readers read autobiographies in a doubly referential manner, attempting to model their lives in whole or in part on that of a favoured autobiographer, as well as readers who read them for 'a good read', or to explore how X or Z construct their lives and selves, or indeed to find the fractures and displacements of women's subjectivities. But how do the readers of autobiographies who write in these collections read them? We know at a formal theoretical analytical level only. This formal theoretical approach rules out of bounds a more personal reading that includes something of the intellectual autobiography of the reader, such as Judith Okely

(1986) provides in her biography of Simone de Beauvoir. The second theme in this metanarrative is then *a full refusal to challenge generic boundaries*, so protecting the formal and highly conventional academic stance of editors and also of contributors.

The third theme is also concerned with reading. The readings of autobiographies provided are highly specialised ones, and this is even more marked editorially, with the emphasis firmly on theoretical approaches to the self and to writing. However, reading remains invisible as a topic for serious theoretical discussion. Reading is instead taken as a theoretical pre-given, a transparent act in relation to a totally active text which is apparently productive of one obvious and incontrovertible reading. What is needed instead is a discussion of reading as an *active* engagement with a text and so as a viewpoint contingent upon the epistemological and ontological position of a reader and thus of her autobiography, such as has taken place within ethnomethodologically-informed sociology (and see here Smith, 1987, 1990; McHoul, 1983; Lee, 1984; Lury, 1982). The third theme in the metanarrative is then one in which *reading is treated as a non-contingent transparency* – these are exemplary readings in which, implicitly, the class, race, sexual orientation, education, of the reader vanishes; ironically, it mirrors the criticised exemplary claims of canonical autobiography.

Finally, the concern with the writing of a life, rather than the referential qualities of this writing, goes hand in hand with a focus on a very particular kind of autobiographer: not Shirley Maclaine (1970, 1975), Martina Navratilova (1985), Coretta Scott King (1969), Miriam Makeba (1987) or Dory Previn (1976, 1980), nor even Barbara Castle (1980), Golda Meir (1975), Sarah Keays (1986) and Benazir Bhutto (1988), but those autobiographers who them-selves *were/are* writers (and see here Judy Simons 1990 for an explicit discussion of the woman writer as autobiographer/diarist). Consider the litany of those whose autobiographies are the subject of discussion in these collections: the names and work of Emily Dickinson, Gertrude Stein, Maya Angelou, Simone de Beauvoir, Mary McCarthy, Madame de Sevigne, Alice James, Colette, HD, Virginia Woolf, Audre Lorde, Djuna Barnes, Zora Neale Hurston, Maxine Hong Kingston, run like ink between them. Of course there are differences between these writers, and their routes into the canon may be different, but their shared writerly status is still no coincidence.

A concentration on the autobiographies of writers is also a

preoccupation of guardians of the male autobiographical canon, and it results from a concern with 'literary' themes explored with textual sophistication, not the relative textual crudities of the Maclaines, Keays, Bhuttos and Navratilovas[5] of autobiography writing. Most published autobiographies, and those most read, do not have such literary qualities and textual sophistications; and it would be a welcomed relief to find a feminist discussion of the autobiographical that was not immersed in the processes and products of high culture, that took note of the autobiographical equivalents of soap operas and of neighbourhood gossip and recognised their importance in informing many people's opinions as to the proper subjects, styles, themes and emphases of autobiography, and of what 'a life' looks like.[6] Thus the fourth theme within the metanarrative is not its proclaimed concern with a complete genre containing many different kinds of writing styles and approaches, but its interest in a sub-set within the genre produced by 'good' women writers – for insofar as 'ordinary women' appear, they do so as, for example, 'black women' and 'lesbian women', and their autobiographical narratives are looked at collectively rather than individually.

Does this lurking metanarrative of feminist writing on autobiography matter? I think it does. The rhetorical openness of these collections to all strands of feminism, all approaches to theorising the autobiographical, all forms of autobiography, stands alongside a high boundaried approach in which there is a very specific dominant theoretical voice. This voice systematically creates subordinate voices, in which only particular kinds of theoretical readings are provided, in which reading is treated as a transparent and objective activity, and in which only particular kinds of autobiographies are subject to inquiry and inclusion within the developing feminist autobiographical canon. In addition, the accompanying excision/ bracketing/valorising of 'the life' removes from analysis that which is most interesting about autobiographies from the viewpoint of the common reader and, I go on to argue, the feminist theorist.

Writing a history/a life

The 'writing of a life' is the writing of a history, an account of the past by a particular kind of historian known as an auto/biographer. The epistemological issues raised in doing so are those that arise in any historical research and writing process, and they concern the interpretive role of the historian, the fragmentary and incomplete nature of available sources, and the role of writing in the creation of, not a slice of the past, but rather an account of what this might have been. It is useful, therefore, to push forward the discussion of the defining concerns of this book – the relationship between feminism, an individual self, a life, an historical or auto/biographical text, and the general category 'women' – through a more explicit and detailed analytic account of that relationship.

I begin with Denise Riley's (1988) deliberations on 'the category of 'women' in history', which raise a major epistemological debate that confronts all contemporary feminism (see Stanley, 1990b for an extended version of this discussion). This debate revolves around the argument that the category 'women' (as well as the more obviously contentious 'Woman') is 'historically, discursively constructed, and always relatively to other categories which themselves change' (Riley, 1988, pp. 1-2). Riley's argument more than emphasises 'conditioning' or 'socialisation', it disputes the existence of any single foundational 'reality' beneath or within the constructions. Both the conclusion and starting point of her argument is that feminism has gone through continual historical loops in its political arguments and actions, necessarily oscillating between 'equality' and 'difference': it has claimed both that women's difference needs recognition, and that women are equal and should be treated so. Her aim is to provide an intellectual route out of what she sees as the impasse of either under-feminisation or over-feminisation of the category 'women'. Denise Riley's intention is thus to prepare the ground for a feminism that neither accepts any notion of 'real' or 'essential' women (lying, as it were, somewhere beneath present 'distorting' categorisations), nor propounds a supposedly 'neutral' deconstructionism that eschews political commitment.

In a recent interesting sociological commentary on postmodern-ism, Zigmaunt Bauman (1988) proposed that it is best seen as a recovering of nerve and a renewed claim to expertise on the part of intellectuals dispossessed of their former places in the sun. Sociology can move in one of two directions. One is that the discipline should give up such claims and develop epistemologically radically reflexive ways of working from a phenomenological base (become, as it were, a form of applied practical philosophy of everyday life). The other alternative, the one Bauman favours, is to ask different questions but in the same 'epistemological voice'. In his terms and words, we can develop either a 'postmodernist sociology' (the first alternative) or a sociology of 'postmodernism' (Bauman's preference).

My own feminist and sociological preference is decidedly for the more radical first alternative. That is, for a clean epistemological break with foundationalism as the basis of sociology. Thus the appeal of Denise Riley's work, as one of the most convincing feminist arguments for deconstruction and which also, by focussing on 'women' and 'histories', provides the means of drawing together feminism, deconstruction, sociology and auto/biography.

What is conceptualised in Denise Riley's account is a rationale for and a means of achieving precisely such an epistemological break. It argues passionately and persuasively for a radical deconstructionism which can concern itself with the constructions of 'rulers' – and, moreover, with the means of taking apart that category itself, to see these people as they are constructed and as they construct themselves. Riley's discussion is a major contribution to the discussion of epistemological issues within feminism. However, what it silences needs serious debate and equally serious remedial action – intellectual as well as practical – by feminist researchers and writers.

Welcoming 'difference', nonetheless her feminist deconstructionism implicitly portrays as essentialist the differing and sometimes multiple identities painstakingly constructed in the (sometimes very recent) past, by lesbians, women of colour, disabled women and working class women (to name only some). What must it be like to be a black woman, having gone through much to have named oneself thus and to have recovered something of the history of one's foremothers, to have it implied that this is not only not enough but is an intellectual error, an ontological over-simplification, to have done so? As a working class lesbian (for so I continue to name myself this different kind of woman), and thus having gone through comparable struggles to name, I sigh another bitter sigh at yet another although surely unintended theoretical centrism: the resurgance of Theory from those who were once the certificated namers of other women's experiences and who are now likely to become the certificated deconstructors of the same.

What is required – and indeed must be insisted upon by those of us who are black, lesbian, aged, disabled, working class – is that all 'difference' must be seen and attended to equally. In particular there must be an end to the now ritual invocation of 'and black women' as the only difference seen but which actually goes no further than a formula of words that leaves untouched actual relations of power between differently situated groups of black and white women. Moreover this invocation also masks a refusal to see that 'black women' is itself no unitary category, but one internally differentiated on grounds of ethnicity, age, class, able-bodiedness and sexuality, to name no more.

And yet there is much in Denise Riley's argument about the ontological experience of the category 'women' as shaky, as something we inhabit or are forced into only periodically at the disjunctures and fracturings of 'ordinary being' introduced by actual oppressions in our lives. Nonetheless oppression and its struggles should be neither denied nor silenced, nor explained away as a momentary and passing necessity transcended by the greater intellectual rigour of deconstructionism. And my view is that there are alternative 'routes out' of the political oscillations described by Riley, which centre upon reinscribing and revaluing the 'life' of women excised from feminist canonical writing on autobiography. I therefore situate the points outlined above in relation to a particular 'history', that contained in the unedited and unpublished Hannah Cullwick (1833-1909) manuscript diaries, as well as in my edited volume of these (Stanley, 1984a).

While apparently rejecting referentiality, Judy Simons (1990) suggests that diary-writing is a particularly female form, as it enables the secrets and silences of women's lives to be inscribed and, thereby, constitutes a rebellious authorised self. This begs many questions. One is the apparent denial of the primacy of everyday life, the implicit positioning of the primacy of the text. Another concerns the fact that many diaries written by men have the same qualities here assigned to women, that of A. J. Munby being a case in point. Munby was an upper class man with whom Hannah Cullwick was involved over many years, and he too wrote diaries (Hudson, 1972). My focus is on Hannah Cullwick's diaries, not his nor their intertextuality with hers; nonetheless it needs to be said firstly that both sets of diaries inscribe (often shared) secrets and silences but bear a puzzling and unknowable relationship to the actual lives of these two people, and secondly that both thereby constitute a (differently and differentially) rebellious self.

One implication of the essentialist versus deconstructionist debate within feminism is that a deconstructionist postmodern and non-essentialist view of the category 'women' is both new, and also provided by feminists and/or academics. The first is a dubious assumption and can be shown to be so by looking closely at appropriate historical autobiographical materials; and the second is the product of an elitist view of the researcher/researched and theory/experience relationship, which locates the researcher on a different critical plane and assigns theory to her (the researched merely experience, while the researcher theorises that experience). A further implication, worked most fully in feminist writings on autobiography, is that the fractures, silences and disruptions of a non-unitary self can only be recovered from *outside* the text and by specialist, uncommon, readers. And equally I shall take issue with this.

Hannah Cullwick was a thoroughly working class woman who worked from a very young age in a succession of domestic service 'places'. She also wrote diaries during a period (1854 to 1873) in which few other working class women 'spoke' on paper, or at least in a form which has survived for us now to read and think about. Obviously I cannot describe in any detail the features of Hannah Cullwick's working life, and anyway these are better read in her own words. However, it is not inappropriate to characterise Hannah Cullwick as a mid-nineteenth century deconstructionist, for she was as well-aware as any contemporary feminist theorist of the non-essentialist and internally fractured nature of the category 'women'.[7] Repeatedly she makes detailed distinctions between these various fractures in her diaries. I discuss four of these fractures here, although she herself deals with more.

The first of these is that Hannah draws detailed – and differing – accounts of distinctions between herself and other labouring women on the one hand, and her upper class mistresses in domestic service places on the other. For Hannah Cullwick, it is these upper class women who are 'women'. She notes, through many concrete instances, their physical incompetence in domestic labour and other household tasks, but also their often dithery and 'feminine' minds, moods and behaviours. She draws her distance from them as surely as any man convinced of his superiority, for she is certainly (although cross-cut by other factors) sure of hers, noting their incompetence in all those daily skills she so amply possessed.

In relation to this is the second point: the kind of 'labouring women' that Hannah identifies with are not just 'working class women'; no such unitary simplicities of class identification inform her estimation of others. Rather, she is aware of internal distinctions to be made between groups of 'working class women': her own identifications are strongly with the 'old-fashioned' countrywomen in the lower and less 'fine' ranks of female domestic service, who retain more traditional ways of dress, of conduct, of speech and of self-estimation and self-presentation. These 'rough' but also thoroughly respectable working women were freer than most by virtue of their dress, demeanour and conduct: Hannah and her friends could frequent public houses and walk back home late at night without heed or molestation. Both her physical strength and her 'unwomanly' (defined in terms of then-current fashion and self-presentation) appearance and conduct meant that few men seemed to have seen Hannah in 'sexed' terms.

This may seem mere romanticism on my part. However, unless readers totally disbelieve the Cullwick diaries, seeing them as fiction only,[8] it is clear that she did indeed go into 'men's places' and roam at night at will and without 'interference', or, if it was intended, she headed it off in a variety of ways. I think it is difficult for readers now to appreciate two important factors. Working class people were seen in mid-nineteenth century England as a different species, almost not human at all, by their 'betters' – much as colonialists treated black peoples at home as well as abroad at this time and later. Also and consequently it was comparatively easy for women across the classes to 'unsex' themselves, signal theselves as undesirable in conventional heterosexual terms.

Thirdly, an attempt to understand difference in race or ethnic terms is no late twentieth-century monopoly. For Hannah Cullwick, race difference loomed large in her life in one way, and had secondary reverberations in another. In more personal terms, decidedly lower class Hannah struggled both to live and to understand her relationship (which resulted in marriage in 1873, following their meeting in 1854) with upper class Munby. Class was then a matter of a divide, a chasm so wide as to be comprehended only in what were then seen to be racial and thus biological terms for those who attempted to cross it. It was certainly so for Munby and Hannah, given his oddities concerning working women and her feelings about working men who tried to dominate and render subservient working women. It is also important to remember that the category 'race' was then not defined in specifically colour terms: the Irish loomed large in considerations of race and so too did the feckless working class.

Hannah Cullwick and Munby conducted their relationship around complex dominances and subserviences; and the longer the relationship persisted, the more Munby depended on Hannah. The cross-cuttings of 'power' in their relationship are not my concern here (although they are discussed fully in Chapter 6); however, the terms in which 'power' was manifested is. The language, and indeed on occasion the appearance, of race formed a key discourse in which they communicated, with 'black/white' serving as a complicated metaphor for class differences, but with interesting complexities in that the white and 'ladylike' Munby, and the black and 'unsexed' or even 'manly' Hannah, crossed and re-crossed conventional power divides. Invariably in her diary Hannah addressed Munby as 'Massa' (which they took to be the form of address used by black slaves towards those who owned them), and on occasion she used soot and blacklead to actually 'black up', writing in her diary (which was sent to him) about such occasions. But Munby depended upon such external displays to enable him to communicate at all with Hannah, for otherwise she suggests he was mute before her, unable to talk about the everyday of domestic work and domestic relationships she inhabited. In addition, Munby was more incompetent in the everyday activities that compose 'looking after yourself' than any of the mistresses that Hannah half-despised and half-admired. She must have construed him in similarly mixed political and emotional terms, just as black people cannot help doing with white, nor lesbians and gay men with heterosexuals, nor working class people with the middle classes: we know too much about our 'betters', and they little about us.

Additionally, black people, and also representations of black people, had a very real presence in the lives of Hannah and Munby. One example is the 'minstrel troupes' that were such a feature of London street life in the 1850s and 1860s. These 'minstrels' were sometimes black people, but more often were composed initially of white men, then some white women as well, who 'blacked up' to sing in the streets supposedly 'minstrel' songs. Hannah as much as Munby sees these white women as having unsexed themselves: clearly white women can be respectably sexed only by maintaining some reserve in public places, some gendered distinctions in their public presence as compared with men. What remains unclear is whether and to what extent it is 'blackness' that unsexed such women or their unusual public self-displays; I suggest that the two cannot be distinguished in this instance.

It is also very clear that Hannah eschewed relationships with men which entailed publicly legitimated control over her. Early in her diary-writing she says the origin of her relationship with Munby was that he didn't try to dominate her in the way that working class men did. On a number of occasions she notes the aggressive reactions of men threatened by her height and physical strength (sweeping them off their feet into her arms was one means she used in dealing with them). Perhaps most poignantly, Hannah notes in the 1870s that although she felt that Munby should offer to marry her, for this was her due, she thought the need came as an imposition from outside in the form of social opprobrium for an unconventional relationship (she was faced with losing her 'character', the written recommendation that was her only means to future employment) which pushed them in the direction of a more conventional one. She is also very insistent that marriage is 'too much like being a woman', in her words.

As I read her diaries, then, Hannah Cullwick was to a large degree an 'unsexed' woman, one who was loosened although not freed from the fetters of middle class and dependent womanhood, but also one who had determined not to enter working class married womanhood and consequent control over her person by an individual man. She struggled to piece together a 'language' – in her case not only conceptual but literal, in terms of the practical difficulties of communicating at a basic level with Munby as the denizen of a different although contiguous social milieu – in which to speak and write of this. And the metaphor she most often used for doing so revolved around race and its divisions and hierarchies.

In doing this Hannah Cullwick was as proficient a theoriser of her own and other people's experience as any contemporary feminist theoretician. Indeed, I would say more so, for she took as axiomatic a number of things which white heterosexual feminists have been dragged to, in effect kicking and screaming after prolonged protest from black and lesbian women. For Hannah Cullwick 'women' was a structural category to which she necessarily had to relate and respond: but she did so in complex ways related to her class position, her rural background, and also her particular biographical gathering together of her life's experiences and understandings as related narratively in her diaries and in relation to Munby's role in both. We have much to learn from her and other women whose lives admit rumpled complexities, rather than these being removed under the heavy iron of Theory. The complexities of the categories 'women' and 'men' are not reserved knowledge for theoreticians/ researchers; and a detailed examination of other historical or contemporary people's lives would yield similar epistemological and ontological complexities fully recognised by them as I have outlined in relation to Hannah Cullwick.

Elizabeth Fox-Genovese (1988) interestingly distinguishes between black and white women's autobiographies of the nineteenth century: those of white women were 'cocooned' in their albeit troubled acceptance of the tenets and parameters of 'womanliness', while those of black women were permeated by an awareness that by definition they were outside of womanliness and sought political advance of their cause through entrance to it. Sojourner Truth's (Gilbert, 1850/1968) 'ar'nt I a woman?' is both a claim and a challenge, an assault on the citadel of the assumed conjunction of whiteness and womanliness. However, strangely for an approach which emphasises the equal importance of class alongside gender and race, Fox-Genovese's analysis sets up 'whiteness' as gendered but unseamed in class terms. But class fractures of 'womanliness' existed then as surely as colour fractures; indeed, as the case of Hannah Cullwick illustrates, the two fractures are articulated in the same elements of discourse and were seen to have the same origins: a *species* difference between whites and blacks and between the classes and the masses. Hannah Cullwick was both excluded from 'womanliness' by her class and also determinedly drew her distance from it, in not so much ambivalent as highly negative terms. Her position in relation to Truth's challenge is, no she isn't a woman, no she won't do particular things for that is too much like being a woman, no she won't be lorded over by a man like women are. Like many black women (see autobiographies such as those by Harriet Wilson (1983) and Harriet Jacobs (1861/1973) as well as the narrative of Sojourner Truth), Hannah Cullwick's partial and only half-disguised contempt for 'women' as she defined this angrily breaks through the surface of her articulated admiration of those who embodied womanliness.

It is simply inadequate to put all of the weight of a feminist theory of autobiography upon the 'graphing' – the writing. Certainly the writing is crucial and replete with fictive elements and strategies, but without a life that contains fractures, silences, secrets, elisions, excisions, neither would writing about that life contain these elements. These features are not solely created by writing; autobiography writing is not a *deus ex machina* that by itself creates change in a life in particular and the body politic in general. Autobiographical textuality is neither deterministic of a life nor (usually) a complete invention: in autobiography graph is predicated upon bio, writing upon life, and not the other way about.

Thus far I have argued these points through a text in effect 'created' through my editorial activity, and readers might object that this privileges my interpretation of Hannah Cullwick's autobiographical self, her writing and her life. I therefore move on to discuss two groups of autobiographical writings by women who have been prime movers in 'claiming an identity they taught us to despise' (Cliff, 1980): black women and lesbian women. I do this, not by discussing autobiographical accounts by the relatively famous, such as Maya Angelou, Zora Neale Hurston (1942), Audre Lorde (1980, 1983), Ethel Smyth (1919, 1924, 1928, 1934, 1936, 1940), Vita Sackville-West (in Nicholson 1973) or Valentine Ackland (1985), but rather autobiographies of less famous lives and histories. These autobiographies apparently provide ammunition for Stanton's move to excise the 'facile presumption' of referentiality, for their authors make highly referential claims throughout. However, as with Hannah Cullwick, I shall suggest that within the details of the lives so written are all manner of indicators of a fractured, displaced female subjectivity entirely aware of the ontological shakiness of 'women' and indeed of 'self'.

Identities they taught us to despise

Three black women's narratives by Jarena Lee (1836, in Andrews, 1986), Zilpha Elaw (1846, in Andrews, 1986) and Julia Foote (1879, in Andrews, 1986) are spiritual autobiographies located within nineteenth-century Methodist revivalism (and for alternative approaches to understanding these see Humez, 1984; McKay, 1989; Washington, 1987). They provide an apparently strong case for Domna Stanton's rejection of referentiality, embodying as they do a central theme, in their editor's words, of claiming, actualising and legitimating 'an authentic, individually authorized selfhood' (Andrews, 1986 p. 16). In making such claims, each autobiographer uses a variety of markers to guarantee the strict referentiality of her text. Such proof was necessary to legitimate them taking on an 'unwomanly' preaching role; it was demonstrated primarily through the specification of witnesses to various spiritual events, but also by reference to their endeavours in converting the seemingly unconvertible: harsh slave owners, wild and giddy youths, men in opposition to women's ministerial role, men and women given over to hedonistic pleasures.

On one level these are tightly referential and realist texts which promote an essentialist view of an emergent but real self, doing so by trading on a reader's expected knowledge of biblical parallels to the trials and accomplishments they describe. In addition, they display relatively few of the ambivalences to whites that Elizabeth Fox-Genovese (1988) discerns within narratives by former slaves such as Sojourner Truth, Harriet Wilson or Harriet Jacobs, and which provide a radical undercurrent to these women's projects of gaining white liberal support for the black cause. However, looking in detail at the ways the lives of these Methodist women are narrated, it becomes clear that these 'conversion and mission' autobiographies inscribe and explore a much more complex view of self. They also demolish the distinction often made between men's diaries, as public documents concerned with events, and women's as private ones concerned with the self, in precisely the way that Graham et al (1989) note occurs with seventeenth century white Englishwomen's conversion narratives.

Each of these women firmly and repeatedly draws her distance from the category 'women'; and none of them ever reaches a point where they feel they have 'an authentic selfhood', for they are each perpetually aware of their inner fragmentation and self-alienation, and each is perpetually in pursuit of a 'true self' which changes and always eludes grasp. More than this, none of these three Methodist freeborn women use the rhetoric of womanliness which marks the autobiographies of Truth, Wilson and Jacobs: there is no ambivalence to womanliness in these spiritual autobiographies, only out-right contempt for and rejection of it within the family, marriage, Methodism and society more generally.

Before their conversion to active Christianity, Lee, Elaw and Foote experienced a continual sense of being out of synch with other people and their own lives. Jarena Lee's whole life before conversion is summed up in these terms; Zilpha Elaw's early life is marked by depression and thoughts of suicide; and Julia Foote too marks her early life as a cycle of the temptations of a deeply troubled spirit out of line with her fellows. For each of these women, conversion provides a framework within which to make sense of their conviction that there was 'something wrong with them', that their self-alienation had a material basis – in their terms, in the unsettled states of their souls.

However, for none of them did conversion promote any fundamental change in their self-perception, and each of them continued dissatisfied and depressed. What did bring about such a change was, for each, the specifically Methodist rite of 'sanctification'. Sanctification not only allows but indeed insists upon fundamental changes in public behaviours and roles, for it requires people to live daily and outwardly in accordance with their spiritual convictions. Sanctification allows Lee, Elaw and Foote to legitimate in the face of all opposition what was seen as entirely deviant and unwomanly behaviour: public preaching and thus taking on a role preserved for a male church hierarchy. What each of these women seeks and finally achieves is a public voice, a woman's ministry, and their struggles to achieve this brings each of them a good deal of open rejection and frequent attempts to keep them in their 'womanly' places.

Sanctification and a preaching role, however, does not end the self-doubt and self-alienation experienced by these autobiographers. Throughout their preaching careers each continued to experience crises, and the command once more to change their lives and activities. Their moves into a preaching role rather enabled each of them to live out a marginal lifestyle which brought with it some harmony between their inner fragmentation of self and the outer fragmentation of how they came to live. As preachers, each of them chose to live peripatetic lives, moving from community to community across America and, in Elaw's case, into the slave states where she repeatedly faced enslavement and then to a long series of moves in England. Wherever they go, each describes themselves facing jealousies and oppositions from within local groups, usually specifically because they are women preachers. In addition there are always sinners to convert, so their preaching role occupies all their time and energies; and always at some juncture the voice of the Holy Spirit tells them to move on to somewhere different and more challenging.

Santification provides Lee, Elaw and Foote with an iron-tight legitimation of their 'unwomanliness': what they do is demanded by God, is permitted by the scriptures, and only mere men object. They successively and successfully take on their husbands, male church leaders, and other men who oppose them preaching and try to keep them in a woman's 'proper' place. Later the Holy Spirit fulfills the same role in providing legitimacy for continuing with particular courses of action against opposition or doubt. Throughout it is clear that each of these autobiographers is fully aware that their chosen course of action is deemed 'unwomanly' by men who want to keep all public roles within their control and each of them pours withering scorn on male opposition – this is as true of Elaw, who in one passage insists that a woman should be subservient first to her parents and then to her husband, as it is of the more explicitly feminist Lee and Foote.

The mission of each of these women seems primarily to have been among black Methodists, for Methodism of the time was internally racially segregated even at 'shared' events such as the revivalist camp meetings described and participated in by Elaw. Their aim, unlike the autobiographical projects of Sojourner Truth, Harriet Wilson and Harriet Jacobs, was not to engage the active sympathy of white abolitionists and liberals, but rather to justify and legitimate, post hoc, their own chosen public preaching careers including, importantly, to other black Methodist women. In doing so they mark out a privileged role for themselves by virtue of their special spiritual status: in a spiritual hierarchy within Methodism, they are superior to all regardless of colour excepting those men and women equals also sanctified and from time to time inhabited by the Holy Ghost. In this connection it is instructive to note that among those converted, white male slave owners and white men formerly convinced of the inferiority of black people frequently appear in each of these autobiographies.

So far I have stressed the common features of these three autobiographies, but there are also important differences. Zilpha Elaw's longer and more detailed autobiography is also the most seemingly conservative on the position of women, containing as it does a long passage emphasising women's proper subordination within the family and marriage. However, the structural purpose that this passage serves should be noted, for it comes in the form of a lengthy aside from the main narrative immediately before Elaw offers strong justification for her separation from her husband, by stating that when husbands are ungodly then women's clear duty is to resist and reject them. Although the autobiographies by Lee and

Foote both refer to their self-dissatisfaction and self-alienation after sanctification, Elaw's more detailed autobiography also contains the most information on this, for her writing covers a longer period. Jarena Lee's autobiography is much more focussed on stages in the development of her spiritual career than the other two: the emphasis is on conversion, santification and her call to preach, although a section on marriage provides a justification of her separation from her husband and child. Julia Foote's autobiography is more openly a political document and in part is concerned with an autonomous organisation of women within the church; it also takes an open and more militant stance regarding 'indignities on account of colour'.

In spite of such differences, each of these three autobiographies contains similarities of structure as well as of content. In part this is likely to be the product of each other's and similar careers of 'deviant' women within Methodism being well-known to them. However, unlike other unpublished spiritual narratives (such as those now in Graham *et al* 1989), these autobiographies were all self-published in their authors' lifetimes; thus their survival owes nothing to official approval by the church hierarchy nor to being promoted as suitable models for other women's spiritual lives. But in the greater part their survival is likely to be a product of the fact that contemporary women who wanted, for whatever reason and in whatever context, to step outside of conventional 'womanly' behaviour and adopt a public role assigned to men were likely to face similar reactions and similar obstacles. Given the common location of these women within Christianity, it is not surprising that conversion failed to satisfy their restlessness, and that Methodism attracted them, for sanctification provided them with a route into a public life and also an unanswerable legitimation straight from God for their conduct in doing so. It is also not surprising that each of them presents the epiphanies of their lives within the frame of a strong liberationist narative, for this best allows them to justify the choices and decisions their lives had contained.

On only one level are these three autobiographies to be seen as referential and realist texts: they are structured so as to use referential means and realist evidence to support these women adopting a way of living that brought their fragmented and displaced sense of self into harmony with an equally fragmented and displaced way of life. It is the details of their lives as narratively and apparently referentially provided, and then as interpreted by them, that gives present day readers the means of understanding each of these women's 'self', not as a unified, coherent whole, but as, in Denise Riley's phrase, 'ontologically shaky'. In other words, here as with Hannah Cullwick it is a respectful attention to the life, to the excised despised 'bio', that enables the reader to see this fragmented and displaced self not as the construct of an analyst who wrenches it from a text produced by an unaware author, but rather as the substance of her life as understood and textually represented by a very aware autobiographer.

I conclude with the brief lesbian autobiographies known generically as 'coming out stories' and refer particularly to The Coming Out Stories edited by Julia Penelope and Susan Wolfe (1980/1989) and the British collection edited by the Hall Carpenter Archives Lesbian Oral History Group Inventing Ourselves (1989) (see also The Lesbian Path edited by Margaret Cruikshank (1985)). This autobiographical form is highly focussed, like the spiritual autobiographies, and it turns on the epiphanous moment of 'coming out', that is, a full realisation of oneself as a 'lesbian woman' (and see Chapter 9 for a different discussion of this); and this in turn is seen as their writers' key means of making sense of what had seemed incomprehensible confusions of self and thus as a route to a 'true' self post-coming out.

Biddy Martin (1988) has offered three stringent criticisms of such narratives. Firstly, within them a tautological and essentialist view of self-identity is promoted, in which there is a linear move to a 'real' identity that seemingly was always there and known but not named because it was apparently unnamable; and this self now contains no distortions, doubts or displacements. Secondly, lesbian feminist theoretical and other literature now forms a set of constraints within which experience has to be located and modelled: this actually constructs experience and identity and renders both the individual and collective past homogenous and not diverse. And finally, the assumed relationship between reader and autobiographical subject is a mimetic one: these are exemplary lives, role models to be read as paradigm examples of lesbian lives. The conjunction of 'lesbian' and 'autobiography' begs many questions, as Biddy Martin suggests, among them the implication that sexuality more than frames a life, it gives it its central meaning; and also the presumption of referentiality between life and writing, which is seen as the organising principle of such collections.

While agreeing in part with these reservations, I think that the point of coming out stories has been missed. This is to act as a form of contemporary myth-making, but a myth-making in subtle ways undermined by particular qualities of the assumed mimetic relationship between writer and reader. These coming out stories are preoccupied with the absence of an everyday language in which to understand lesbian women's feelings and desires, and thus with a literary and political re-shaping of language and thus consciousness.

Readers of coming out stories are, as Martin notes, almost invariably lesbian feminist women in contact with some kind of 'community': and, as their readers well know, this is actually a diverse, disagreeing, fragmented collectivity as well as one capable of unity and agreement. Such readers are active readers, knowledgable readers, readers capable of transforming the coming out stories back into the oral and dialogic form of collective story-telling they so clearly derive from. I am not suggesting that these women constitute the only active readers – as I have argued, all readers use often very varied means of reading in an active way. Rather my argument is that these particular readers of these particular texts achieve their active readership by reading between, above and beyond the lines, for instance by adding another time-phase to them, one beyond the 'happy end' quality they typically have, in reaching the epiphany of coming out and then ending. These readers know 'what happens next' and that the euphoria of coming out becomes a three-dimensional and complex daily reality in which problems continue, including within the nature of 'lesbianism' itself as within all other modes of living. There are interesting parallels as well as differences between the coming out stories and Audre Lorde's autobiography, *Zami* (1983), for this also determinedly constructs new mythologies as well as transforms old ones, infuses them with new meaning: black, lesbian, feminist, take on new resonance as this life history of an emergent 'woman-identified woman' unfolds.

Coming out stories have a clearly affirmatory quality of 'self and like-minds against an oppressive world' which makes them sisters-under-the-skin to Lee, Elaw and Foote's spiritual autobiographies. They share the same basic structure: here a pre-realisation doubt and confusion followed by naming, then doubts and difficulties, followed by coming out and entry into a new life-style and community; and in the spiritual autobiographies a pre-conversion doubt, confusion and self-alienation, followed by conversion and naming, then doubts and uncertainties preceding sanctification, and this initiating an entirely different way of life with its resultant difficulties and oppositions but also with support from a community of like-minds. Also both kinds of autobiography centralise self-alienation, lack of self-knowledge and coherence, and the lack of a language not only to understand but also to speak of self in ways that make more sense. In addition, both see the emergent more authentic self as beset by the negative reactions of others, sometimes militant and prohibitive reactions, but with all the new self-knowledge providing a defense, as much ethical as emotional, against such reactions. And lastly, beneath the stylistic, temporal and other differences, both of these kinds of autobiography are essentially ethical in their organising principle and claims. That is, both are concerned with achieving a greater degree of self-authenticity in the face of what are presented as a diversity of unjust oppositions.

The main differences concern the explicit continuance within the black spiritual autobiographies of self-fragmentation, doubt and displacement, and the textual removal of this in the coming out stories by a series of closures that provide their 'happy end' quality by, literally, making the endings to such stories in the subject's arrival in community, identity and so forth. The political purposes of the spiritual autobiographies require the continuance of self-doubt stilled, calmed and used by God through the Holy Ghost, while the political purposes of the coming out stories require that the achievement of lesbian identity should appear to foreclose doubt and displacement while also retaining experiential complexity. In both cases, understanding these different pieces of writing requires the reader to have knowledge gained from outside of the text: common readers' active readings, unlike the close readings of academic textual analysis, make good use of the extratextual.

Two different kinds of coming out stories – those of separatist women and those of lesbian women who are not feminists – highlight some details of narrative that permit or even encourage a more active reading by speaking to the fractures and displacements that Biddy Martin argues, erroneously in my opinion, are removed from them.

Separatist coming out stories reveal the non-unitary nature of 'lesbian community', one of its discordances. Within these stories there is a specifically separatist naming, coming out, community and identity, which may grow out of a more generic sense of lesbianism but is nonetheless positioned as precisely a difference. Feminism is also treated as a separator from other lesbian women, and indeed feminism of a separatist kind is seen as a mark of theoretical and practical opposition within feminism. Silences within texts are not simply absences; depending on the reader, silences can sound, can have immense consequentiality for how a particular text is read and interpreted. One of the silences of separatist coming out stories is that what are described as experiential differences – differences in emotional perception and feeling – also have considerable ontological and epistemological consequence, for the entire nature of 'reality' and one's relationship to it is thereby changed (as with 'the getting of feminism' itself indeed). These differences have rocked feminism from the days of the 'lavender menace' when lesbianism was taboo and heterosexuality an assumed iron law, through to present-day theoretical and methodological divisions concerning the nature and status of cultural and revolutionary feminisms within the feminist body politic. Relatedly, another of these silences concerns the actually marginal status within lesbian feminism of separatism, and the often entirely negative and dismissive reactions to those women who identify as such.

One way to read these coming out collections, then, and particularly the Penelope and Wolfe collection (1980/1981), is as an attempt to heal such divisions while recognising and promoting difference: as positioning separatism with other minority forms of identification within lesbian feminism among a wide spectrum of diversity, rather than the crude marking out of puristic role models that Biddy Martin claims. Another related way to read them is as a set of emphases on the complexities of the processes both of naming/ coming out and of the style of living that results. Many of the writers, for instance, actually conclude with problems and difficulties intertwined with 'happy end' features – happyish endings.

Both collections, but particularly *Inventing Ourselves*, contain coming out stories from women who do not identify as feminists and from women whose feminism came long after coming out around a stereotypical 'butch' and 'femme' mimicking (or parodying) of heterosexuality. For these women, coming out as lesbian perforce meant a separation from other women by virtue of departing from the presumption of heterosexuality; and it thereby took considerable courage, particularly when sub-cultural convention required those who rejected femme/feminine styles and behaviour thereby to publicly – because sartorially – show their difference to a hostile world. And of course here too 'community' was marked internally by separations and fractures, including between butches and femmes, a relationship capable of being every bit as hostile and mutually damaging as that between heterosexual men and women. 'Role playing' is precisely that, and one of its qualities has been the sometimes transitory and always complex nature of butch and femme modes of interaction. In other words, these roles are at least as ontologically shaky as is 'women' itself, and anyway public presentations of self can be multiply traversed by more private departures from role. Other fractures here include those derived from divisions between women who live openly – in dress or self-presentation or both – as lesbian and those who seek, apart from in particular times and places, to 'pass' as heterosexual; and between those who have a political analysis of lesbian oppression and those who accept this as a somehow deserved condition of life. In addition and increasingly so, there are divisions and separations brought about by the existence of lesbian feminism with its own, frequently diverging, analyses of the political situation of lesbianism and of the relationship between feminist women and those who reject feminism or find it an irrelevancy.

It is easy to dismiss coming out stories for their lack of sophistication in theorising 'self' and its relationship to collectivities and identities. To do so is not only to overlook the fundamentally political character of these collections and their attempts to show the wide diversity of 'lesbian experience', it also misses their dialogic quality and active engagement with active readers. This dialogic quality, and their assumption that the writer is a representative of a collective experience, marks their similarity to the Latin American women's testimonios discussed by Doris Sommer (1988), although they differ in that the testimonios assume a readership of different people who do not share their experiences. However, close attention to the specifics by which these slices of lives are narrated reveals hints and more than hints of fractures and disagreements. In addition an active because involved reader – the reader for whom these collections are intended – produces a dialogue with the coming out stories, supplying not only a more complex 'what happened next' time dimension to them, but also a continuing and knowledgeably critical engagement that stands the reader's experience alongside that of the writer as a means of assessment and a source of additional and/or conflicting information.

The presumptive feminist

'Presumptive': Giving reasonable grounds for presumption of belief; warranting inferences.

Readers read autobiographies for complex reasons and in complex ways – and including readings of the same autobiography on different occasions. One of these ways involves referentiality, and I can see no good reason other than theoretical fashion for summarily dismissing referentiality on the part of reader or writer or both. Moreover presumptions of referentiality are most certainly not facile, for they engage and make use of both the structure and the content of autobiographical writing, and thus referentiality deserves close analytic attention of the order that feminist canonical writing on autobiography devotes to self or 'auto' and to 'graph' or writing.

The autobiographical writings these theoretical collections are predicated upon do contain writing about a life as well as about the constitution and understanding of a self (that is, narrative and interpretation cannot be prised apart), and within them claims are typically made for the distinctiveness of the writing self as a female subject. And the differences of women's lives matter, not differences from an assumed exemplary male life, but rather differences from each other. Whatever else, a comparative referential reading of Ellen Kuzawayo's Call Me Woman (1985), the Sistren Collective's Lionheart Gal (1986), Miriam Makeba's Makeba: My Life (1987), Audre Lorde's Zami: A New Spelling of My Name (1983) and Coretta Scott King's My Life With Martin Luther King Jr (1969), should tell the reader something of the vast material differences within 'women's lives', here those of black women, while also emphasising that their authors recognise some commonality of experience or understanding that marks their subjects as precisely both women and black women at the level of living as well as at the level of writing.

Moreover, referentiality is more complex and interesting than is suggested, and as I have discussed earlier in this chapter it is often if not invariably constituted out of closures built around and upon gaps, fractures, alienations. A feminist theory of autobiography requires equal theoretical attention to 'the life' because doing so creates analytic troubles for current theoretical work. Not the least of these troubles is the power of the narrative that underpins 'a life' in autobiography. The narrative form is highly seductive, for all the time it engages a 'go on, what happened next?' response. Narrative form embeds certain conventions, marking points, that readers expect and look for, and the who, what, when, where and why of a narrative are among them as much as (typically if not invariably) a linear chronological structure. Analytic reflection within autobiography – the 'pure form' loved by so many critics – engages readers on a very different level. Perhaps it is more complex, sophisticated and to some more interesting; however, it is equally important to recognise the complexities of narrative and the very immediate way it engages the interest of the reader. Narrative is comparatively easy and pleasant to read and this has been influential in its dismissal as a qualitatively less significant writing form. The autobiographical writings of Hannah Cullwick, Jarena Lee, Zilpha Elaw, Julia Foote and lesbian women in coming out stories all show that narrative has its own complexities, largely deriving from those in the life that is being narrated, but textually inscribed through the complex inter-twining of narration and interpretation. In spite of taxonomies of autobiographies which determinedly treat these as distinct forms, in practice narrative or story-telling autobiographical writing and inter-pretive or hermeneutic autobiographical writing typically occur within one autobiography. Readers, common readers, know this complexity to 'a life', for it is this quality which engages our attention and interest.

The feminist reader as she has been constituted within the collections about autobiography I have discussed is a specialist theoretical and deconstructionist reader whose reading is contingent upon these and other facts of her intellectual and other autobiography. However, the contingency of her reading practices is effectively denied in this work, which is rather authoritative, certain, canonical. But the presumptive reader is a common reader who both does and does not know her place: she rejects her removal from the act of reading in canonical writing, and she knows her centrality to the system of the production and consumption of written lives, for without her this dynamic market would not exist.

The common reader recognises the power and importance of referentiality in autobiography writing and is capable of reading in an active way, recognising both the fragility of 'the self' and its constitution in and through the everyday behaviours, events, per-sons, of the life. Moreover, this reader is not inviolate but engages in a subtle process of exchange with what is read: noting and diversely using the similarities and differences of other lives inscribed in autobiography in constituting the referents of both a biography (her interpretation of the autobiography read, her emphases and omissions constituting another 'life' to stand beside the autobiographer's own), and the changing content and form of her own autobiography. At this point I move on to discuss in a more direct way the practical as well as theoretical links between biography and the autobiography of those who produce it. Although I have stressed the role and the activities of different kinds of readers in this chapter, I presented my own reading practices in very much a take it or leave it fashion. The following chapter amongst other things offers a re-reading of some of my earlier work on the case of Peter Sutcliffe, the so-called 'Yorkshire Ripper', and thus begins the task of examining reading in greater depth; however, my main discussion of reading is contained in Part Two and in particular in Chapters 5, 6 and 7.

Notes

1 The discussion of Denise Riley's work in this chapter appeared in an extended version in 'Rescuing 'women' from feminist deconstructionism' in *Women's Studies International Forum* 13:1/2:. An earlier version of the discussion of black women's spiritual autobiographies was given at the 'Feminism and Postmodernism' conference organised by Mary Evans at the University of Kent in November 1990; I am grateful to her for the opportunity to speak there.

2 And in doing so she thereby shares Lejeune's formalist prescription of autobiography as necessarily including a disposition on the inner meaning of self, the 'story of the writer's personality'.

3 An aim shared by a recent collection of Englishwomen's autobiographies of the seventeenth century edited by Elspeth Graham *et al* (1989).

4 I am assuming here that such collections are read sequentially rather than selectively, including their introductions. Thus although I have made this reading of them, readers' varying reading practices may produce alternative readings.

5 Navratilova's autobiography is ghost-written; Philippe Lejeune is one of the few writers on autobiography, in his later and less formalist work, to recognise the particular interests and problematics raised by this and related kinds of 'impure' autobiographical writing.

6 A related point here concerns whether we read differently ghost-written memoirs and autobiographies such as Navratilova's, and also how the notion of 'self' within these should be analysed, for certainly one of the indicators of autobiography as distinct from fiction – that there is a synonymity between the writer, the protagonist and the author whose name is on the title page is absent from them.

7 I have been seen (cf Swindells, 1989) as imposing present-day feminist meaning on a life which was, as seen by this commentator, antithetical to this, and doubtless will be again for what I write here about 'deconstructionist' impulses in Hannah's diaries. I discuss this criticism of my work in Chapter 6; and I try to provide evidence in this chapter to bear out my 'deconstructionist' interpretation of her writing.

8 The relationship between Hannah's diaries, Munby's life and my editorial work has been critically discussed in both Julia Swindells' chapter (1989), and in the editorial introduction to the Personal Narratives Group's (1989a, 1989b) edited collection, *Interpreting Women's Lives*. I respond to these criticisms in Chapter 6, which discusses my work in editing Hannah Cullwick's diaries in more detail.

A biographer manqué

Biography and fellow-travellers

There are many forms that writing a life can take. Certainly there are
the four outlined by Carolyn Heilbrun (1988a, p. 11): The person
can tell their life themselves in an autobiography; they can tell it in
what they may choose to call fiction; someone else may write it in
what is called biography; or the person may adopt a variety of
autobiographical, biographical and fictional motifs as the groundplan
of actually living a life. However, to these I would add at least the
following five forms:[1] Someone may write a person's biography in
what they choose to call fiction – and I would include here Thomas's
The White Hotel (1981) and Keneally's *Schindler's Ark* (1982). Someone
may 'collect' a life history, often focussed on particular themes or
dimensions, in what is called oral history or social science; and in
sociology two well-known examples are Clifford Shaw's classic life
history *The Jack Roller* (1930/1966) and Robert Bogdan's more recent
The Autobiography of Jane Fry (1974). Someone may focus on a single life
in the absence of a life history within social science; a good example
here is Brian Masters's book about the serial sexual murderer of men
Dennis Nilsen, *Killing For Company* (1985), which uses Nilsen's prison
notebooks as its source materials in order to recover an autobiographical account of Nilsen the man as well as of the crimes he
committed (a related example being my work on Peter Sutcliffe, the
serial sexual murderer of women known as the 'Yorkshire Ripper'
(Anony Ms, 1984; Stanley, 1984b; Wise & Stanley, 1987 pp. 98-
113)). Someone may edit for publication a person's written words in
a diary or letters; and I discuss editing Hannah Cullwick's diaries
(Stanley, 1984a) in Chapter 6. And perhaps most crucially, each time
a reader, each reader, reads one of these forms of life writing, they
place their own emphases, make their own omissions, produce their
own interpretations, draw their own conclusions. Each reader of
written lives is a biographer, producing their own authorised version
of that life; and a more formal approach to active readership is
provided in Chapter 7, which offers a reading of Cronwright-

Schreiner's *The Life of Olive Schreiner* (1924a). Moreover, different readings by the same reader can produce slightly or even very different versions of the life; reading, after all, is a complex business, as complex in its own way as writing; and this chapter offers a series of re-readings of my work on Sutcliffe.

Apart from the first two of Carolyn Heilbrun's ways of writing a life, all the above are forms of biography. That is, there is an authorial presence which stands between the subject and the reader: a novelist, a biographer, an editor, who shapes, selects and presents. Indeed, even within autobiography, and in spite of formalist definitions, there is no necessary referential identity between the author and the key character they write about. Another way of making this point: telling apart fiction, biography and autobiography is no easy matter, for these forms of writing a life do not exist each in a hermetically-sealed vacuum: rather each symbiotically informs both the form and the content of the others, and they also inform the living of lives. And these epistemological and ontological complexities multiply when we take into account not only written fictions but also those derived from film, radio and television, for soaps such as *Dynasty, Dallas, Neighbours, Coronation Street* and *East Enders* are more real, have more everyday realism, for many people than documentaries about ecological issues, world political summits and major human disasters, which are presented using all the tropes and artifice of drama and fiction. And when spoken and more renegade versions of lives are also taken into account, and their intertextuality with these other accounts of lives recognised, then any claim that 'biography' is a hermetically distinct genre becomes impossible to maintain.

However, this is not the way that biography is presented conventionally. Rather it is treated as self-sealed; and the biographer as apparently absent from their text other than at particular sanctioned moments. Canonically the biographer is a voice which is detached, Olympian: everywhere and nowhere in the statement of a narrative and the announcement of events and occurences, and present only in the drawing of conclusions. This is very different from how autobiography is seen. Increasingly over the last twenty years autobiography has been subject to keen analytic attention to its form as well as content. There is now a willing acceptance of its creation of a written self, of the role of fictive devices in doing so, of the part played by different narrative structures, of the impact of the statement and disruption of chronologies (Eakin, 1985; Olney, 1980; Bruss, 1976;

and in feminist terms, Jelinek, 1980; Benstock, 1988a; Stanton, 1987; Brodzki & Schenck, 1988). Succinctly, there is now a poetics or theory of autobiography, pieced together from a variety of other theorising, some aspects of which I discussed in the previous chapter.

However, writing on biography is stuck in a timewarp, protected from and resistant to the winds of change; its practitioners remain sealed off from taking seriously ideas and analyses drawn from theorising autobiography and from related discussions of the nature of 'the subject' within psychoanalytic theory and 'the self' within postmodernist theory (although see here various of the essays in Iles, 1992). There are good reasons for this, although not quite good enough, in biography's own autobiography: in its parentage, its upbringing, its endowments, education, development, and in the company it keeps.

The dominant canonical variety of biography has its origins in nineteenth-century high positivism – the professionalisation of biography and the concommitant concern with the tracking down and presentation of fact about the subject. Boswell (1934) is an ambiguous forerunner, because he has now been unmasked as a rampant interpretivist (Dowling, 1978); Froude (1882, 1884) is an interesting and complex precursor; John Foster (1844, 1874a, 1874b, 1875), commissioned handsomely to write on Goldsmith, Landor, Dickens, Swift, Cromwell and others, represents the first full-flowering of the professional biographer and Michael Holroyd (1968, 1971, 1974-1975, 1988, 1990, 1991) its latest British bloom.

Of course there are other strands within biography, some very different indeed. For instance, there is psychoanalytically-influenced biographical writing such as Sigmund Freud's *Leonardo Da Vinci* (1947), Eric Erikson's *Young Man Luther* (1958) and Jerrold Siegel's *Marx's Fate* (1978). A smaller and presently less influential strand also exists, of what Ira Bruce Nadel (1984) calls 'meta-biography', such as A. J. A. Symons's work on Corvo (1934) and Brigit Brophy's on Firbank (1973); as well as a more analytical although minor strand of sociological biography that includes Steven Lukes on Emile Durkheim (1975), David McLellan on Karl Marx (1973, 1989) and more recently Simone Weil (1989), Reinhart Bendix on Max Weber (1977), and Helmut Wagner on Alfred Schutz (1983). And even within this dominant form other 'voices', in the form of the insertion of modes of narration drawn from these other strands, speak within the resulting text: the purity of Gordon Haight's life of George Eliot (1968) is both the apotheosis of the canonical form and rarely matched by other biographers. However, it remains true that biography is seen as a kind of science or at least as having many of the attributes of science. Certainly many of its practitioners – at least in public – seem to see themselves as sensitive scientists who write with style; and the leitmotif of professional biography remains the concern, apparently expected by both readers and writers, with accuracy, objectivity, detail.

What is needed is a critical response to these conventional pieties and assumptions in the form of a developed theory of biography influenced by cultural politics and feminist theory. Within this, as within the poetics of autobiography, the author, here the biographer, would be firmly located as an active, indeed a determining (even if not totally determining), presence at biography's centre. The key is the argument, the insistence, that 'writing a life' in a number of forms – biography, autobiography, editing diaries, fiction, life histories – entails a similar set of problematics solved, or at least approached, in similar ways; and that analytically understanding and appreciating these requires a focus on the how of writing rather than only on what is written. This requires moving away from treating the narrative and the narrator as transparent, instead turning the attention of readers towards authors and their artful practices in shaping a life and so guiding a reading. The defining feature of biography is on one level the documentation of a life, but wrapping this round so closely that most of the time readers and commentators fail to notice it, is the equally defining fact that biography is a literary act of composition: the production of a written text and the dependence of the author on the conventions and tools of an 'appropriate' language, a formal language shared with other authors working in apparently quite different genres.

I move on to sketch out what such a theory might encompass by stressing the generic properties of all forms of life writing. To indicate this genericism I use the term 'auto/biography', a term which refuses any easy distiction between biography and autobiography, instead recognising their symbiosis; and it also collects into it social science and other apparently 'objective' ways of producing and using life histories of different kinds. In the later parts of the chapter I examine more closely some aspects of the ramifications of writing biography for the autobiography of the biographer; and I do this with reference to my failed biographical work on the case of Peter Sutcliffe, the so-called Yorkshire Ripper.

Towards a theory of auto/biography

Auto/biography is not and cannnot be referential of a life. Memory is selective: paradoxically, a defining feature of remembering is that most things are forgotten or exist half-submerged to be occasionally and unpredictably propelled to the mind's surface – each of us a Proust transfixed by a madeleine. Also constructing a life – piecing together various kinds and forms of remembrances of a self's past – is itself highly selective: selecting in what fits a framework, selecting out what appears not centrally relevant. Thus auto/biography is more properly to be seen as artful construction within a narrative that more often than not employs a variety of methods and tools which imply referentiality. Authorial authority is itself constructed within this narration by the production of facts, statements, quotations from letters or verbal sources, even reported speech and sometimes reported thoughts: in biography Richard Ellmann on Joyce (1959/1982) comes to mind, in autobiography Maya Angelou (1969, 1974, 1976, 1981, 1986). In other words, the auto/biographer signals clearly their competence and expertise by a variety of markers which readers know are to be taken as indicative of such; and the impact of this is cumulative in reading auto/biography, such that interpretations and conclusions are written as if they are inevitable products of their underpinning mass of announced fact. However, 'the facts' are actually what Hayden White (1978, p. 125) has called 'congeries of contiguously related fragments'. A telling example is that even a lengthy chapter which deals with one focussed event in a life is necessarily highly selective of what is included. In the narration, occurrence may logically follow occurrence, and the former appear to have been causal of the latter, but in life these will have been separated by a multitude of behaviour, speech, thought. It is the interpretation of the auto/biographer which assigns consanguinity to them. However, the narration implies, persuades, insists, by its structure that these and only these occurrences are directly related and meaningful; and its main means of doing so is the (apparently) chronological nature of what is told: order and development are implied by chronology, and so too is causality.

These authorised facts are actually authorised *fictions*, the picking out of specifics related by the interpretive understanding of the author and presented as generic unfolding truths about the subject. They 'work', gain their authority and apparent impregnability, through two closely related narrative forms, which Tzvetan Todorov (1977) refers to as the narratives of contiguity and of substitution. A narrative of contiguity is a representational narrative built up through the statement of facts, events, persons and so forth; it is linear – a history in the strict sense of the word – and it links through contiguous placing in the text. A good example is what Brain Masters (1985) does with Nilsen's notebooks, pulling together into a contiguous narrative material which careful study of his references shows is actually drawn from different notebooks, written at different times, addresssing different topics. A narrative of substitution, by contrast, is concerned with promoting interpretation and understanding; it uses figurative language to stand for a point of view established through contiguous narrative; it is circular in its argument, relying heavily on metaphor. A good example is the way that Michael Holroyd (1988) uses different names to stand for particular phases of Shaw's unfolding character as contiguously built up: Sonny precedes George precedes Bernard Shaw precedes GBS.

Certainly the use of tropes is important in the structuring and impact of auto/biography, even if these are not always quite as discussed by Kenneth Burke's *A Grammar of Motives* (1955) and more recently used to stress the tropes-laden nature of anthropological ethnographies (see Clifford and Marcus, 1986; Marcus and Fischer, 1986; Geertz, 1988). However, as the example of Holroyd's Shaw suggests, tropes are inevitably hitched to contiguous narrative. But which is the horse and which the cart depends on particular examples. Often, for example, metaphor can drive an entire factual narrative – Cronwright-Schreiner's (1924a) *a priori* insistence on Olive Schreiner as a genius who was a wayward child, Boswell's (1934) coupling of 'portrait' and 'monument' in relation to his biography of Johnson, Gordon Haight's (1968) view of George Eliot as absolutely needing a man to lean upon – which, once read, floods a reader's understanding of the rest of the text. And similarly so with irony, which deliberately and completely structures all else in Edmund Gosse's *Father and Son* (1907/1983) and undermines the surface pieties invoked about his father.[2]

But of course writers of the same subject's life frequently disagree, not only about complex matters such as the interpretation of character and motive, but also about apparently more simple, but actually more fundamental, matters such as which events and persons were important to the auto/biographical subject or sometimes even whether they happened or not. For instance, from reading *Orlando* (1928) and her diaries and letters, I think Virginia Woolf clearly felt that Vita Sackville-West was a person of great significance in her personal and writing life; and this importance is accepted by Phyllis Rose (1978), demurred over by Quentin Bell (1972a, 1972b), and blandly denied in a dismissive few lines by Lyndall Gordon (1984). Moreover, the grounds on which at least some biographers take issue with their autobiography-writing subjects focus on their treatment of what the biographer takes to be key fact and in particular its absence or claimed mis-representation by autobiographers: the fussing over Colette's (1922/1929) fictionalising of aspects of her own as well as her mother Sido's life, the picking over of Henry James's (1956) chronological misplacing of the fire in which he claimed injury and thus the grounds of his failure to fight in the Civil War, and discussions about the reasons for Zora Neale Hurston's (1942) failure to treat issues of race, racism and white patronage with sufficient (in present-day terms) outrage and overt anger, are three such instances.

For most biographers, and I would say also for social science producers and users of other kinds of written lives, facts tend to be if not all then certainly crucial, while autobiographers have other ends and purposes in what they write and how they write it. However, as I have argued concerning the construction of a narrative of contiguity, this difference between biographers and fellow-travellers on the one hand, and autobiographers and fellow-travellers on the other, is more apparent than real. Contiguous narrative is a fabrication in both senses of the word: both an artifice, and also the weaving together of separate strands to make a fabric, a whole. It is also useful to remember that 'the facts' are not 'there' to be discovered or uncovered – they are a result of temporally and structurally located epistemological changes which enable different things to be 'seen', to be comprehended. Froude's (1882, 1884) loving portrayal of Thomas Carlyle as having faults was greatly disapproved of; to have discussed his probably celibate marriage with Jane Welsh Carlyle was at the time unthinkable.

The facts, then, are a product of their time and place as well as of their author. They are also (although in the theoretical literature on auto/biography this is never mentioned let alone discussed) a product of their *readers*. Reading is both active and a process; it also relies heavily on intertextuality. Texts are certainly not inert and how they are structured certainly intends a preferred reading (Smith 1983, 1990), and the active text is a focus of ethnomethodological and feminist attention within sociology. However, readers are also *active* readers (McHoul 1983). We may be textually persuaded, cajoled, led and misled; but we can, and we do, also scrutinise and analyse, puzzle and ponder, resist and reject. Readers, then, form a discriminating audience, one with its own understandings; and it is a fragmented audience – not an 'it', 'the audience', at all, but rather a large number of people who multiply engage in its largely solitary virtues and vices. But also authors have in mind 'the reader', 'the buying public', in writing lives for publication: Froude could not have written about, even if he could think about, the celibate marriage of the Carlyles without this having produced either the refusal of publication or his ostracism by his peers and the reading public of the day. This may be so, but it is worth remembering that many seditious things *were* thought and written and published by the supposedly stodgy Victorians: feminism, socialism, anti-racism, anti-colonialism, sexual liberation and sexual subjection were all dis-courses being made and promoted at the time of Froude's half-hints. In other words, writers may make assumptions about readers and their values which will not stand up under close scrutiny and which are designed to make the resulting textual product appeal to as many potential consumers as possible.

One of these assumptions concerns characterisation in auto/biography. The vast majority of auto/biographies of all kinds and shapes contain a limited range of character: a cast of one under the limelight supported by a few bit-part players who come and then typically go in the relative darkness around the star. Biographies are generally less limited in this respect, but even here the subject is always centre stage, other people always peripheral. How unlike life and yet how absolutely central to the auto/biographical project. Auto/biography has at its heart a project which is concerned with the artful construction of a self-in-writing, a self which can be as it were looked in the eye. Using Roland Barthes's (1975a) distinction, auto/biography turns on a tripartite pivot: the self who *writes* constructs a self who *was* (an other self for biography, a past self for autobiography); but there is also a self who is, outside of the text as it is written, who continues to grow older and to change after it is completed but who is prototypically unmentioned.[3] And as I discussed in Chapter 2, Barthes' *Camera Lucida* (1980) is a good albeit disguised example of this dislocation or plethora of selves.

Running counter to the emphasis on the single essentially ungendered exemplary self in auto/biography are claims that women's autobiographies are different, less ego-focussed and more concerned with self located in a network of others. Following Estelle Jelinek's (1980) argument Mary Mason (1980/1988), for example, proposes that, instead of the drive to ego-fulfillment which characterises men's autobiographies, women's autobiographies tend to adopt one of four very different structures. She says that in these four patterns:

we can discover not only important beginnings in the history of women's autobiography... but also something like a set of paradigms for life writing by women down to our time... Nowhere in women's autobiographies do we find the patterns established by the two prototypical male autobiographers, Augustine and Rousseau; and conversely, male writers never take up the archetypal models of Julian, Margery Kempe, Margaret Cavendish, and Anne Bradstreet. (Mason, 1980/1988, p. 21)

These four 'paradigms' involve the autobiographical self being defined through a relationship with an other, and they consist of self defined in relation to: a single transcendental other, such as God (Dame Julian of Norwich); a transcendental other and a worldly relationship with a loved other (Margery Kempe); one other loved person (Margaret Cavendish); and a collectivity of others (Anne Bradstreet).

The grounds for Mason's argument and those influenced by her (e.g. Friedman, 1988; Marcus, 1988) are not essentialist ones, but rather that such supposedly distinctive patterns of life writing are the product of material differences in men's and women's lives within partriarchy. Even so I find it unconvincing. Autobiographies by, for instance, F. Scott Fitzgerald (1936) and Henry James (1956), seen as being as archetypical of male ego-focussed writing as those by Augustine and Rousseau, actually exemplify the dependence of their subjects on others: Fitzgerald in 'The crack-up'on the friends who unknowingly supplied the constitutent elements of his post-breakdown self; James in his *Autobiography* on the omnipresence of brother William, taller, stronger, clever, more handsome, more successful and continuingly 'other' to James's always fragile autonomy. Also examples of autobiographical writing by men can be found to fit the four 'female' modes identified by Mason: Edmund Gosse's (1907/ 1983) autobiography defined through his relationship with one other, his father; Pierre Teilhard de Chardin's (1962, 1968, 1969, 1970) letters, which pivot on his relationship with the transcendental other of God/Christ; Leonard Woolf's (1960, 1961, 1964, 1967, 1969) autobiography, in which he positions himself within the overlapping collectivities of 'Bloomsbury', socialism, Fabianism; and Cecil Beaton's (1973, 1979) diary in which his self is intertwined with his mother and Greta Garbo.

Male examples of the four paradigms ascribed by Mason to women only exist in plenitude. And conversely, many examples exist of autobiographical writing by women who are as ego-focussed as Augustine and Rousseau: Marie Bashkirtseff's (1928) autobiography must be the prime example because of her important influence on women's autobiography writing by the generation immediately following its publication; but more recent examples include Rosemary Manning's two autobiographies *A Time and a Time* (1971) and *A Corridor of Mirrors* (1987) , and the recently decoded *Diaries of Anne Lister* (Whitbread, 1988). Being 'ego-focussed' is often no bad thing and nor is it necessarily synonymous with being selfish or uncaring of others; and certainly it is no bad thing for women struggling in a social context in which to be so was/is taboo: how else would Florence Nightingale, Elizabeth Barrett, Marie Bashkirtseff, Zora Neale Hurston, Anne Lister, Rosemary Manning, Maya Angelou, Simone Weil, Simone de Beauvoir, have become what they did?.

Making Barthes' apparently simple distiction between the self who writes, the self who was, and the self who is, immediately challenges the central myth of auto/biographical writing, the myth of a single, coherent, stable and gradually unfolding inner and indubitably real essential self. Auto/biography smooths out of sight doubts as to the nature of the self – or at least those selves who write or have auto/ biographies written about them, if not the selves of common readers – by treating its reality as an *a priori* truth. Again, there are always exceptions, but mostly exceptions which prove the rule. For instance, Fitzgerald's 'The crack-up' may concern his breakdown, but it is also a strategy for re-building a self, or at least the re/semblance of a self, out of a job-lot of other men's characteristics. And Rosemary Manning's (1971, 1987) two autobiographies confront the same dilemma and adopt a very similar strategy; she too struggles

for, and obtains, a (real) self – real for all practical purposes. Both
Fitzgerald and Manning survive, more whole than before; both
contribute, albeit complexly, to the mythology of self which informs
auto/biographical practice.

The 'projects' of the autobiographers mentioned above is on one
level easily recoverable from material provided in the text (e.g.
Lister, Bashkirtseff, Fitzgerald, Beaton and Manning) or from a
combination of this and externally-available information (eg. James,
Gosse, Woolf, Teilhard de Chardin, Neale Hurston). Similar projects
can be discerned in the work of many women autobiographers:
Colette exorcising her betrayal of Sido by reconstructing a house and
a garden before the fall; Maya Angelou constructing the black
woman warrior triumphant; Carolyn Steedman (1986) speaking to
her mother by constructing a new biographical form for those –
women, working class people – excluded by the assumptions and
form of the convention, and Gertrude Stein (1933, 1938) completely disrupting auto/biography writing.

Biographers are committed to projects concerned with accounting
for the proceses of self-creation. There are some forty or so 'serious'
biographies of George Eliot, as many if not now more of Virginia
Woolf. There are three main grounds, or mixtures of them, that
these congeries of biographers use to justify their own particular
activity, and these reveal the project that underpins each author's
work. These are, firstly, the uncovering or discovering of new factual
information (as with Ina Taylor (1989) on Eliot's girlhood and
marriage to John Cross); secondly, writing about aspects previously
'unseen' following an epistemological shift (as with Susan Chitty's
(1974) discussion of Charles Kingsley's combination of sexual and
religious mortification beneath a bluff matter-of-fact exterior, or
Louise DeSalvo's (1989) account of persistent child sexual abuse in
the Stephen household and Virginia Woolf's varied writings about
this); and thirdly, conviction of a new and illuminating interpretation of character, events, work or all three (as with feminist re-
working of Woolf's character, life and work in the face of much
disapproval from the 'Woolf mainstream'). Other interesting examples of biographers' projects include Michael Holroyd's (1968)
calculated matter-of-factness about Lytton Strachey's gay relationships and self-perception as a sexual outsider; Ruth Dudley Edwards'
(1976) determined breaching of the mythology of Patrick Pearse the
shining perfect Irish martyr, and Wendy Webster's (1990)

gendering of Margaret Thatcher's constructed armory of being 'the best man' in the British Conservative government from 1969 to 1990.

Biographers are at least as active as autobiographers in the re/de/ construction of self in the writing of a life; are at least as fertile in their inventive use of, indeed construction of, 'the facts'; and at least as adept in their deployment of a range of fictive devices (Eakin. 1985) in establishing authorial authority and factual status for their writing. By the notion of 'fictive devices' Eakin intends at least two meanings: firstly that fictions and fiction-making are central con- stituents of the truth of any life; and secondly that story-telling is the fundamental property of all writing about a life. As the title of Dennis Petrie's (1981) edited collection proposes, biography is necessarily Ultimately Fiction.

If not novelists, biographers are certainly adept in the use of fictive devices. Biographers just like autobiographers are writers, albeit writers bound by a perceived duty to produce some kind of factually-located account. They too select, omit, invent a narrative form, direct the reader's interpretation of the subject, interpret, conclude. Biography is not the representation but the re-making, not the reconstruction but the construction, in written form of a life. However, biographers as writers are typically as omnipotent and absent as Godot, for they are the central character of, although not in, their text. The author in biography writing is an almost invariably absent character although an active controlling presence. There are three typical 'voices' available for the biographical author through which different kinds of biographical discourse are produced (Nadel, 1984): participation, detachment, and analysis. These voices might be characterised as the speech of participation, the thought of detachment, and the whisper of analysis, for each is differently and characteristically modulated. Nadel uses the examples of Boswell (1934) for participation, Lockhart (1837-1838) for detachment, and Strachey (1918) for analysis; and recognises that many biographers mix these voices or discourses. Although this and Todorov's notion of two narrative styles are both interesting ideas, they cannot easily be tied together, in the sense that contiguous narration permits of each voice as does the narrative of substitution. It also remains doubtful how far Nadel's account of biographical discourse can be taken. For instance, both Boswell and Virginia Woolf, whose Orlando (1928) Nadel in a later passage presents as the most radical of departures from the biographical canon, are examples of a participatory stance, both adopting dramatic/expressive stances; and yet Boswell's work on Johnson supports and insists upon realism, while Woolf's on Orlando/Vita Sackville-West ironises, undermines and flagrantly rejects a realist position. The realist or anti-realist intentions and writing of the auto/biographer seem to me more useful in gauging authorial voice than a focus on stance alone, although clearly both are important.

The largely denied perspective of the author in biography becomes central in a poetics of auto/biography. Recognising this authorial centrality disrupts the supposed omnipotence that positivist ideas assume. If the author is a fabricator, then the reader can unpick, re-stitch, and re-fashion. Disrupting authorial omnipotence can take a number of different forms. One of these is for readers to require, and authors to produce, what Nadel calls 'meta-biography'; that is, for biographers to locate themselves as a character within the text: and his main example is of Symons's *The Quest for Corvo* (1934). This is not, as might be supposed, to turn every biography into standard autobiographical writing. It is rather to produce 'intellectual autobiography', focussing on factors involved in the genesis and development of the writer's understanding and interpretation of the biographical subject or subjects. That is, it focusses upon biographical *processes*, rather than the *product* of these alone. And as with this necessity in biography, so it could be productive of a different stance within autobiography. Mary McCarthy's *Memories of a Catholic Girlhood* (1957) is an interesting precursor of this approach, containing more analytic fibre than the average autobiography for a readerly digestion to take hold of through her continual questioning and disruption of facticity in her 'descriptions' of the past. It is this feature of intellectual autobiography and its symbiotic relationship with other aspects of the biographer's feelings and thoughts that I pursue in relation to my work on the courtroom and media-constructed and promoted biography of Peter Sutcliffe, the so-called 'Yorkshire Ripper', and the two pieces of writing that finally emerged from this, in its original terms *failed*, research process; I also discuss it again in Chapter 9, 'Is there a feminist auto/biography?'.

Mr Normal meets The Beast, or how 'The Yorkshire Ripper' became Peter Sutcliffe, by Anony MS[4]

Some events in the life and times of Peter Sutcliffe

A roll call of the dead and maimed:

July 1975	Anna Rogulskyi attacked
August 1975	Olive Smelt attacked
October 1975	Wilma McCann killed
January 1976	Emily Jackson killed
May 1976	Marcella Claxton attacked
February 1977	Irene Richardson killed
April 1977	Patricia Atkinson killed
June 1977	Jayne MacDonald killed
July 1977	Maureen Long attacked
September 1977	Jean Jordan killed
December 1977	Marilyn Moore attacked
January 1978	Yvonne Pearson killed
January 1978	Helen Rytka killed
May 1978	Vera Millward killed
April 1979	Josephine Whitaker killed
September 1979	Barbara Leach killed
August 1980	Marguerita Walls killed
September 1980	Upadhya Bandara attacked
November 1980	Theresa Sykes attacked
November 1980	Jacqueline Hill killed
January 1981	Peter Sutcliffe found with Olivia Reivers and arrested
May 1981	Peter Sutcliffe tried and convicted for the murder of 13 women and the attempted murder of 7 more

And also remember this...

1 During the investigation of the deaths and attacks for which Peter Sutcliffe was later arrested, tried and convicted, several hundred women told the police they thought that their lover/spouse/father/brother/son was the so-called 'Yorkshire Ripper'.

2 At football matches and in pubs, when the police canvassed for information about 'the Ripper' massed gatherings of men chanted in praise of him and his activities.

3 Public opinion (sometimes called the mass media) took very little notice of the attacks or killings until so-called 'respectable' women were involved. Until 'public opinion' became concerned the police appeared to take very little notice either.

4 Most murders of women are sexual murders and the dead bear the same marks as Sutcliffe's victims: torsos battered and stamped upon; nipples bitten or sliced off; vaginas raped with knives, brooms and broken bottles; uteruses mutilated and often partially or completely cut-out.

5 Peter Sutcliffe was a considerate and loving husband and son who hated
and feared 'women' because our existence gave the lie to his feelings of
superiority.
6 What Sutcliffe did in the north of England other men do the world over.

Is this the start of something big?

COSMIC BATTLE ON HERLAND FRONTIER
Today a battle is being waged by the combined forces of Law 'n' Order,
Decency, Family Life, Manhood and Virility somewhere on the borders of
The Good Life. The enemy are the loathsome Harpies of Herland.
    The Harpies are trying to castrate our menfolk, destroy the fabric of
society, run off with our women and poison the minds of those too young
to recognize their evil ways.
    It has been rumoured that some of the Harpies *are* our women, but the
American President has released the information that Soviet spies have
infiltrated The Good Life and spread this filthy perverted communist propaganda to weaken our iron resolve. (From *The Daily Oppressor*, 23.12.1999)

STOP PRESS
 A report from our war correspondent: Devastating clash on herland border
stop spokeswoman Lois Lane tells of her sudden conversion to harpy-hood
stop she and wonderwoman release previously classified information stop
claim they know real identity of The Beast stop released Beast's real name stop
all hell broke loose stop outraged manhood conducted berserker onslaught
stop many killed stop manhood spokesman said Lois Lane statement
destructive stop retaliation fully justified stop. (From *The Daily Oppressor*,
23.12.1999)

Who is The Beast?

    The unknown killer known as The Beast has sexually maimed or killed a
few hundred million women and children of both sexes over the last five
thousand years alone. His latest victims include three red terror gang
members who were orally, anally and vaginally raped before being
strangled in their cells, some nuns from a hill station school ditto and
partially burned, the dismembered person of some woman or other found
in her own blood in a metropolis bathtub, and a nice 87-year old who was
shat on and had her nipples burned before being raped by three young men
and then dying from a serious blow to the head.
    The deaths of seven assorted children cannot be detailed because they
were too young to count and anyway they smiled at their assailants. The
nuns were innocent and therefore count (except one who once mastur-
bated), while all the others went out or stayed in without a man to protect
them and don't count either.
    A police spokesman said yesterday 'We are determined to find who The
Beast is. We will not give up in our struggle with him, his continual evasion
of arrest insults us. We are searching mental hospitals and the files of all

psychiatrists and psychologists for a hugely tall and stupendously muscled man of magnificent intelligence who salivates heavily, pants continually and wears a hat saying 'I'm The Beast kiss me quick before you die missis". So far we have not interviewed anyone fitting this description. Until we find him all women are advised to sit inside locked steel boxes and hand the keys to any passing male.'

The latest theory being worked on by the medical profession is that The Beast is a Superhero or Titan who has gone to the bad because of malsocialisation caused by a deprived early herohood at the Beginning of Time. Dr Hands Eyesken claims that such crimes are always linked to high rise housing and a domineering working mother. A paper by Wimp deMan criticizing Eyesken's position points out that at the Beginning of Time housing was low. Eyesken's rejoinder, given in an exclusive interview, is that there are always mothers and His Mother Did Him Wrong. (From Glorry Wailer's column, Old Statesman Christmas Issue, December 1999)

A somewhat fishy course

The divide and rule principle I:
Have you ever noticed that men come in two types? There are the Mr Normals and The Nasties. We all get warned about The Nasties: don't talk to them in the streets or take sweets from them; slap their wandering hands and reject instantly their indecent proposals; and so on ad nauseam even unto death. And they still get us there on the cold privacy of the slab; and we're even guilty of that for dying with holes between our legs. Remind me to have mine bricked up if ever I show signs of dying. I want to die hygienically, untouched by inhuman prick.

The Tale of Mr Normal:
He does it on 'Impulse', the advertisement says so. He's going down this escalator and she's going up another. He smells her as she goes past, that headysweetsmellingfromthesprayofherperfume. A tasty little dish to set before and before you can say 'off with his briefcase' he thinks 'my taste buds bud, a meal is in prospect boyo'. He goes down the escalator, buys some flowers and runs up the steps to follow this dish. He catches her with consummate ease, for she's hobbled with a skirt and crippled on fingerthick heels, what's called fair game for a running man the hunter with this lethal bouquet. In front of her he bares his teeth and thrusts into her face the stunning flowers. She's stunned he notes her name and number birth date address weight IQ and political affiliations. She moves off, still dazed. He stands and shows his teeth some more while swallowing heavily. Impulse they call it, that deliberate making of decisions and then carrying them out, just as long as you don't take more than about four months over it.

The divide and rule principle II:
Have you ever noticed that there are two types of women? There are Bad Girls, who grow up into Sick Bitches or Silly Cunts, and Good Girls, who become Wives and Mothers and then get put into good homes when

they're old. They're differentiated because Bad Girls can't tell the Mr Normals from The Nasties. This is both a moral failing and so chosen, and what they're all really like anyway and so determined; both ways they deserve what they get.

The dish of the day

Song of the dish:
> Hip hip hooray
> I'm the dish of the day
> I like it, I love it, I'm happy forever
> I wash me, I clean me, I'm nice fried or stewed
> I'm not very bright and nor am I clever
> But boy am I tender when served in the nude

Thinks the dish:
I couldn't get work as a brain surgeon, which is all I'm trained for, and it's a job, hell it's a job. And no, before you ask, it's not demeaning at all to lie in a dish surrounded by boiled carrots and broccoli having gravy hurled at me.

Revenge of the dish:
Arnold Scrunge, aged 41 and $3/4$, ate the dish of the day yesterday. Since then it has been repeating on him. Every time he burps or farts the ghostly sounds of the song of the dish are heard. He was admitted to hospital last night after being assaulted by outraged Manhood punishing him as a traitor to the cause.

Your B/bill:

> Armageddon,
> Christmas Eve,1999

Dear Susan,
Hoping this finds you as it leaves me. We're stuck in the mud here at Armageddon and some very peculiar goings on have been going on. First Lois Lane turns up and denounces Superman as male supremacist racist right wing uptight and into fascism with a have a nice day smile. Then Wonderwoman renounces her American citizenship saying that women are citizens of nowhere with no country nor even any memorial to their countless dead.
Then they both give a press conference and say they have conclusive proof that The Beast is ...wait for it, Mr Normal!!!
Have you ever heard anything like it? I mean, we all know there are two types of men. Anyway, our gallant boys of the free press have refused to print such stuff, so doubtless you'll get this censored. But, just in case, I know you can be trusted not to tell.

> With love from Bill xxxx

Nowhere,
Christmas Day, 1999

Dear Bill,

You were too dear. Enough is enough and no more, no thanks, so over and out.

Goodbye, Susan

PS Did you know I was a Harpy?

PPS I might just see you stuck in the mud at Armageddon as I fly over with the rest of the Harpies.

PPPS Everyone knows who The Beast is.

PPPPS No tip – you were terrible, all tough and gristle.

How 'the Yorkshire Ripper' became Peter Sutcliffe, or did he?

Some problems in mind travel:

Mr Normal, our fearless hero, plunges into mind travel as ducks to blancmange, forwarned and forearmed like Bluto with the one Absolute Truth: 'Never, repeat, never meet yourself anywhere in mind, for then you may see who you really are. You don't want that and nor does anyone else. Anyway, if you did Life As We Know It might have to end unless we could figure out something else to do' (from *The Absolute Truth* 31.12.1999)

Mr Normal seals the capsule hood, smiles at all around and vanishes....While he's gone a woman has her head smashed in with a brick in a sock in the next street....He reappears, smiling, and kisses his wife.

Mr Normal seals the capsule hood, smiles at all around and vanishes....A city away a woman with half her head smashed in is fucked so the listening men think her choking and her moans are of pleasure....Our hero returns, smiling, to his lovely wife.

Mr Normal seals the capsule hood, smiles at all around and vanishes....Some streets away a woman gets in a passing mindcraft and her fate is sealed with the capsule hood....Home comes our hero.

Mr Normal seals the capsule hood, smiles at all around and vanishes...flashes into sight eyes cold and hard...vanishes...flickers into sight and a woman enters the craft...more flickering and vanishing....Somewhere in another city we hear The Beast is caught. Meanwhile search parties comb all mind for the missing Mr Normal.

The case of the vanishing man

In the court there is this thing – huge with gnashing teeth, lolling purple tongue and hideously deformed face. A woman runs forward, revealed as a Harpy, and snatches at him. A mask is torn and his face shows clearly. It is, it seems to be, it can't be, some claim it is, the missing Mr Normal. Sligo MD etcetera, Mrs Normal's psychiatrist, tells of her former secret Harpyhood and how she turned him Funny, always making him Wash His Organ Before Coitus. He had No Chance and the Voices came. 'The Harpies claimed it was Mr Normal wearing nothing but the face of Mr Normal with the police and gutterhounds thinking it was the mask of The Beast', shouts

Sligo in triumphal roar, 'but all along it was The Beast wearing the mask of
Mr Normal wearing the face of Mr Normal wearing the mask of The Beast'.
He leaps forward and tears from the face of Mr Normal the face of Mr
Normal and we see the face of... Mr Normal. All mind shimmers. Men
scream in self horror and women pack their leaving bags.

The sirens begin their silvery screaming 'mindtornmindrepairmind-
repairmindrepair' over and over. Suddenly a voice like glue from a most
expensive agency, accompanied by tunes from Tchaikovsky, seeps into our
ears and wraps around the torn and bleeding pieces of mind. 'I could tell
you a story perhaps, but it's time for the whole truth, a usual sort of case
but you must be given the complete picture in the public interest, well he
killed them yes but there were extenuating circumstances, he said so
himself, most of them were fair game for a running man, the others he
thought were the others, game for him, and anyway God had got himself
involved by then and I mean, you can't go too hard on God can you now?
that's understood of course, and then, his lovely wife was odd, not really
normal, a sick bitch in fact, and like to like, except that it was she who
made him like that, so then he got a little beastly, I know the shrinks didn't
come over very well, half gone themselves just between us two, I mean nice
enough but not men of the world, very gullible, but there's a lot in what
they say, everyone who has spent any time with him will tell you, except
the deceased ha ha, most of them have lost their tongues cat got them ha ha,
anyway and then she, so he, then she, while he, and another she, then he,
for she, all the time he, now he, goodbye she, and then he was All Beast for
that Sick Bitch while Mr Normal not Mr Normal anymore, nice and sleepy
now so snuggle down right down in the warm close our little peepers sweet
dreams good night Good Girls. Come on Boys out to play at midnight, 31
December 1999'.

Twenty theses, gift wrapped

1 All women are Harpies, we love to feel the wind in our wild hair as we
sweep and wheel in the open sky in our minds.
2 We disguise it in fear for our very being.
3 We lose our lives and our being in disguising ourselves.
4 All men know we are Harpies.
5 Therefore we are not men.
6 So they hate us for being different.
7 Difference is what men were made to destroy.
8 But women give life to men as well as Harpies.
9 Ergo women have to be retained until expendable
10 And anyway, hating makes men feel good, there, present, correct.
11 Harpyhood has to be controlled if it can't be destroyed: so they lie: we
love you (we hate you but we need you); so they cheat: you can't do
without us (we deny you the chance to find out); so they steal 1: you
haven't minds like ours (we took them from you as much as we could); so
they steal 2: you haven't the strength we have (we cripple and maim you to

make sure); so they steal 3: you haven't time to do and know (we take it from you as our guarantee).

12 All men are born just mouths and bums but grow up more than a little beastly.

13 Because for reasons imperfectly understood they can't tolerate difference or otherness.

14 Which has to be destroyed or denied or they think they don't exist.

15 But otherness has to exist (they scream in terror) or they wouldn't exist either.

16 So they smarten up The Beast, push him out of sight and hope he doesn't crawl out at inconvenient moments.

17 The world is full of men who pull aside their shirts to show each other the size of the sniggering Beast inside.

18 But we know he's there, in fair man and in foul.

19 Keep your shirts buttoned tight boys for the Harpies hunt tonight.

20 Our hunt has no prey but it does have a place and a consequence; the place is everywhere and we go with the light; and the consequence is that we leave you alone in the dark, each of you alone with your very own raping, murdering, insulting, selfish, foul-tempered, pampered, sniggering, sulky, harassing, hungry little Beast. Goodnight, boys.

The practice of auto/biography

Like many women in Britain, in the north of England in particular, I followed the unfolding horror story of the murders and attempted murders assigned to 'the Yorkshire Ripper' with both fear and fascination. Fear for my safety and that of other women known and unknown to me, because most feminists recognised from the outset that this man killed not prostitutes but women, women vulnerable to attack, Any Woman. Fascination because of the extraordinary activities of the press following the murders of Jayne MacDonald in June 1977 and Josephine Whittaker in April 1979, dubbed by the media the first 'innocent' victims of the Ripper; because of the signal incompetence of the police derived from structural reasons (that the murderer could be Any Man) which seemed completely to elude them; and in particular because the biography of 'the Ripper' built up in the activities of media and police-as-reported-by-the-media was the antithesis of what feminist analysis proposed the murderer would be like and what the causes of his butchery were.

For some years until the arrest of Peter Sutcliffe I followed national and local press reporting of murders of women allocated to the Ripper and also murders of women not so allocated. I collected press cuttings, tape recorded radio and video recorded television news and other programmes. I talked to friends and acquaintances who were journalists and psychologists and who had had dealings with the police 'hunt'. The arrest, trial and conviction of Peter Sutcliffe brought with them extraordinary events during the trial, such as the appalling and illegal antics of the press in buying some witnesses and harassing to the point of persecution those (like Sonia Sutcliffe) they could not buy; in the attempted collusion of defence and prosecution to have an insanity plea accepted without trial; in the examination and cross-examination of Sutcliffe and his 'God made me do it, they deserved to die' narrative; in the mind-bogglingly incompetent evidence of some of the psychiatric 'expert witnesses'; and in the tacit agreement of both defence and prosecution that some victims deserved to die less than others.

Existing feminist analyses of such events by Wendy Hollway (1981), Lucy Bland (1984) and Nicole Ward Jouve (1984 in French and 1986 in an English version) seemed insufficient on a number of grounds. Media accounts were treated in a cultural studies framework by Lucy Bland as representational of not only the trial but also the events of the attacks and murders and the characters and behaviours of persons discussed or examined in court; Wendy Hollway's analysis suggested in a reductionist psychologistic fashion that all men could and probably would engage in similar activities to Sutcliffe as well as also treating media accounts as directly representational of actual events; and Nicole Ward Jouve argued out the literary semantics of the case and proposed a romanticised version of 'the north' and 'the moors' which for me de-politicised in disturbing ways these acts of horror. My approach continued the work I had started earlier, ironising by taking apart media accounts as precisely accounts and not as representations, with the planned end of obtaining the transcripts of the trial and of using textual analytic means (Lury, 1982; Smith, 1983; McHoul, 1983; Boulos, 1984; Stanley, 1984b) to unpack the work of judge, defence, prosecution, defendant and witnesses in producing 'a trial'.

I tried to track down a trial transcript. However, the case had not gone to appeal and only the court shorthand writers possessed such a thing – but in shorthand, so that obtaining a transcription would have been prohibitively expensive. There was then an interregnum of nearly two years which involved the final decline and death of my father in a context in which repeated strokes led him to become violent – violent towards women, to my mother in particular but also to me and an elderly neighbour. His doctor and male social worker both, separately, denied this was happening and proclaimed my father's right and 'need to discipline his women' (words actually used to me). All this had a tremendous impact at many levels, including emotionally, politically and analytically, not least because it seemed so clearly an echo, indeed a loud echo, of those other events of the Sutcliffe case which continued to engage my interest and concern. This concern was brought to a new height with the publication of Gordon Burn's ...somebody's husband, somebody's son... (1984), Patricia Highsmith's review of it, 'Fallen Women' (1984), which appeared in the London Review of Books, and Sonia Sutcliffe's review of it in The Guardian (1984).

Through my father's hospitalisation, I continued trying to obtain a copy of the trial transcript. I heard about a journalist who had been in court, had her own shorthand transcribed, went away to write about the trial – and had a breakdown. I tried to contact her but failed. By this stage I could no longer sit with my back to doors and experienced day- as well as nightmares about the case, so I had a good idea of what she had gone through. A legal friend suggested I contact the defence solicitor, because they sometimes use a privately (ie not from the official court shorthand writers) prepared transcript.

My father died. Half-way through a sabbatical, I prepared to write about the case using media accounts if a transcript was unobtainable. At my desk, carefully positioned to keep the door in view, I was startled when the phone rang to hear Mrs Sutcliffe on the other end of the line. The details of the conversation elude me now, although I remember saying I would send her a copy of the one thing I had written so far, and also a copy of Highsmith's to me libellous implication that Mrs Sutcliffe had colluded in her husband's activities; and I remember her saying that the various 'exclusive press interviews' were complete media fabrications, that she had given no interviews and nor did she intend to. I had previously felt sympathy with her as yet another of Sutcliffe's victims and some awe that she could survive such a revelation about a person she had loved and lived with. Alongside these responses I also felt fear: fear that now Peter Sutcliffe might get to hear my name, know about my phone number, be able to gain access to my person should he ever escape or be released; a fear I knew was a product of the media hype exponentially increased by my own imagination, but a fear that remained.

I had nearly finished writing about the media accounts, Gordon Burn's book, Patricia Highsmith's review and Sonia Sutcliffe's review (Stanley, 1984b), and when ready dispatched a copy of my textual analysis of particular features of Burn's book and Highsmith's review. Its intention was to trace out the workings of the 'ideological three-step' (Smith, 1974a; Marx & Engels, 1968) involved in the production of ideas as material practices. The paper deals with other media fabrications and outlines a future programme of writing for a book, one chapter of which would be concerned with examining in detail how the press in its so-called 'exclusive interviews' went about according a character, motives and behaviour to Mrs Sutcliffe.

In writing and mulling over those events, I came to certain conclusions about the nature of serial murders such as Sutcliffe's (a conclusion Masters avoids making in his book about Nilsen): these men killed because they found they could, and it then became a hobby for them. I found this convincing and disturbing, not because it was something I saw as any simple product of patriarchy, but because I could so easily apply it to *me*. I found myself unable to avoid gauging situations and persons for the ease with which I could kill and get away with it, from my nearest and dearest to complete strangers. I probably became both unnerving and boring by relating my theorisings about how to murder to other people. Such thoughts went on for a long time, and were eventually put on ice and at the back rather than the everyday front of my mind when I stopped writing and planning to write about sexual murder. This was occasioned by Mrs Sutcliffe's response to my paper.

My writing about the case I felt to be highly sympathetic to Mrs Sutcliffe and the predicament she had been placed in, in particular that for many people she would always be seen as complicit in Peter Sutcliffe's crimes. Highsmith's review proposed this in a malignant way – although not as venomously as occurred more recently in *Private Eye*. My concern was to analyse the ways in which media accounts sought to discredit her for their own gain. I was, then, startled to find that she thought my planned work would do precisely what the media had done: invent a point of view for her to bring her into more public attention and opprobrium. I considered a careful response, explaining the actually ironising intent of what I planned to do. In the end I abandoned both replying and any further writing about the trial or the murders. The theorisings about murder went on, however, fuelled by conjecturings about Peter Sutcliffe possibly knowing more and now negative things about me. However, there was still much in my mind that had to be not only spoken but written, confronted on paper so that I could 'see' by externalising my thoughts; one night I woke up at 2 a.m. and wrote the piece that precedes this section, Anony Ms's 'Mr Normal and The Beast'; it was the only other published product of the original planned set of research.

Finally I gave way to being told that working on these kind of materials was making me unbearable – including to myself. Eventually murderous thoughts and worries receded, every now and then resuscitated when I teach or write about associated matters. I still find it fascinating as well as horrifying.

At this point I suspend my narrative, and suggest that the textual analysis of Burn/Highsmith, the Anony Ms piece (reproduced in this chapter as the most ambiguously autobiographical thing I wrote on the case), and indeed the narrative I have just provided, should be subject to the kind of analytic attention I argued for in the early sections of this chapter. That is, each of these pieces of writing is the product of a biographer manqué. Each is concerned ultimately with the biography, and claims made about the biography, of Peter Sutcliffe; each is a fabrication; is riddled with 'fictive devices'; employs different forms of narrative structure and voice; intends particular kinds of reading directed towards different kinds of audience; and each has a describing, interpreting, analysing, selecting, omitting, creating, active biographer at their heart.

There are (at least) four levels or stages to my failed/displaced research activity. First, as a reader or consumer I read and watched and listened to media reporting of the case of the Yorkshire Ripper. I consumed actively, using a variety of feminist, sociological and personal tools, in an analytic engagement with these different kinds of text. I placed my own emphases on what was included, repaired absences as best I could, made my own omissions from what I was presented with; and I produced not only one but a number of readings through doing so. Among these at a meta-level were: all men could do such murder, most men would never under any circumstances; all women are vulnerable to rape and sexual murder, most women are not because of the steps they themselves take to avoid danger as much as possible. Among them at a micro-level were: the details of the ways in which both texts and readers are active; and the means by which ideology is produced through material practices. Second, I began to focus on a single life – that of Peter Sutcliffe – but one I treated as exemplary of men who sexually murder women and the accounts they and others produce to explain their activities: I did so not as a conventional biographer (say Gordon Burn) might do, focussing on a reconstruction of family and personal history, but as a feminist sociologist, and so dealing with the social processes by which biographically-oriented accounts are produced, structured and used, and the means by which these can be analytically engaged with and deconstructed. Third, as a woman and a feminist I used biographical, autobiographical and fictive elements of the case as part of a groundplan for living my life as safely and as honourably as possible. Finally, as Anony Ms I wrote an auto/ biographical piece presented as part of the genre of speculative fiction but actually deadly seriously and as a resolutely factual account embedded throughout by fictive forms and devices. And I wrote it for a specifically feminist audience, one which could be trusted to read through the fiction to the fact as active engaged readers.

Beyond stating these four successive kinds of reading and writing activity, there are other more specific points to be made about these pieces of writing which tie them to the theoretical outline produced earlier.

Biography does not take place in a self-sealed unit within a biographer's life; it always has autobiographical implications, if for no other reason than that of spending some years of your life immersed in the details of another person's; for instance, Michael Holroyd has written of 'taking up residence' with Lytton Strachey for a period of years. However, if an auto/biographer's feelings about 'the subject' or parts of their life or work are strong (strongly negative, strongly positive), then there will be autobiographical implications beyond this mundane 'spending much time together' level. Victoria Glendinning's (1983, 1988a) very different response to Vita Sackville-West and to Rebecca West, for instance, is palpable for it has intellectual – textual – reverberations as well as more personal – extra-textual – ones.

The intellectual reverberations of my planned but largely aborted sociological work on the Peter Sutcliffe case appear in the analytic arguments of my textual analysis of Burn's biography and Highsmith's review. However, at the time this planned work ended there was still much to be said, much of the horror and also cold revengeful anger that needed expression. Stymied of an 'academic' way of expressing and using these feelings, I turned to a quasi-fictional account. The name 'Anony Ms' was not intended to hide my identity as author but rather to signal clearly that any feminist could have said the self-same things. However, it should not be supposed that the Anony Ms piece represents my 'real' feelings about the case, and the more academic writing is a false because a muted expression of these. Not only do *different* writers of biographies of the same person disagree, but also the *same biographer* holds different opinions, different views, different conclusions, about their subject. And so with each of my different writings on the Sutcliffe case.

Moreover, the differences between these apparently different genres melt under the glare of scrutiny. The apparent 'fact' of the narration opening this section is actually a fabrication of selection and omission, of weaving together contiguously related elements and not directly related ones, for in the time-gaps between the steps outlined lie a host of events, behaviours, persons, not 'seen' in this account. The facts, like the fictions, are a product of their time, place, author, author's frame of mind, reader. The author as writer is central to each, uses approximately similar means of putting across an argument, making a case, telling a story; it is the 'voice' and its modulation that differs starkly.

The difference in voice and modulation is consequential for how these different pieces of writing are read. The textual analytic setting out of an argument through detailed examination of precise words and phrases wrapped around with forty or so references, some of which are used in detail in the text, is unmistakably 'academic', a modulation albeit intruded upon by the less dry and more 'there' presence of feminism as a point of view on the events of the case, as a supplier of intertextual arguments and references, as a framework for conclusions to be lodged within. However, the telling of the narrative tale is made in a detached voice, the author is apparently removed from the story thus unfolded; its events have a 'here they are, no question about it' closure to them that makes it difficult if not impossible for readers to engage with. In contrast to both, the Anony Ms spinning of a hag-iography of the case eschews authorial authority in its rejection of detachment and evenness of modulation;

but by doing so it claims a different kind of authority, one which depends upon the assent of its readers to the basic premises and stance which underpin it.

But matters do not end here, for cross-cutting these different voices and modulations is another related issue concerned with stance: the narrator has a detached voice, there but emotionally untouched; and the hag-iographer is Any Feminist, not one particular one, and actually speaks things with which this particular author does not always agree – I wanted them to be written, whether I agreed with them or not. Only the analyst speaks in my own voice within the text, and only in this piece of writing is biographical product closely linked to its intellectual process of production, thus revealing to readers the artful acts of literary composition of not only Burn and Highsmith but also myself as author. The analyst is deeply ironic in approach; the hag-iographer as well as the narrator is a realist through and through. The self who was, the self who writes, the self who is. Only in the more analytic piece is the gulf between 'the self who writes' and 'the self who is' breached. In the two other pieces 'the self who is' is removed, hidden from readers behind detachment in the one and impassioned involvement on the other.

Passionate participatory prose is not always what it might seem nor what is often claimed for it, for the Anony Ms piece is driven throughout by a narrative of substitution in which metaphors are used to gloss the enforcing on readers of unargued conclusions. The key metaphor concerns The Beast and his relationship to Mr Normal (otherwise known as Hyde and Jekyll), but there are others with equally powerful effects. Authorial authority is achieved very efficiently by these means, as long as the basic premises of the piece are shared by readers. Paradoxically, only in the 'analytic' piece are readers treated as intellectually involved equals and a part of the process of analysis, while both this and the Anony Ms piece share a rejection of the particular realism implicit in the narrative account. Of course each of these pieces of writing have different projects, and this accounts for the mixtures of voices, means of claiming authority, stances towards the reader, positioning of the author, within them.

The project that I claim for what has appeared in this chapter has had different dimensions: to begin to introduce the same complexities into the reading of biography and its fellow-travellers as have already been introduced into the reading of autobiography and its fellow-travellers; to stress the generic features of the forms of writing a life by theorising neither autobiography nor biography but *auto/ biography*; and by doing so to dispute realist forms of writing, both in relation to assumptions about 'the self' and also about 'the author' and her activities in producing a written life.

Notes

1 However, even the augmented list omits: CVs, plays and films about historical figures (Joan of Arc, Antigone, Ruth Ellis, Queen Elizabeth I), autobiographical poems ('The Prelude', 'In Memoriam'); and also all the many forms of spoken auto/biographies are not included.
2 An irony missed by Gosse's most recent editor Peter Abbs (1983), who instead reads this as an unconsciously inscribed minor sub-text to the book.
3 Even McCarthy's (1957) *post hoc* interventions, for example, have behind them yet another 'self who is' outside of the text.
4 This section of the chapter was originally published in *Women's Studies International Forum* 7 pp. 19-23 and I am grateful for permission to republish here.

Part II: On (auto)biography

Introduction

The chapters in Part I were concerned with autobiography and with my role as an active reader of autobiographies; and they also emphasised that 'autobiography' and 'biography' are not generically distinct. In these chapters I argued that focusing on the reflexive role of the writer opens up analytic possibilities which greatly promote active readership. The chapters in Part II which follow are concerned specifically with *biography*, particularly with setting out a framework for, and some of the analytic tools of, a feminist theoretical engagement with biography, and they deal with my work as a *writer* of biography.

I argued in Chapter 3 that feminist theoretical interest in life writing has been almost exclusively concerned with autobiography, making use of prior theoretical work which has stressed the role of fictions within autobiography and its possibilities for challenging referential claims for the consanguinity of the self in the text and the self of a life. Biography offers a considerably tougher challenge, for its present-day mainstream form and content derive from positivist and foundationalist origins and assumptions. However, as Chapter 5 suggested, the boundaries between autobiography and biography are rhetorically constituted, for the actual practices of both centre upon textual construction, the artful fabrication in written words and perhaps also photographs of a self and a life, and are thus shared in common. Chapter 5 outlined the basis of a feminist theory or poetics of auto/biography which traverses generic divisions between biography and autobiography, treating the rhetoric of separation as a topic for analysis within it. Various of these themes are developed in the chapters of Part II, by developing analytic approaches to them around examples from my own work as a biographer.

I became a feminist biographer, a writer of biography, because as a reader of biographies I found that these operated as would-be closed texts, pieces of writing which did nothing to promote a questioning active approach to reading them. Also some particular biographies – Derek Hudson on A. J. Munby (1972), Ruth First & Ann Scott on Olive Schreiner (1980), David Mitchell on Christabel Pankhurst (1977), Phyllis Grosskurth on Havelock Ellis (1980), and Yvonne Kapp on Eleanor Marx (1972, 1976) – wrote about their subjects in ways that confronted my other reading about these people and their times, and thus raised questions in my mind that I had to have answers to. The more I read biography, and the more I puzzled over these questions and the biographical research I started carrying out, the more I became convinced that as a reader there were fundamental problems with the coventional form that biography takes. My own practice as a biographer eschews this conventional form, as I discuss in the following chapters.

The conventional 'microscope' model of modern biography suggests that biographic truth lies in the amassing of irrefutible verifiable detail and its presentation on paper: the Victorian triple-decker revisited. One consequence is that the biographer as a collecting, selecting, interpreting omnipresence is textually denied: the facts once assembled speak for themselves, biographers merely draw conclusions from them. Chapter 6 challenges this view, proposing the actually symbiotic relationship of the 'intellectual autobiography' of biographers (that is, their analytic interpretation of the biographic process) and the biographies they produce (that is, their textual construction of a biographic product). It does so in relation to my editing of the diaries of Hannah Cullwick, arguing that the reflexivity involved in centering the role of the biographer opens up the processes of biography and thus its product to readers, who can thereby assess, reject, conclude differently when the textual products of biography are relatively open in this way.

Biographies are ideological accounts of lives in which specific incidents, behaviours and attributions of character are divorced from the specific contexts these arose in, to constitute and confirm a more general and apparently trans-situational biographical self. This is then used to read back in the life, as an explanatory framework for understanding and drawing together otherwise unrelated *ad hoceries*. Chapter 7 looks in detail at one particular example of this process, a biography of Olive Schreiner, which produces biography as a material ideological product. I argue here that *all* biographies (not simply 'bad' ones) use precisely the same textual means; and that one strategy is for readers to develop analytic means to deconstruct biographies as ideological accounts. These focus upon reading, rejecting the view that texts are determinant of one authorially intended reading only.

Another important convention within modern biography is the focus on a single 'unique' subject. This focus strips from a subject's life the multitude of others it was peopled with, and sees them not as an equal among their fellows but as someone different in kind. Thus

this de-socialising of the subject is not seen as consequential in producing a highly particular – and individualised – 'knowledge' about
them, but as merely a product and proof of their 'greatness'. In Chapter
8 I outline a number of alternatives which are concerned with emphasising the importance of friendship networks and patterns within
feminist biography. However, I also stress that even when friendship
networks, such as those of Olive Schreiner or Emily Wilding
Davison, are recognised as important, the different ways that friendship may be conceptualised produce different viewpoints and emphases. Three particular examples – Emily Davison's friendship with
Mary Leigh, Edith Lees Ellis's romantic or sexual relationships with
other women, and four women correspondents who wrote letters to
Edward Carpenter about 'homogenic love' – show the interpretive
complexities in reaching conclusions about historical relationships
such that these can be unproblematically named and assessed.

Chapter 5 was concerned with re-reading auto/biographical texts,
and with the different kinds of readings set up by different kinds of
text, in relation to my work on Peter Sutcliffe. It is against this grain
that active reading takes place, focussing on both the textual means
(both content and structure) by which particular kinds of readings
are intended, and also silences, the absences from a piece of writing.
Chapter 6 develops this theme of analytic re-reading in relation to
my editing of the diaries of Hannah Cullwick. Here I emphasise that
both 'editing' and 'writing' are activities that construct a fabricated
text for readers to consume: editing may not inscribe an author's
words in quite the same way as writing does, but the effect is of a
text produced by the editor/writer, not by the original author or
diarist.

Although both Chapters 5 and 6 are concerned with active
reading, with reading and re-reading against the grain of the
structure and content of auto/biography, Chapter 7 looks in close
detail at the means by which one kind of active reading can take
place, here focussing on a particular piece of writing, Cronwright-
Schreiner's biography of Olive Schreiner. Although texts may be the
determinant products of acts of writing/editing, they are rarely if
ever totally closed texts: active reading is always possible, the voice
of the reader can be made to become the dominant voice, thus in
effect constructing another and ultimate text, one composed by the
reader's selections in and out, emphases and omissions, rather than the
writer's.

Finally, it is important to re-emphasise that the chapters in Part II are an extension of my concern with the role of the active reader, even though their substantive focus deals with writing. Writers of auto/biography start out as readers and forget these origins at their peril.

Biography as microscope or kaleidoscope? The case of 'power' in Hannah Cullwick's relationship with Arthur Munby[1]

A model biography

The conventional model of biography production is one which can be likened to the effect of a 'microscope': the more information about the subject you collect, the closer to 'the truth' – the 'whole picture' – you get. This need for 'more information' can take the form of amassing detail about the subject's life and work, or the form of psychological insight which is seen to 'reveal the subject'. My work on Hannah Cullwick[2] originated in reading the edited diaries of A. J. Munby (Hudson, 1972); and in producing a biography of her I found that the microscope approach was inappropriate, in part because of its enshrining of referentiality, it part because it misses out from biography many of the salient factors which helped me to understanding this complex woman and her equally complex relationship with Munby.[3] It also denied the sometimes uncom-fortable fact that 'biography' and 'autobiography' are inseparable dimensions of the same experience. I may be 'the biographer' of Hannah Cullwick, but this biography, like that of Peter Sutcliffe, necessarily became a part of my autobiography. In order to 'write biography' I had to deal in the currency of 'intellectual autobio-graphy'; and a more appropriate and less scientific metaphor to describe my way of working is to see biography as a 'kaleidoscope': each time you look you see something rather different, composed certainly of the same elements, but in a new configuration. Effectively, then, I describe an existing and living relationship between me, Hannah and Munby: I am a part of the (historical?) process I am concerned with; and its relationships encompass and engage me as well as the other two participants.

I have made two assumptions about being the biographer of Hannah Cullwick that need unpacking. First, although I edited Hannah Cullwick's diaries for publication (Stanley, 1984a), rather than 'wrote a biography' of her, I have assumed that the result is indeed biography. Strictly speaking I am the editor of Hannah Cullwick's words rather than the inscriber of my own. However, this apparently simple statement belies the close relationship between editing a text and writing one. 'Editing' involves a high degree of selection in and out, of what words, what passages from what diaries, and also what photographs, are to represent 'her'.[4] In addition, editing necessarily involves a high degree of interpretation of the 'character' of the diarist, her behaviours, their meaning and consequence, in the Introduction and notes, but also and most tellingly (although seemingly 'hidden' in the apparent facticity of the 'she wrote it, this is the real Hannah Cullwick' text that results) in the ways that what is selected constructs a particular reading of this subject. In addition, much of writing a text of one's own involves editing: omitting some passages, putting in new ones; indeed the editing is more stringent here: changing sentences, odd words and phrases, whole passages. A result is that an 'other' text can come to be so familiar, so worked, as to seem mine, the editor's; while 'my own' text (like for example this book) can come to seem quite other to me and indeed to the text as first written. Thus although I am not arguing that writing and editing biography are exactly the same, I am suggesting that both are generically 'biography' and that there is a considerable degree of overlap; and it is this rather than the differences (which centre on the act of writing itself) which I deal with here.

Second, although I have never written 'an autobiography, in the strict sense of the word', I have assumed that producing a biography has an impact on (written, spoken, thought) autobiography; and this in its turn (if indeed the ontological impact can be separated out temporally) has tremendous analytic consequentiality. 'Doing biography' changes how you think about yourself, and this in turn changes how you understand the subject; and both impact more widely on how the auto/biographer sees and analyses other social persons, events and processes.

These two assumptions are unpacked in what follows, and a range of detailed evidence and argument is used to demonstrate precisely why they are not merely allowable asumptions to make, but central to the production of biography.

On writing fiction/research/biography/ autobiography/history (delete as appropriate)

Early in her writing career, when she was about 24 years old, Virginia Woolf (1985)[5] looked for a woman's voice from the distant English past that would speak the close detail of the fabric of women's lives. Not finding one, and being even then a redoubtable woman who had no truck with conventional distinctions between 'fact' and 'fiction' and 'time past' and 'time present', she made up not just one such voice but two in her fictitious review, by the fictitious historian Rosamond Merridew, of the equally fictitious fifteenth century diary written by fictitious Mistress Joan Martyn. In doing so she composed her three interlinked sources – the review, the research that the review was based on, and the diaries that the research turned up. And each of these was written in such a way that the actual writer, the time present Woolfian writer of artful fiction, stands in subtle yet commanding presence between us and the 'them' she created.

I dwell on Woolf's work although writing about another and actually factual set of nineteenth century diaries – a 'real' woman's voice from the less distant past than Joan Martyn – because there are interesting parallels between what Woolf was doing and my own concerns.

Woolf gave life albeit of a fictional kind to Rosamond Merridew and Joan Martyn because there were overpowering intellectual and political reasons for calling these women into existence. Her autobiography was at the centre. She had the need, she created; they lived as a consequence of her; but, as with all good fiction, they took on something of an independent textual (and intertextual) life of their own – limited perhaps but still believably complete. Autobiography and fiction, then, are more than close relations: twin sisters under the skin of a different textual guise.[6]

But this essay is no simple fiction. Here fiction and history and research and biography and autobiography are entangled. And as for which is the 'real' name to apply to this piece of writing, Joan

Martyn may not have 'really' existed but she ought to have done: Woolf gave her a life she would have had if patriarchy (to use a simple shorthand for many complexities) in time present as well as time past valued everyday life and the voices, of both sexes, that speak its changing events and thoughts. Virginia Woolf 'preserved' a voice that never 'was' because what actually happened never appeared on paper or was never preserved.

This chapter deals with a woman's voice from the past, an insistent and often discomforting voice: that of Hannah Cullwick. Hannah Cullwick indubitably 'really' existed and wrote diaries. So says Arthur Munby and Trinity College, Cambridge, and Munby's biographer Derek Hudson. I too accept this reality, authenticated by the tangibility of diaries in a non-Munby hand and the provable existence of an historical Hannah Cullwick complete with photographs and a death certificate. But I have found this real Hannah Cullwick to be a more unlikely and certainly politically far more contentious woman than Joan Martyn. Also, as any devotee of Munby and his diaries can vouchsafe, Munby is a brilliant recounter of 'fact' − the facts of the clothes working women wore, the jobs they did, the money they earned − but he is brilliantly dubious about himself. He fragmented his self in his life and re-created it in writing his diaries with a wholeness it had never had in the living. So, it is to the trustable untrustable compiler of fact spinner of tales Munby that we rely upon for ultimate proof of Hannah as a real-life writing woman.

But the paradoxes multiply, for I, the biographer of Hannah Cullwick as the editor of her manuscript diaries and in another sense of Arthur Munby as an interpreter of his, have created for readers these two persons in my presentations of them. And each presentation in turn is not so much a faithful reflection of 'her' and 'him' as it is a rough guide to my states of knowledge and insight or lack of them, my 'intellectual autobiography' for the period and purpose in question.

These remarks are designed to point up the uncertain contours of the landscape over which we roam, those of us so foolhardy as to succumb to the siren song − 'just editing', 'a short book', 'a little talk' − of biography and her older broader and less individually quirky sister, history.

The name of this relationship is ...

We use titles or 'glosses' as simple ways of describing and summarising a variety of different kinds of relationships. 'He's a colleague', 'she's my lover', 'this is my mother', 'he is my husband'. We use them to explain in summary form the relationship between us and another person so signified. But at the same time that we daily use these titles, we also know that they are rather like icebergs: beneath the simple one-dimensional tip lies the complex ninety-nine per cent, which can contain a welter of shifting and often antithetical thoughts, feelings and emotions. The lover we desire and love can also enrage and annoy; the enemy we fear can also fascinate and teach us much; the husband who cares for us can also constrain and confine.

Moreover, all relationships, unless they are dead and sometimes even – or especially – then, have histories: they begin, they grow, and, most of all, they change as we and the other person/s change, grow older as we ourselves do; and our histories, our personal biographies, for good and for ill lie within these histories of present and past relationships. The lover, the enemy and the husband, after all, can be different ways of glossing the 'same' relationship at different or even the same points in time.

Here I am concerned with one such relationship, that which exists between me and Hannah Cullwick. One title or gloss for this relationship is 'biography'. Another which describes its earlier period is 'falling in love'. By this I mean neither 'lust' nor 'love' but precisely that transient but enthralling state we call 'falling in love': a feeling of high excitement, a welter of emotion and, standing over both, an absorbing fascination with the smallest insignificant detail of this woman's life and times. In writing about this I make some points which are significant for what 'feminist biography' could and perhaps should look like. I summarise them here while the next section of the chapter adds flesh to them.

The first point to make is that there is and can be no neat divide between different forms of writing, for each is dependent on the transforming medium of the writer and her states of consciousness, what I term 'intellectual autobiography'. The conventional model of biography is that it is a kind of microscope for revealing 'the *real* X or Y'. This view of biography is lacking, even though rhetorically it can be made, by fair means and less, to appear as though it is not. 'Doing biography' in any of its sub-forms is intimately connected with the biographer's own autobiography and to omit this is to deny readers much of the information they require to produce their own 'biography of' from their active readership.

Second is that conventional biography sees the rich complexity of a person's life as an embarrassment, an obstacle to finding the real person who must be there if only you look hard enough and do it 'properly'; and, in writing biography, biographers have developed efficient ways of reducing complexity to manageable proportions. The end product is a genre which all too often pronounces 'she was like this (and not like that)'. A feminist biography, indeed *any* good biography worthy of the name, should instead firmly grasp the cup of plenty that a person's life and their contemporaries' views of it represents: 'she was like this *and* like that' should be its motto.

Thirdly, my particular interest is with how those of us who see the necessity can investigate and write about the competing versions of a life seen from the perspectives of different observers and participants, including our own. Through focussing on the processes of producing a biography these versions are made available, and indeed accountable, to the reader as essential elements in constructing an interpretation of the subject's life, times and work by means of a rigorous explication of 'intellectual autobiography'. By this I mean making visible what is conventionally hidden to readers: the shifts, changes, developments, downturns and upturns in the way that the biographer understands the subject with which she deals.

To recover and write about this process is always to deal with 'history', for the act of biography is temporally located: this person with this particular personal and intellectual history in this time and place who understands, in now this light and now that, first one and then more facets of this other person as seen by that person, their friends, their enemies, the indifferent. The biographer is indeed temporally located; and of one thing we can be sure: time moves on, and memory ensures that we take what *was* into what *is* and *will be*. Because of this we accumulate layers of understanding – and misunderstanding. The snake, and people, may shed physical skins: our minds accumulate them, layer upon layer.

Any overt look at the contours and contents of the biographer's mind – especially her *changing* mind – tends to be seen as inadmissable evidence. Judith Okely's biography of Simone de Beauvoir (1986) tentatively admits her own 'subjectivity' into the erstwhile 'objectivity' of biography; while 'meta-biographies' like Symons's *The Quest For Corvo* (1934) or Germaine Greer's *Daddy we hardly knew you* (1989) remain rare, whatever status they have in theoretical writings about biography. The 'objectivity' of the dominant strand of biography is better seen as a realist title for a set of practices for producing ideology – the ideology known as objectivity – and I discuss its production by looking at Cronwright-Schreiner's biography of Olive Schreiner in the next chapter.

Life is 'subjective' because we necessarily see and understand through our own consciousness. This is certainly a *social* and not an individual consciousness; but it can never be an 'objective' one, for by definition it derives from particular 'subjectivities'. The subjective/objective dichotomy is itself an ideological product: two opposing glosses on pretty much the same thing but worked up rhetorically and presented differently. To counter such ideological practices requires, not the definition of more titles and the production of bigger and better glosses, but instead a careful analysis of the *research and writing* processes that produce the natural as well as the social sciences. It is within such an analytic scrutiny that 'intellectual autobiography' is located.

My fourth point concerns the necessity of not confining feminist biography to feminist heroes. There is a need for realism and for eulogies in biography; however, these should not constitute the totality of feminist biography, which must be able to encapsulate innovations in *form* as well as content. Certainly I have been challenged and fascinated by Hannah Cullwick, a working class woman who devoted herself to an upper class man and in doing so acted out endless games of servitude and mastery with him. I have also learned an enormous amount about feminism from her; and I am equally sure that my feminist ideas have developed as much from the Peter Sutcliffe case discussed in Chapter Five as from 'right-on' people, experiences and writings.

If feminist biography is confined to the politically right-on, we will lose the challenge of making sense of the right-off. In particular a great deal about sexual political power can be learned from contemplating the co-existent dimensions of 'power' and 'powerlessness' (what absurd absolutes) in the relationships of the Hannah Cullwicks and Arthur Munbys of this world (and their many variants). My fifth point is simply that biography in its feminist form can show us as quite no other kind of writing can that 'power' and 'powerlessness' are complex matters, most certainly not two poles of a dichotomy but often co-existent in the same piece of behaviour done by the same person at exactly the same moment in time.

I now draw these thoughts together and give them concrete form through a discussion of the 'hows' and 'whys' of my changing ideas about 'power' in Hannah Cullwick's relationship with Arthur Munby. Because of the limitations of the written word in capturing the more elusive aspects of intellectual life, I describe these changes as temporally distinct states of understanding, whereas it is only *post hoc* that they (seemingly) separate. At the time my thoughts were more indistinct: there all right but much like a country explored under dark. Moreover, although the changes I describe were successive, what followed did not make redundant or in any way falsify what went before. Each of these changes is still plausible; more than this, all of them (and doubtless more that I haven't experienced) are necessary to any rounded view of 'what happened' and 'what it was like' in the relationship between Hannah and Munby.

Accumulating layers

I first came across Hannah Cullwick's diaries serendipitously: I bought a remaindered copy of Derek Hudson's *Munby: Man of Two Worlds* (1972) (the best thirty pence I ever spent), which is composed of extensive extracts from Munby's diaries linked narratively by Hudson. I was at least as fascinated by its all too brief mentions of Hannah's diaries as I was by Munby's. Galloping through the book one afternoon and evening, by its end I had decided to find out who was working on Hannah's diaries and, if no one, to edit them myself. I was prepared for disappointment. I couldn't believe that anyone could know about and not be working on them: I realised the rarity of a working class female voice from that period writing untranslated by the well-meaning middle class. The next morning I rang Trinity College, Cambridge, and obtained a list of three or four people already working on the diaries and made an appointment to go and take a preliminary look at the Munby collection.[7]

I duly went to the library. From even my first excited dippings into two or three diary items I was enthralled, and not just by the great rarity of Hannah as a working class woman speaking in her own voice. More than this, I really hadn't been prepared for the fact that Hannah Cullwick was so present in the text as a *presence* and indeed as a power. I felt an immediate respect for this woman and knew there could be no writing-off the things she did and wrote as either a complete subservience to Munby or a kind of 'false consciousness', no matter how dubious they might be to my personal taste.

I related to Hannah Cullwick's writings with what Virginia Woolf (1931) calls 'real' as opposed to 'fictitious sympathy'. Real sympathy in Woolf's terms is characterised by the sharing of experience. Hannah Cullwick and I shared a poor working-class background, an experience (in my case very much briefer) of 'service' and the vagaries of the upper[8] classes, a liking for and valuing of manual labour. And beyond this there was also rumour of a similar secret relationship with an upper class man in my parental great-grand-mother's life, life in service for my maternal grandmother and her many sisters and also my mother's older sisters.

Almost immediately, however, this first impression of respect for Hannah was bracketed away. Two interlinked factors had this effect. One was the view of 'Hannah the creation at the wish of her 'Massa'' that Derek Hudson outlines. The other, much more influential, was Leonore Davidoff's (1979) discussion of the diaries of Hannah and Munby, for Davidoff was a feminist whose other work I already knew and respected.[9]

The position I accredited to a combined Hudson/Davidoff view[10] was: Munby was a man of power by virtue of his superordinate position within the sex, race and class dichotomies that characterised Victorian society at the time, and through the way he used his relationship with Hannah and other women to create the reality of these dichotomies in his everyday life. This series of dichotomies was begun by male/female and expanded to overlay upper/lower, clean/dirty, white/black, Munby-Massa/Hannah-slave; and they fixed Hannah as subordinate within each of them, for they composed an interlinked hierarchy.

At the time I failed to perceive any sharp divide between my initial response to 'Hannah, woman of power' and this view of 'the subordinate Hannah'. I seem to have subordinated my understanding to the constructed Hudson/Davidoff one. I set up a hierarchy in which the dominant view was theirs. Mine, not in books nor by an 'expert', was bracketed away as a kind of false consciousness I would grow out of with greater familiarity with the combined diaries of Hannah and Munby. However, greater familiarity did no such thing. Much hard work and voluminous reading later, in the period just before sending the finished manuscript to my publisher this 'power-less Hannah' view shifted considerably. What occasioned this were two interlinked factors.

One was my much greater knowledge of Hannah and her diaries. Having read the whole of these and most of Munby's manuscript diaries, I had become aware that I knew more about the woman and her writing than anyone living or dead had done bar Munby him-self.[11] I was now immeasurably more confident that my 'Hannah, woman of power' first layer view was textually confirmed. The other was that this greater knowledge had not closed off all problematics – indeed, it had opened up various mysteries. One concerns why Hannah left her home with Munby in 1877 some four years after their marriage in 1873 and the precise nature of the 'rows' they had, one of which was the immediate cause of the breach and which Munby characterised as 'shameful words and foul spewings'.[12]

The resulting third view synthesised the two prior ones. Here I saw the question of 'power' in the relationship between Hannah and Munby in almost neutral terms: he 'had' power in some ways and she in others. At times in the published book I almost seem to cast the relationship in egalitarian terms. For example, I say that:

Her relationship with Munby certainly involved her in the outward shows of subservience. But woc betide him when he overstepped the mark – her mark – and took her behaviour as indicating that he truly was her master. (Stanley, 1984a: 17)

and added:

similar instances of her 'naughtiness' abound ... This naughtiness, Hannah's answering back, I take to be another demonstration of her fundamental independence of mind, an independence albeit mediated by complex and sometimes disturbing emotional ties and dependencies. (Stanley, 1984a: 18)

The general picture I had in mind was of a complex relationship and certainly one in which Munby had and used power so as to shape Hannah's life – but also in which Hannah had resources such as to produce Munby's dependence on her and to effect immense consequentialities in his life. A complete interdependence, then, in which both had and used different sources of power vis-à-vis the other.

I am of course using 'power' here as another gloss or title, one standing for a multiplicity of ways by which one person can control, confine, compel, constrain, influence, cajole another into being, doing, saying. And by far the majority of these ways are not peculiar to Hannah and Munby. I observe them around me in much more apparently humdrum relationships, including my own and those of other feminists; and of course by 'relationship' I don't necessarily mean a sexual one but any relationship based on mutual ties.

So far I have made reference to: the published and unpublished diaries of both Hannah and of Munby; Derek Hudson's, Leonore Davidoff's and my published writing about these. Indirectly because of the example of Hannah and Munby, directly because at this time I was also immersed in reading Virginia Woolf's letters and diaries, I began to keep a diary of my own on something like a regular basis. My previous diaries had been a bit like the life of Hobbesian man: nasty and short; they had come to an end because I missed entries and then gave up. Such is the stuff of personal revolution: if the diary of V. Woolf, one of the incomparably great diarists, could contain gaps so too could my humbler one. Not being a 'soul' diary but more a 'weather, work and writing' one, mine contains many puzzlings about Hannah and Munby; and from now on I refer to it as another source of data about my thoughts about their relationship. I shall also refer to a research notebook I kept while reading the Munby diaries.

As the text of The Diaries.... was being finished, some eight or nine months before the published book appeared, another and fourth layer of complexity was already accumulating; indeed hints of it are to be discerned within the published book. After the row of 1877 when Hannah left, she returned to and worked in a variety of jobs in Shifnal, the Shropshire market town that was her birthplace. However, she also returned to 'service' on a number of occasions, although she had enough money saved not to make this an economic necessity. There are various letters from her to Munby when she lived in Bearley near Stratford which make often painful reading even after 100 years.[13]

In these letters, Hannah expresses her unresolved dissatisfaction with the outcome of their relationship, and her searing unhappiness because of the suffering quite literally engendered. As she says, she lives alone against her will, but even though: 'I tell everyone I talk to as I've always been a servant & how much I like the work, you know

I have suffer'd enough through it to make me hate the name...'
(Stanley, 1984a: 297).

Here, at the end of the Postscript to the book, I make no bones
about suggesting that in the last resort it was Munby who dominated
and whose decisions and insistencies produced this final solution to
the problems inherent in the relationship. Just before quoting the
letter, part of which appears above, I say that their living apart but
with long visits from him to Hannah two or three times a year was
in a way a resolution:

> But this was made possible for Munby only after he had set up still more
> separations and divisions in his life .... He thereby regained control over the
> relationship, a control he had lost when Hannah became an everyday
> presence in his life and much too real for him to be able to cope with.
> (Stanley, 1984a: 296)

However, at the same time that this fourth view crept into the
final pages of the book, I was also moving towards a fifth view, and
one far closer to my first response to Hannah. In August 1982 I was
just about to complete the manuscript. In my diary on a number of
occasions during this month I argue strongly that *Hannah* was the
controlling power for good and ill in both their lives. I portray
Munby as merely responsive to the most consequential of the stances
she took up – that is, her insisting on remaining a servant and
refusing ladyhood. Her 'downfall', as expressed in the Bearley letters,
I see as the consequence of Munby's escape from her controlling
presence. For example, I say that:

> I used to think that Hannah was 'taken up' by Munby & used by him
> something rotten ... I then came to think ... that that wasn't right, that she
> used him as he did her, he was as dependent on her as she on him ... But
> now ... Now what I think is that Hannah was an immensely powerful and
> self-willed woman who ... would never bend the knee ... in the sense of
> being determined by another ... My betting is that M. wanted a short mild
> dalliance, but met his match in someone who knew a lot better than he
> what she wanted ... And then, I think, & with visions of social disgrace
> zooming towards him, Munby wriggled & squiggled like a little snared
> beastie, & escaped ... I feel, I don't know, that Hannah was determined,
> stubborn, bloody-minded, a kind of unyielding wall of a woman, who in a
> sense played Munby like he was a fish on the end of her line. (Tuesday 25
> August 1982)

But, as I also note, interpretations of character and the meaning
of relationships are precisely that – *interpretations*. As such they are

dependent on and emanate from the interpreting consciousness, and thus the intellectual autobiography, of the researcher and/or biographer and/or reader:

But as for wherein lies all this about H. as a 'wall' of a woman trapping the initially eager, later fearful, still later wriggling and tiggling Munby – it lies in me. It lies in me putting together this & that, a mood & a way of phrasing something. It lies, therefore, in me and how I feel about it, H. & Munby and their lives & their relationship with each other, as of this point in time. (Tuesday 25 August 1982)

It will be apparent that I had re-recognised Hannah's power: what I now saw as her effective long-term domination in the relationship. And I had also come to feel sorry for Munby, as the wriggling 'little beastie' imagery suggests (a snared rabbit was what I had in mind). But, as I have said, times and interpretations change. In the early summer of 1985 I began a complete reading of the Munby diary in manuscript. Before this I (as other researchers) had relied on Hudson's excellent book to guide my reading of the primary material (a point I return to, for it had unexpected consequences).

One reason why Munby's diaries are so important for researchers interested in women's work in the nineteenth century is that, along with a great deal else, Munby 'collected' groups of women workers. Each collection of 'spottings' would represent the fad of the moment – which might last for a period of months, or, as with the pit brow women (John, 1980), years. So that, once one dustwoman, woman brick maker, agricultural labourer, or acrobat, makes her appearance, readers can be assured that more will follow hard on her heels. Munby would just happen to find himself walking near a brickyard employing women in Buckinghamshire, just happen to be on the walking home route of dustwomen who worked on the various tips around the inner London of the day, just happen ....

However out of the ordinary Munby's obsessions with working women might be, his 'collections' can be assimilated within a portrait of a not entirely sexually politically objectionable man. Hudson says from his reading of the diaries (and my own confirms this) that whatever the inner motivations and feelings of the man, his outward behaviour to these women – *as he related it, of course* – was careful, courteous and, apart from the desire for information from them, non-exploitative.[14] But Munby made another 'collection', one which is very much harder – I have found it impossible – to assimilate within a view of 'Munby sexually politically just about OK'.

Derek Hudson notes Munby's interest in cases of disfigurement from disease or accident, particularly lupus cases (TB of the nasal bone structures in which the nose and sometimes the upper lip became gangrenous and then dropped off). Sometimes with financial as well as medical help the victims survived; in several cases, in particular that of Harriet Langdon, a working class bonnet maker by trade, Munby provided this and indeed other practical help. So far, so good. However, reading Hudson's mentions of some of these cases among the extracts from Munby's diaries is a different experience from reading the original manuscript diary entries in a number of respects.

For one thing, these entries are indeed a 'collection' made over a specific time period. I found it quite mind-boggling to find one disfigured woman 'just happen' to crop up, following another, following another. Indeed, once the first few had occurred, I found myself looking for the next: I began to conduct my reading of the diaries around a framework provided by 'Munby's thing about disfigurement'. I made notes on by no means all members of his other 'collections', but I did on the entirety of this: like Munby, I too began to wait for the next 'spotting'. And Munby goes to great pains and sometimes travels great distances to make his 'spottings'.

For another, there was a price extracted for Munby's kindly sympathy (in short supply, let us not forget, for women with stinking rotting faces and no noses or upper lip) and practical help in Harriet Langdon's case. This 'price' was a photograph he obtained of Harriet, albeit a photograph he destroyed later as he prepared himself and his diaries, letters and photographs (again, of unparalleled historical interest with regard to working women) for death. And there are suggestions that there were other photographs of similarly disfigured women.

And yet another difference concerns the character of Hannah's and also Harriet Langdon's supposed 'difficultness'. Hannah was supposedly 'unaccountably' jealous of Harriet Langdon and was once (see Stanley, 1984a, p. 201) furiously angry with Munby about her. For a number of years beginning in 1861, Munby concerned himself closely with Harriet Langdon's welfare. On Tuesday 14 October 1862 he went to see her. His diary for that day – not in the published extracts – contains the following:

And yet, as she sat there, & I looked on that ghastly useless face ... it seemed conceivable to me that a man might even love such a one ... In such dream of pity ... I kissed her forehead: for reverence and because it was the only part of her countenance that was not diseased and loathsome. (Munby's diary, Tuesday 14 October 1862)

My reaction appears in my Munby research journal as a large heavy exclamation mark that speaks volumes.

Derek Hudson's view, in his published edition of the Munby diaries and expressed again in conversation in May 1986, is that Munby's concern was only and entirely chivalrously helpful to Harriet Langdon and the other disfigured women. Originally I accepted this. What I now began to put together was the fact that the surely significant 14 October 1862 entry was absent from the published diaries, but later entries in which Munby records Harriet Langdon's 'difficultness' are included. For example, Harriet thought Munby should still spend as much time with her as he had earlier and give her more attention while he was there; and she was given to 'outbursts' and went on at him when he tried to bring visits to an end.

Munby became a skilled and circumspect recorder of events and persons in his life. However, we need to remember that what appears in his and every other diary is a selection, one made according to the interests, needs and understandings of the particular diarist. Succinctly, it is an interpretation, a construction. From Hannah's diaries, it is clear that on occasion Munby simply omitted what he found it difficult to acknowledge. My exclamation mark covers my conviction that a missing part of the Munby/Hannah conundrum had fallen into place. Hannah's and Harriet's reactions alike could be sensibly explained through Munby's behaviour. I think it likely there were more kisses (at the least), more expressions of 'reverence', and a great deal more attention given to Harriet than Munby records. She, even more than Hannah, embodied for Munby the 'subordinate' end of the various dichotomies referred to earlier. Indeed she extended and expanded these in ways he would have found irresistible: the double dichotomy whole/subject and deformed/object becomes added to the others.

I felt disturbed at Munby's emotional intrusion into Harriet Langdon's life and his objectification of her through his use of her disfigurement to feed his sexual political and class 'needs'. His account of 'the kiss' made me angry, both for its own sake in rousing unfulfilled hopes in Harriet Langdon, and for the other women's lives he may have similarly intruded upon. There were further implications for how Munby might have thought of working class women in general and Hannah Cullwick in particular. Perhaps for Munby *all* working class women were disfigured, Harriet Langdon only more obviously so than his collections of general servants with large red hands, dirt-covered dustwomen, tall muscular milkwomen, and so on. 'Dirt' and the effects of hard work on hands, face and physique I now thought might be admired and found enthralling by Munby not because they represented something admirable in their own terms (physically competent womanhood capable of fending for itself economically as in other ways), but because he interpreted these effects of hard work as precisely *disfigurement*.

So what does this suggest about Hannah? I considered and accepted the possibility, even probability, that she might represent a case of 'super-disfigurement' for Munby because of her willingness to dirty herself, redden and coarsen her hands with hard manual work, vis-à-vis other working class women; and that Harriet Langdon was probably a case of 'mega-disfigurement' for obvious reasons.

These thoughts also made me annoyed on my own behalf: 'I had been sorry for this exploiter of misery' was the essence of my annoyance. So then, by mid 1985 there was yet another sixth accumulation to my understanding of the dynamics of power between Hannah and Munby: he a perverted even if subtle exploiter of working class women and Hannah with Harriet Langdon a victim of this. But later there was a seventh-layer accumulation, re-asserting the 'powerful Hannah' view.

As I began writing the first version of this account, I was aware there was one particular loose-end I needed to tie up: I wanted to talk to Derek Hudson about Munby's obsession with disfigurement, his relationship with Harriet Langdon in particular. When I met him he suggested that I should visit the not too distant Wheeler's Farm at Pyrford in Surrey. This was the 'little cottage' Munby rented from the late 1870s until his death and which was the main home of his retirement.

Derek Hudson is a charming and insightful man who produced an amazingly accurate guide to the voluminous totality of the Munby diaries. My admiration for his work stands intact. However, I was in no way prepared by the printed word for how different in social class terms he was from me, and also that he was undoubtedly of a lower class than Munby. Clutching my small, scruffy working class past tightly to me, I found myself unable to be explicit about my reactions to the Harriet Langdon episode in the face of his gentlemanly and old-world courtliness and his complete conviction of Munby's chivalry.

In the days that followed, and as I pondered my response to this meeting, I became aware of the extent to which I had 'normalised' Munby in class terms. The 'embourgeoisement of Munby' had occurred by my taking him down a class or two, to cast him as rather like the – in my terms then – very upper class people I had worked for as a nanny when I left school at 16. Before this meeting I don't think I had really appreciated just how vast was the social gulf, chasm, between Hannah and Munby. It was not only this meeting that brought about this effect, but its conjunction with my visit to Wheeler's Farm. Munby's 'little cottage' was in fact large and very imposing and no 'cottage' at all. Before my visit I couldn't imagine Munby's friend Vernon Lushington, the High Court judge who was its previous tenant, living there; now I could. In my diary I put it like this:

yesterday I saw Wheeler's Farm ... That, with the meeting with Derek, was a truly salutary experience for me. Somehow I had 'normalised' Munby – seen him as a kind of more peculiar X.Y. What Derek and Pyrford did was bring home to me just how posh Munby must have been ... Munby might never have been very wealthy – but, for one thing, you didn't have to be to live very well, and, for another, it wasn't money that counted ... Munby really must have been of a different world... (Wednesday 16 April 1986)

This realisation of the class and social chasm between Hannah and Munby explained to me many of the problems they undoubtedly had in communicating with each other: Hannah, proficient on paper, 'dried' before Munby and was often almost mute while with him; Munby doubted the (to me) obviously smart Hannah's ability to understand anything of the complexities of life and seemingly told her very little about either his life or feelings and thoughts. My diary is clear about my conclusion: 'He, I am sure, was the one lacking in comprehension, filled with a haze of his own difference, importance and social power' (Wednesday 16 April 1986). And I draw this conclusion because of the difference between 'real' and 'fictitious sympathy':

I feel so much more comfortable and knowing of Hannah and her diaries ... in spite of all the differences I know Hannah's life from the inside, whereas to Munby I am always a stranger. This is not because he was a man per se, but that the life of working class girls and women still brings with it the same kind of perspective, on work and indeed on life. I may be 'educated', but not as Munby was, for I take nothing for granted that he did. (Wednesday 16 April 1986)

The effect of such thoughts was the seventh-layer accumulation. I was filled with admiration for Hannah's ability behaviourally to cross this class and social divide when she put herself out to do so, and to work out for herself a sophisticated analysis of the difference and relationship between the 'being' and 'doing' aspects of class. This is the 'dual vision' of subordinate groups; and as well as the possession-in-use of women, black people and gay people, it is also the possession-in-use, historically and contemporaneously, of the working class. For Hannah too this knowledge was a practical knowledge, a thing of use, and not only in her relationship with Munby but also with the many other members of the employing upper classes with whom her life intersected. She used this knowledge to resist, effect, influence, control -- she used it to achieve empowerment.

A few weeks later as I was putting together my notes to write about this, I summarised my thoughts about the meeting/Wheeler's Farm experiences thus:

Effect of both -- again: admiration of H. -- her strength of character, that enabled her to cope as she did: but then she knew such people from the underside ... And what an underside Munby had! And, come to think of it ... totally oblivious that the rows and 'foul' language were from her rage at having him insist on the show (?) of hierarchy & superiority, when Hannah was treating him as an equal .... (Saturday 19 May 1986)

Some concluding thoughts

In this chapter so far I have discussed some of the complex interminglings of 'biography' and 'autobiography'. There have been a chronologically-expressed series of changes in my thinking about a biographic subject, Hannah Cullwick, whose life I concerned myself with in great detail. But I am not saying these are progressive stages in thinking, that the later and then the last changes represent 'better' or 'superior' thoughts on the topic of power in Hannah Cullwick's relationship with Arthur Munby. There is no realist hierarchy expressed or intended.

Nor am I claiming that either Hannah's or Munby's diaries are
referential: at various points I emphasise that they as well as I are
constructing, not reflecting, a social world and its events. However, as
the discussion above so clearly shows, immersal in this intertextual
world leads to a predominantly referential reading, even though
alongside it at all times stands my allegiance to a quite different
epistemological frame. One factor in this is what in an earlier chapter
I referred to as the pull of the narrative flow: the chronology carries
the reader along, as does the large degree of mutual corroboration
between the two sets of diaries. However, another and more
important factor relates to my position as a very particular reader of
these two sets of diaries. Here I am not a 'common reader' but a
highly specialist one; the common reader is dependent on me, on
the selections I have provided, even though of course they are able
actively to read these and disagree with my interpretation, as Julia
Swindells (1989) and through her the Personal Narratives Group
(1989b) have done.

My view of these people and events is a product of a wider
reading: of all the diaries of Hannah, not just the published
selections; of Munby's complete manuscript diaries; of their correspondence; of Munby's other letters; of his poems; his photographic
collection; my travels to places one or both of them lived or visited.
While I do not want to claim that because of this wider knowledge
my reading is a priori privileged over anyone else's, I do want to make
two other claims. The first is that, as I have shown in this chapter, I
have good reasons for writing as I do about Hannah Cullwick's
relationship with Munby and I reject claims from other people that
their's is the privileged reading – as with Julia Swindells' (1989)
discussion, for example. The second and related claim is that, unlike
the role ascribed to me by the Personal Narratives Group (1989b, pp.
19-23) as inscribing a fixed late twentieth century feminist meaning
on and over Hannah's diaries, I was in fact responding to them at a
particular point in time: however, books have a 'flies in amber'
quality, for like photographs they reduce a process to a particular
moment in time. As I have shown, my view of these diaries and what
they say about 'power' in the relationship between Hannah Cullwick
and Munby has gone through a number of changes – and indeed still
continues to change ten years after starting work on them.

Each of the described ways of thinking about power in their
relationship I have discussed are still as valid now as they were

before other later accumulations took place. More than this, all of them need to be incorporated in a reasonably rounded account of power in this relationship: it simply will not do to reduce Hannah's person or Hannah's diaries or both to being a mere tool of Munby, as Julia Swindells and the Personal Narratives Group seem to do. The relationship between Hannah and Munby changed, as a study of the two sets of diaries in tandem clearly shows. These changes are discernible textually: and while the discerning is a product of my reading, I can provide the details of the evidence which this reading makes use of; it is thus a reading I would argue which is more defensible that the one-dimensional one these other commentators offer.

The one sure thing I know about relationships is that our knowledge about a person and relationship to them becomes more complex over time. The relationship that doesn't do this is a truly dead relationship; and the relationship that does lives in a way that transcends what may be the actual physical death of one of the people involved. This growing complexity must be included in any half-way competent biography. It is expressed by the phrase 'reverse archeology': the accumulation and analytic investigation of layers of knowledge and complexity, not the stripping away of these as but so much debris preventing us from seeing 'the real X or Y' beneath.

I hope I have shown in a practical, and not just penned in an abstract, fashion that an accountable reflexivity is achievable (and only so) by treating biography as a process, not as merely a product which contains a presumed end of process: 'the facts about ...'. This biographic process, as my discussion shows, is firmly lodged within and is symbiotically related to the 'intellectual autobiography' of the biographer: how she understands what she understands. Moreover, this process is by no means ended even with the compilation of a textual product such as the one you are reading at this moment. Not only may I undergo further changes of mind, but your reading/ consumption of written products is itself an active process with further 'change' implications for thinking: about Hannah, Munby, and me, as well as about life, power, the universe and everything. Which brings me back to the topic of power.

'Power' is neither simple nor unchanging. Its distribution between my protagonists of course changed many times over the fifty years or so of their relationship. Also power is not a 'thing' which, if one person has 'it', then another person has not. 'Power' is a process

effected, and affected, by a multiplicity of means: in Hannah's
relationship with Munby, through the writing of diaries and letters
and the giving and receiving of photographs, among others. And
understanding 'power' in this relationship is precisely *understanding*: an
act of comprehension on the parts of the writer, and thus a
dimension of *how* she understands, using *what* evidence, and *when* in
her relationship with her subject/s. And it is also an act of
comprehension on the part of the reader, who similarly selects,
omits, emphasises according to a framework of comprehension, but
who necessarily proceeds from what the writer provides.

The majority of recent feminist biography is composed by
conventional biographies but written about women. They could have
been written by *anyone*; it needed no feminist to write them, just any
competent biographer. The encapsulating of process in biography
through the inclusion of the biographer's intellectual autobiography
would, for me, construct a more feminist approach to biography.
This is not because I hold any *a priori* claims for its greater 'reality' –
that it is somehow 'truer' – but because the privileging of what is
often written of (and written off) as 'subjectivity' – the workings of
mind as displayed on paper – opens up for analytic scrutiny matters
which seem to me key for a feminist theory and practice of
autobiography. A reflexive biography rejects 'the truth' in favour of
'it all depends', on *how* you look and precisely *what* you look at and
when you look at it. This is the 'kaleidescope' effect that the chapter's
title refers to: you look and you see one fascinatingly complex
pattern; the light changes or you accidently move or you deliberately
shake the kaleidoscope and you see – composed by the same
elements – a somewhat different pattern. All biographers know this;
usually they keep quiet about it for fear of publishers, including
feminist publishers, who won't publish a 'failed' biography that
doesn't come up with 'the real X' but instead a series of Xs.

Writing biographic processes makes visible the existence of
something usually invisible and effectively denied. It helps break
down the strict power divisions that conventionally exist between
writers (here are the facts, take them) and readers. It facilitates
readers making up their own minds, so making reading a truly active
process. You, reading this now, may find one of my versions of
power in the Hannah/Munby relationship more plausible than
others, you may want to combine them all as I have done, you may
want to reject them in favour of a version of your own. I think I have

given you a better basis for whatever you do than the monolithic approach of most biography writing.

Notes

1 This paper was first given at a 'Writing Feminist Biography' day conference held in the Sociology Department at the University of Manchester and appeared in *Studies in Sexual Politics* no.13/14. A later version appeared in *Women's Studies International Forum* 10:1:19-31. What appears herein has been substantially reworked; and I am grateful to those people who gave me detailed comments and especially David Morgan.

2 Hannah Cullwick (1833-1909) was born in Shifnal, a market town in Shropshire, and died in the same place. In between she worked as a pot girl, kitchen scullion, char, cook, maidservant and maid of all work among other jobs. In 1854 she met Arthur Munby. Their relationship lasted for fifty-four years; they married – reluctantly – in 1873 and lived together secretly from just before then until 1877. Hannah wrote her diaries from 1854 to 1873.

3 Arthur Munby (1828-1910) was an upper-class author and poet who worked for many years as a clerk for the Ecclesiastical Commission. However, his main occupation was his abiding interest in working women and in collecting – and recording in his diaries and notebooks – information about their work, their dress, and their lives. Munby was truly a 'man of two worlds', for he compartmentalised his life so that almost none of his friends or relations ever knew about this 'other' of his worlds, about his relationship and then marriage with Hannah Cullwick in particular.

4 See here Stanley 1986 for a discussion of the issues involved in selecting photographic representations of Hannah Cullwick in and out of the published diaries.

5 Written in 1906, first published in a journal 1979, first book publication 1985.

6 Again, I am not suggesting that there are no differences between fiction and auto/biography, any more than I was earlier that there are no differences between editing and writing biography. Rather, it is the degree of overlap and its consequentiality for a feminist theory of auto/biography that I am concerned with here rather than difference.

7 For more details of the actual editing, see Stanley, 1984a and 1986. The manuscript diaries of Hannah Cullwick are in the Munby Collection, held in the Wren Library at Trinity College, Cambridge; and I remain grateful to the Master and Fellows for permission to publish the edited Hannah Cullwick's diaries.

8 I am aware that strictly speaking, using present-day measures, Munby was not 'upper' class; however, both he and Hannah used a two class model – the upper classes and the lower classes; Hannah was indubitably lower class, Munby indubitably not, and they both treated him as upper class. I prefer therefore to use the terms used by Hannah and Munby to describe their class relationship, not that of present-day history/social science.

9 I discuss the ways in which our thinking sometimes overlaps and sometimes differs in Stanley, 1984a, especially pp. 18-20.

10 I'm not saying that either would necessarily agree with this view, rather that this is what I understood and combined from their work.

11 He read her diaries but not she his; and shifts and changes in Munby's life of which she remained unaware had consequences for Hannah herself.

12 The 1877 row and its aftermath is discussed in detail and its components teased out in Stanley, 1984a, pp. 287-97.

13 There is a gap in anything by Hannah in the Munby collection over a long period

following the row: what Munby preserved recommences around 1882, with these letters.

14 It has to be remembered that this view derives from Munby's own reporting. His subjects, with the exception of Hannah, do not speak with their own voices. Before any easy condemnation of Munby for textual inventiveness, readers should remember that the subjects of radical research, such as Paul Willis's (1977) lads and Sally Westwood's (1984) women factory workers, are equally subservient in textual terms.

7

How Olive Schreiner vanished, leaving behind only her asthmatic personality[1]

Widows' and widowers' biographies

It has become a truism that Victorian 'widows' biographies' are hagiographies: written lives stripped of the unattractive and unacceptable behaviours and characteristics of their famous dead husbands.[2] These are essentially public documents, key elements in constructing the mythology of public men, not a post-Stracheyan modernist deconstruction of such myth-making. One instance here: Frances Kingsley's *Charles Kingsley: His Letters and Memories of His Life* (1877) omits the scourgings that formed an essential part of Kingsley's and her own tortured religious and possibly also sexual experience that Susan Chitty's (1974) biography explores. Lytton Strachey's *Eminent Victorians* (1918) represents symbolically a break from this past tradition, as the putative start of a modernist 'warts and all' approach, although this is perhaps more literally represented by Froude's *Carlyle* (1882, 1884). But whatever its precise point of origin, modern biography stands on one side of a divide and hagiography on another.

Present-day readers, then, are well-schooled in treating many past biographies as ideological productions, and few biographies from the Victorian period and before would now be treated as unproblematic sources of fact about their subjects. Interestingly, widowers' biographies have escaped these strictures, perhaps because there are so few of them, perhaps because of the tacit sexism in the opprobrium heaped onto widows' but not widowers' pieties. A case to stand alongside the one I shall discuss in this chapter is John Cross' *George Eliot's Life as Related in Her Letters and Journals* (1885), suppressing as it does aspects of Eliot's character he found difficult to come to terms with, specifically her sexual appetites and demands on him. However, in the case of Samuel 'Cron' Cronwright-Schreiner's biography

of his wife, the feminist novelist and theorist Olive Schreiner[3] (1855-
1920), critical judgements are still suspended by many people, who
treat The Life of Olive Schreiner (Cronwright-Schreiner, 1924a) and
accompanying The Letters of Olive Schreiner (1924b) as effectively
primary source material about this woman. I discuss my reading of
his biography in this chapter, for it constitutes an important element
of my work as a biographer of Olive Schreiner[4] and has greatly
influenced my theoretical ideas about auto/biography.

The chapter is concerned to accomplish three closely linked tasks.
Firstly, to suggest that this particular widower's biography with its
presentation of Olive Schreiner as damaged and socially isolated is
sexually politically motivated. Secondly, to examine the textual
means Cronwright-Schreiner uses to accomplish this negative characterisation of Olive Schreiner while centering conventional pieties
about greatness, reverence and husbandly devotion. And thirdly, to
locate these textual practices in a wider analysis of the concrete
means used to produce 'ideology': that is, to rescue an analysis of
ideology from what is, ironically, the actually idealist representation
of it by many latter-day marxists – although not, as I shall suggest,
by Marx himself. I hinge the first and third of these concerns to a
detailed explication of the second.

I focus on how an 'asthmatic personality' is assigned to Olive
Schreiner by examining The Life in depth, examining the elements used to
assemble this personality, the evidence used to locate and 'prove'
these elements, and how they are linked to constitute a stably structured
personality rather than being read as one-off events and behaviours.

In examining this authorised view of Olive Schreiner, I discuss
episodes and behaviours given special explanatory significance,
which cohere around seeing her as a 'divine child'. The authorised
view depends on the reader trusting the biographer's goodwill and
intentions towards his subject; and assuming in particular: (i) that he
provides readers with all the relevant evidence available, (ii) from as
many as possible of the important persons in the subject's life, and
(iii) that the conclusions drawn are fair – that is, that the evidence is
sufficient to allow these conclusions rather than any others to be
reasonably drawn from it.

My argument is that the biographer's goodwill is not demonstrated by his text: his manifest account is rather different from the
stated intention. This would not matter, apart from morally, except
that Cronwright-Schreiner's (C-S) biography has been immensely

influential on later views of Olive Schreiner (OS). Much of the original evidence he used no longer exists and so later writers have until recently[5] necessarily relied for many 'facts' on what appears in these two sources. In addition, the common reader does trust the biographer's goodwill and so the text he produces; thus it is important to explicate the means by which his negative and ideological account can stand as an apparently objective and loving one.

Although I argue these points in relation to a detailed examination of one particular biography, the argument is a more general one. All biography consists of *post hoc* highly selective ideological accounts of particular selves, for the means used by C-S and the effects produced are, by and large, those typical of all biographical investigation and textual production. All biographers construct a framework or character to explain their subject and assemble around this particular contextually-specific behaviours which are then read off as instances of general attributes and character traits. This chapter is thus to be read as a particular demonstration of this general argument.

(a) Compelled to take up the task[6]

In the opening paragraphs of The Life (pp. vii-x; from now on page references will appear without a 'pp.' prefix) C-S spells out his task as OS's biographer. Firstly, he situates his role as one chosen by OS herself: 'she said to me, that, if a biography of her had to be written, she would like me to do it, and, failing that (for any reason), her old friend, Havelock Ellis' (vii).[7] Secondly, he disclaims any positive wish to write the biography: it fell to him by default because Ellis 'found himself unable ... and ... hoped that I would' (vii); then, feeling that if he did not do so 'some unauthorised life would appear, necessarily incomplete and almost certainly gravely incorrect' (viii), he felt 'compelled to take up the task' (vii). Thirdly, his claimed ability to produce a more complete and correct biography depends on OS's 'incredible' personality and his supposedly strictly factual representation of this within The Life.

C-S describes OS as 'a woman of genius, so strange and incredible' (vii) that he wouldn't have believed such a person could exist before he met her, for she could be compared with neither 'normal nor even abnormal persons' (viii). He suggests her personality would be misunderstood and misrepresented 'unless the only person who ever had an opportunity of knowing her thoroughly' (viii) described it; thus he insists upon a uniquely privileged knowledge of a uniquely different personality. Then he underlines The Life's status as 'an unusually complete record': it was produced with the help of, and seal of approval from, Havelock Ellis, who 'after myself ... more than anybody else, knew Olive best' (ix).

These claims for The Life's strict facticity and OS's 'unusual' personality (ix-x) are summarised in four major points in the final paragraph of the Preface. C-S states that every conceivable effort was made to assure The Life's correctness concerning incidents related and the 'unusual' personality dealt with. He insists that 'In so far as so complex and baffling a human being can be known, I repeat that I am the only person who can be said to have known her' (ix). The entire contents of the book – every opinion, deduction, story or event – is included on his 'sole undivided responsibility' (x) and is thus authorised by the status self-assigned as a uniquely knowledge-able biographer. This status is further legitimated when he finishes with 'I have been inspired throughout by my heart's love, by profound admiration and deep reverence' (x): his motives 'through-out', he suggests, have been exemplary and beneficent.

Thus the Preface, short though it is, advances powerful claims for the scrupulous motives and specialised knowledge of the biographer, for the correctness of the resultant biography with regard both to matters of fact and the interpretation of the personality of its subject, and for the baffling and odd, unbelievable unless you had experi-enced it, personality of Olive Schreiner herself. These claims predis-pose readers to accept what the biographer says about his subject, to take its facticity and fairness on trust and in the light of his 'inspiration' by love, admiration and reverence. They thus predis-pose a particular reading of the text that follows.

I focus on the 'how' of assemblage, the methods used in piecing together these claims. C-S produces a number of major character summations of OS; I have divided my analysis of his methods at these same junctures.[8]

(b) Olive ... correctly portrayed for the first time

The first chapter of The Life deals with the origins of the Schreiner family, with OS's missionary parentage, her father Gottlob's lack of worldly wisdom, her mother Rebecca Lyndall's cleverness and disillusion, her possibly Jewish ancestry on her father's side, and potted histories of her sisters and brothers. It contains, like most other chapters, extracts from testimonials, reminiscences and letters supplied by various people that C-S considers 'relevant witnesses', and also some family 'Reminiscences' that OS herself wrote. Here OS's 'personality' is discussed by comparison with her mother and through reference to 'Olive's power, ... her extraordinary intensity ... her serious, direct, merciless intelligence ... great presence ... powerful gestures, the blaze of eye and explosive energy ... the ringing vibrant tones ... when Olive was aroused' (22), which C-S summarises as 'There was something almost awesomely elemental' (23) about her.

Chapter II deals with OS's childhood and early girlhood in the then Cape Colony of South Africa and is particularly concerned with the reactions of those who knew the young Olive. A timetable of 'lessons' with her brother that she wrote in her journal at age fourteen in 1869 is described as an idealised fantasy, something she could never have adhered to and 'a way she had almost to the last' (72). From this the first lifelong trait in her personality is discerned: her lack of realism then disappointment and misery when confronted with reality.

Various relationships of later importance to OS are introduced: with the Cawood family and especially Mrs Erilda Cawood; and subsidiary relationships with members of other families met through working as a governess. OS's first governess job was with the Orphen family. The young daughter of the family later, as Lady Crewe, provided C-S with a description of OS at that time as in a nervous state, which C-S insists 'was, I have no doubt, her normal state' (78), as well as being beautiful and having a gift for telling the children thrilling and exciting stories. Mrs Hemmings, with whom she stayed *en route* for the Orphens, says that OS took open dislikes to some people; while Mr Blenkins, who met her at the Hemmings', describes her as 'small, dark, Jewish-looking, beautiful, brilliant and very eccentric; she was unlike other people' (79).

From these retrospectively written accounts of OS at fifteen and embarking on her first employment some hundreds of miles from her family and living among strangers, C-S concludes 'Here we see Olive, as she really was in her nervous organisation, correctly portrayed for the first time' (79), and suggests she would have been

like this in infancy and was certainly like it 'into old age' (79). Here
he establishes the second lifelong trait in OS's personality: its
normally highly nervous, disputatious and eccentric disposition.

C-S then describes OS's meeting with Willie Bertram, a young
man met in 1871 who was one of the origins of 'Waldo's Stranger',
an important but mysterious character in her novel The Story of an
African Farm (1883) (The SAF). At this point the third lifelong strand in
OS's personality, her 'exaggeration', is discerned. C-S states that OS
said that Bertram was exactly like 'Waldo's Stranger', but 'She was
prone to use superlative and absolute words, which should not be
taken literally' (83). He then outlines his different view of Bertram's
appearance and character.

The Reverend Robinson knew OS in the early 1860s. In 1923, in
his late eighties, he provided C-S with a reminiscence, part of which
mentions OS's lack of formal education; C-S's rejoinder constitutes
the fourth lifelong trait in her personality. The statement that she was
never at school should not be taken 'quite literally' (88); but he feels
confidant that she owed nothing to 'schooling': her mind worked on
a contrary tack to that required for 'teaching' to occur, for 'she
would question or dispute everything ... She would not accept
statements ... merely on authority' (88). He suggests that OS was in
a sense uneducable, for her mind could not be 'taught' by ordinary
means.

The fifth lifelong trait in OS's personality (90-95) links her
asthma with the other traits. The asthma, C-S says, first occurred
following a difficult and uncomfortable journey from Kimberley in
late 1870 or early 1871, and he describes it as a 'kind of neurosis,
connected with a special excitability of the nervous centres' (91)
which couldn't be accounted for by her experiences on the occasion
in question. A few pages later he quotes Havelock Ellis's version; this
involves the same difficult journey but culminates in OS's relatives
not caring about her discomfort and experience of an intense pain
which caused her collapse when she ate. He is quite adamant in his
judgement: 'I do not think (it) should be construed literally' (94),
while a footnote is equally insistent that the details are incorrect: she
did not go home from Kimberley, as she had told Ellis; 'As to her
asthma, I adhere to my account' (94).

Chapter II ends with C-S tracing early mentions of OS's novels in
her journals, while Chapter III begins in 1874 with her arriving at
Colesberg to be governess to the family of George Weekly, where

she refused to give any religious instruction[9] (she habitually did so, and had her wages lowered as a consequence). She was tyrannised and sexually harassed by her employer, who refused to pay her wages when she left. After quoting to this effect from a note Ellis had made on a contemporary letter OS had sent to her mother, C-S makes his first major personality summation of OS (100, 102).

In spite of, indeed almost because of, her genius and intellect, he concludes that OS was 'in many ways peculiarly unfitted for the struggle of life'. Her intellect didn't work well in practical ways, he says; he is also adamant that it 'actually unfitted her for almost all kinds of work, except the expression of her ideal world' portrayed in her writings. He adds what he describes as OS's 'inability to judge people' and her spontaneous outgoing liking for people until her suspicions were aroused. This is followed by her 'powerful expression, if only in face, of her powerful, often violent and rapidly varying emotions', her absent-mindedness, and her 'strangeness and glaring unlikeness to her people'. C-S concludes that these and the other 'strange traits' of her genius should have made her family greatly anxious in sending her out into the world, for she was 'as ill-qualified for the work-a-day world as almost anyone could be' (all the above quotations from p. 100). The effect of OS's personality on her close friends, C-S says, was that she had to be 'shielded and protected' (102).

Thus far C-S has described OS's 'genius' as one where her mind was non-linear and resisted conventional 'schooling', rejected orthodoxy and asked persistent awkward questions derived from her different intellectual framework. He connects this with other perceived personality traits: her lack of realism and its particular manifestation in exaggeration, her unlikeness to other people; and these are wrapped around by 'neurosis', made concrete in her asthma. Her 'intellect' too is seen as closely bound to these traits: unorthodox, eccentric, outside or beyond of what was 'normal' or even 'abnormal', and given material expression in her various literary works.

Superficially, this may seem plausible. However, the same 'facts' can be interpreted differently, providing different conclusions. One example is OS's claim that she had effectively no schooling. C-S's objections are pedantic and make great play of a few months of her sitting in on classes in her brother Theo's school after she left home but before working as a governess. Relatedly, her 'failure to learn from conventional schooling' is better seen as the reaction of someone whose intellect was formed through self-education, who treated 'learning' differently from those who had been through the 'conventional' (i.e. white male) educational mill – like C-S himself.

In addition, it seems astonishingly competent of an uneducated fifteen-year-old to launch herself with success as a governess. It seems even more admirable that she managed, alone and unaided, to rescue herself from a rapacious and violent employer, and no slur on her judgement that she failed to realise his oppressiveness prior to working for him. Her supposed inability to judge character seems unrelated to what has appeared in The Life so far.[10] Nothing discussed has shown her 'unfittedness' for everyday life, indeed quite the reverse. Also the only specific episode providing evidence for OS's violent expression of emotions is her failure to be polite to a woman she disliked and who expressed similar reactions to her – and here Mrs Hemmings in fact ends her reminiscences by saying that '"I do not blame her, for Mrs — was very unpleasant"' (79).

Furthermore, OS's other supposed personality traits – her lack of realism (her list-making of lessons), her exaggeration (the insistence on Willie Bertram being 'just like' the character of Waldo's Stranger, and the differing stories of the first occurrence of her asthma) – are also capable of explanation other than that C-S prefers. For example, surely OS is not the only fourteen- or fifteen-year-old to draw up idealised and unrealistic lists; and surely OS cannot be the only person to provide somewhat different accounts of how major ill-health started. That C-S finds these things so odd suggests more about his character than it does about the 'uniqueness' of OS's, for he writes with a pedantic literalness that treats all departures from what he sees as self-evidently obvious facts as sinful deviance.

C-S also makes categorical claims concerning the fixed nature of OS's personality and its behavioural components. For example, following his deduction of OS's 'usual nervous state' from people's reminiscences, he concludes that this was the correct portrayal of 'her' as a personality, rather than of a particular mood or of one facet of her behaviour among others. Indeed, he insists that she was definitely like this throughout adulthood and probably like it in infancy also. But an equally plausible view is that C-S is so utterly convinced of the facticity of 'OS's asthmatic personality' that he sees it in everything, and including in behaviours, events and situations that readers might well interpret differently if they came to them 'cold', rather than through the 'personality' already presented in the Preface by such an apparently reverential biographer.

(c) The whole woman was 'the divine child'

Chapter III covers 1874, when OS arrived in Colesberg as governess to George Weekly's family, to early 1881, when she left the Cape Colony for England. The opening pages (99-102) deal with her sexual harassment by Weekly and then the personality summary already referred to. It then moves to early 1875/76, when she worked for the Fouche family and during which her friendship with the Cawood family, particularly Erilda Cawood, was closest.

Here too narrative and retrospective knowledge is interspersed with recollections collected by C-S, particularly from the eldest Cawood daughter, who remembered OS as small, dark, beautiful and eccentric, 'but I don't remember storms of violence or emotion' (114), a phraseology which suggests she was explicitly asked about this. Then OS worked for the Reverend Martin's family from 1876 to early 1879. C-S considers this period of the greatest significance, for while at the Fouches' OS wrote most of *Undine* (1929; finished soon after this but not published until her death), and whilst at the Martins' she wrote a substantial portion of *The SAF* (1883) and began the novel published unfinished after her death as *From Man To Man* (1926) (FMTM).

After describing the first drafts of the novels, an occasion when she sat up with Mrs Martin and her sick baby is discussed (119-26). C-S adds that this was 'probably not' an episode she wrote to Ellis about in 1888: 'This story, Ellis thinks, is fairly creditable in its details'; however 'But, for myself, I doubt the whole of it' (126). No reason whatsoever is provided for introducing the journal entry in the first place, nor for why Ellis was asked to judge its facticity, nor C-S's own more damning judgement.

In early 1879 OS left the Martins' to teach the Cawood children for three months, then in summer 1879 returned to the Fouches with more money and better teaching facilities. Although leaving the Cawoods on good terms, soon afterwards Erilda Cawood sent an impassioned letter denouncing OS's 'Freethinking' and that she had occasioned an 'almost idolatrous love' (136) from her. C-S characterises OS's reply as restrained, but also insists that those who knew

her could perceive in her reply 'the sustained agony she had endured
and the hold she had regained over herself after a storm' (137).

C-S then discusses journal entries, one of which mentions
Goethe's *Wilhelm Meister*. When he read and discussed it with her he
found 'to my surprise ... she had not read the whole book' (140).
Discussing this and other admired writers, he suggests she assimilated 'large lines of thought' (140), but never obtained knowledge
of the details. He then outlines her failure to grasp any language
other than English, though he notes she could read an 'easy' writer
like George Sand in French and also notes her verbal though not
written proficiency in Afrikaans.

The last part of the chapter (141-48) deals with the first references to *The SAF* in OS's journal, her plans to go to England and her
relationship with Dr John Brown, then practicing in the Cape
Colony, and Mrs Mary Brown, to whom the second edition of *The
SAF* was dedicated.[11] C-S summarises the part that OS's time in
England was to play — she imagined life there bringing to fruition
many hopes and dreams; but although it brought much happiness, it
also brought 'untold mental and physical agony, and was to break
down even her Herculean constitution and handicap her in all her
subsequent literary work' (145). Connectedly, C-S refers to OS's
cherished hope of becoming a doctor, a link with the Browns; and
then outlines their role in helping revise an early draft of *The SAF*
(146-48). A footnote here notes Mary Brown's mention of OS's
almost illegible writing; C-S suggests that very different writing
could occur on the same page and 'varied with her mental and
emotional states' (146), implying these changed as rapidly.[12]

Chapter IV deals with the period 1881 to 1889. Its opening pages
refer to her visit to brother Fred's school in Eastbourne and to the
Browns' in Burnley, but are mainly about her move to Edinburgh
and the collapse of her plans for medical training, including as a
nurse in a women's hospital in London. A letter to John Brown
provides explanation: her fear that 'I shall find myself a great fool
when I come to measure myself ... with other people' (150). C-S's
view is that systematic study was impossible, for 'these things were
outside the scope of her splendid intellect' (151); and OS could
never work closely with others for they misunderstood her and she
them (150). Nevertheless, OS herself identified physical illness as
defeating her medical and nursing plans; and after which she
accepted 'scribbling' as the only career she was fitted for (151).

The next part of the chapter (152-159) deals with attempts to get *The SAF* published, which it was by Chapman & Hall in 1883. A year later OS and Havelock Ellis first corresponded (he wrote a critically admiring letter about *The SAF*) and then met; and his recollections of her when they first met are included (160-64).[13] C-S attaches much importance to Ellis's knowledge of OS in the Preface, and his use of Ellis as a judge of her veracity frames these recollections as particularly authoritative. I deal with two passages: one (161-2) which discusses OS's intellectual character on arriving in England and changes to this in middle age; the other (162-63) her overall 'nature' and its relation to the external world.

In the first passage Ellis says that when OS first came to England she was shy and diffident except when roused by indignation at injustice (161), but in middle age became 'dogmatic' and 'intolerant of contradiction', admitting mistakes – 'as often happened' (161) – only with great difficulty. He suggests that OS judged people as either good or bad – 'all confusing nuances ... were alien to her' – as an essential part of her 'childlike simplicity' (161-62). The second passage links OS's intellectual stance with a more general account of her as 'simple, strong, primitive, and passionate' (162): she worked within the imagination and was rarely accurately adjusted to the external world. He summarises this as combining a 'feminine disposition' and a 'masculine powerful intellect' with being a 'helpless child' – a 'divine child'.

This account of Ellis's views of OS is completed (168) by two arguments from C-S. Firstly, he emphasises how closely and for how long she and Ellis were in frequent correspondence, including after her return to the Cape in late 1889, and that their relationship was 'of great value and highly prized' (168) by her. Then, secondly, their correspondence is seen to demonstrate how her asthmatic reactions led her to move from place to place 'in search of relief, mental and physical' (168); and this constant movement was part product, part producer, of 'her dread of strangers, her helplessness, her impracticality and her unusual temperament' (168-169).

A brief account of OS's movements in England from 1884 to 1886 and a list of some of her reading follows (169-73), including a short quotation from Edward Carpenter's (1916) autobiography, *My Days and Dreams*, which is the only mention of their long and close friendship in *The Life*.[14] Carpenter outlines his first meeting with OS in 1885 and describes her as beautiful, vivacious, quick-minded and passionate and the years 1886 and 1887 as ones of great suffering for her (171).

The remainder of Chapter IV covers OS leaving England for Switzerland and Italy, her inability to judge character in life, and suggests that in her novels 'every character she drew was a phase of her own myriad self' (174). C-S then contrasts OS's productivity and physical health before leaving the Cape with her illness and emotional agonies in England: if she had stayed in virtual seclusion on the karoo, she would have completed her unfinished novels and done other great work and her 'genius' would have come to 'a full and glorious fruition' (176). As it was, during her six years in England 'She was able to complete but little work' (175), she had failed in her promise. The final section of the chapter contains memories of OS by W. T. Stead, editor of the the *Pall Mall Gazette* (181-82), the critic and poet Arthur Symons (184-90), the sociologist and philosopher Herbert Spencer (190-91), the poet Robert Browning, the painter G. F. Watts (191) and the politician William Gladstone (191-193).

Chapter V deals with the years from 1889 to 1894, and thus OS's return to the Cape and her meeting then marriage with Samuel 'Cron' Cronwright. I begin with OS's meeting with Cecil Rhodes, then discuss the lengthy assessment of her appearance, personality, behaviour and relationships that C-S makes in dealing with 1892, when he first met her.

Because of asthma,[15] in early 1890 OS moved hundreds of miles out of Cape Town into the higher land of the karoo near Matjesfontein. She lived here during the summer for a number of years, leaving it for, mainly, Cape Town during the winter; during this time she met then orchestrated her literary and political opposition to Cecil Rhodes (201-5, 208-16). C-S perceives Rhodes as a 'perpetual child' who was yet a man of strength; 'She admired strength' (211) and C-S says that OS had 'said with tears' (212) that he and Rhodes were alike in stubborness. He then outlines how OS became disenchanted with Rhodes, summarising the 'two phases' of her supposedly unrealistic positive and then unrealistic negative views of people in relation to Rhodes; thus: 'without any real evidence, she had idealised him ... On personal contact, however, she was ... painfully disenchanted' (214).

In discussing OS's role for many as a quasi-religious figure, he notes her views on death and conventional Christianity and says that

in discussing her Freethinking he is 'compelled ... however reluctantly' (226) to say something about himself (226-33). He portrays
himself as of medium height, stocky, muscular, strong and athletic,
and thwarted by family economic misfortune in his intellectual/
professional plans. From early childhood he rejected 'just stories' in
favour of things that were 'true'. As a young ostrich farmer, his
reading of The SAF in mid 1890 affected him in an 'extraordinary'
way, particularly an allegory dealing with spiritual struggle that
embodied his own religious struggles and rejection of Christianity.
He then wrote to OS expressing his admiration.

C-S's first meeting with OS was in December 1892 at the
Cawoods' (233-34). She looked shy, nervous and like a 'wild
creature'; the next thing that struck him was her strangeness and the
size and brilliance of her eyes; also that she 'showed her timidity
more on that occasion than I have noticed it since with others'
(233). Although noting his attraction, he is insistent that there was
no 'falling in love'. He saw her immediately as 'the divine child' and
had never seen anything like her. He says he wrote a description of
OS soon after her death, which he then substantially reproduces
(234-41). This forms his second major account of OS's personality,
drawing together the various elements touched on before.

OS's physical force and vitality in 1892 at age thirty-eight (and
eight years older than C-S) is outlined and her appearance detailed
(234-37). C-S suggests that twenty years of asthma meant that he
could have only a faint idea of what she must have been like as a
young woman; and even less idea would be possible for those who
knew her only in 'the last few sad years' (234). C-S spends over a
page describing her 'violent' and 'unusual' throwing around of her
arms and fists when in a 'tensity of emotion ... to which the average
mortal is stranger' (236). In various ways her physical appearance –
her gesticulations, her large and intense eyes, her 'ringing and
vibrant' voice – is linked to her personality as someone 'So unlike
other people', who lived at a nervous pitch 'incredible ... to the
ordinary person' (237). The difference between OS and 'ordinary
people' is emphasised as of kind rather than degree, and her
supposed explosive nerve storms presented as a normal part of her
living pattern. A very long paragraph (238-40) then portrays OS's
inability to spell or punctuate, absence of 'business' ability, lack of
musical ear, failure to stand loneliness, and use of a baby language
with those she was most intimate, including with C-S 'much to my

puzzlement and happy amusement at first' (239), as her being part child and part a woman with a 'masculine' intellect. This complexity made her deeply baffling. She was, C-S says, not good at 'the practical application of her theories to public, or, often, to private life' (239), and she often misunderstood people and manufactured 'facts' to her convenience. He also notes that on her 'great side' OS had flashes of insight and a great command of language, and she fought against all oppressions for those who suffered; but was herself 'a perfectly helpless human being' (239) in the face of any intrigue or hostility and 'The pity was that so little could be done for her' (239).

This summation concludes by returning to C-S's first meeting with OS, in which she disputed and argued every topic with him: 'I was not accustomed to that sort of thing!' (240). He describes their conversation in a return visit as being like a 'great fight' which made his blood surge 'even now'; he was outclassed by this 'dear little woman' (241) although he later did better.

This is essentially the same view of OS's personality advanced earlier. In it OS's eye-catching presence is contrasted with how she must have been 'before asthma' in her youth, and with her 'last sad years'. However, C-S, in whose 'factual description' this appears, was in fact never witness to these last years except for some brief weeks during 1921: its source is likely to have been Ellis.

In *The Life* Havelock Ellis refers to OS's increasing 'intolerance' and 'dogmatism', but neglects to provide instances of behaviour or events which demonstrate either. Other evidence, from Ellis's (1940) autobiography, *My Life*, suggests a major clash occurred between them over Ellis' movement from pacifism to tacit support for English militarism in the First World War, and OS's rejection of what she saw as his hypocrisy. There was also, although again Ellis does not mention it, disagreement about OS's support for Edith Lees, Ellis' wife, during the period of his relationship with Margaret Sanger and later during Lees' illness and then death in near destitution from diabetes.[16]

OS's years in England also saw what other sources suggest was her social and political triumph. The blanket 'strangers' that C-S says she dreaded were specifically stylish society women who despised her intellectuality and lack of 'womanly' social skills; she was, however, ordinarily assured in her dealings with the radical intelligentsia, although retaining a great need for solitude and a rejection of any hint of 'competition', including for affection. In addition, OS's years in England (both in the 1880s and from 1913 on) witnessed her major involvements with women, in close and loving friendship intertwined with feminist and socialist political action. However, OS the political radical appears nowhere in *The Life*, so that, for example, the feminist and socialist basis of her friendships with Eleanor Marx and Constance Lytton, both briefly mentioned by C-S, vanishes, as does her increasing militancy on questions of race in South Africa.

No details of C-S's private life are provided, although there are clues in the passages which deal with the verbal exchange or 'fight' in which C-S was 'almost angered' by unaccustomed contradiction. OS was in other ways 'timid' with him, he says, though not with others. He constructs a particular status relationship between them (she, most famous woman in Africa, timid with him), and therefore between him and other men (she not timid to other men and Rhodes = a hierarchy of C-S over other men including Rhodes). There are additional instances in which C-S status-ranks others. Initially, for example, he presents himself and Ellis as jointly knowledgeable, then (around 126) he summarily dismisses a 'judgement' about OS's behaviour made by Ellis. Readers are surely intended to read this in the light of C-S's 'uniquely knowledgeable' status *vis-à-vis* OS; the result is to demote Ellis's knowledge below that of C-S.

A persuasive alternative to C-S's 'reluctantly compelled' account is to see him as a factually-inclined, physically-oriented, narrow-minded, intellectually and professionally disappointed man helped in his spiritual struggles by an older and internationally famous woman to whom he wrote a fan letter, by whom he was later overwhelmed, angered and challenged, and whom he wanted to dominate. The 'two phases', of unrealistic admiration then total disenchantment, seem more appropriately applied to C-S's painfully ambivalent response to OS than hers to Rhodes or anyone else. I outline contributions to this alternative view in what follows.

(d) Her inability really to work

The remainder of Chapter V (242-72) deals primarily with OS's response to her future husband (242-49). She associates him with two of the central characters (Waldo and Lyndall) in *The SAF* and feels that he is "a part of myself" while also warning him against

ambition and desire for power achieved through compromising his
principles (245). Extracts from various early letters to him emphasise
her hopes and dreams for him.

OS left South Africa for England in May 1893, writing that they
must think of each other as brother and sister, 'nothing more' (255).
By late August she again accepted the possibility of marriage and
asked "Do you think it would be very strange if we were
'Cronwright Schreiner?" (256). His surprise was not, he says,
'because of the departure from conventional custom' (256) but
because of other people's likely reactions, though he agreed. In
England the reactions of OS's (unnamed) women friends to C-S's
photograph and her description of him as 'a man who can knock
eight men down with his fists' (257) was first shock and then, as OS
danced around the room mimicking him doing so, shrieks of
laughter.

She returned to Cape Town in October 1893 with particularly bad
asthma. Her letters to C-S focus on the theme of her hopes for him:
'Only promise me ... you will satisfy my ideal of the great strong
unselfish man ... there is the hero' (258). In November she was
paralysed with indecision and 'dare not act' about their relationship
and asked him to 'think it all out with that brain of yours so clear
and strong' (259).

OS and C-S married in February 1894; immediately afterwards,
OS wrote to friends and relatives of her happiness and peace (262-
65). C-S sums up the tenor of their life on his farm. He ran the house
as well as the farm and she had nothing to do but give the servants
orders 'to leave her free to do her literary work' (265). However,
she did no writing, being prostrated by asthma every night (265),
which he links to the farm's location. Three months later, when C-S
was at a farming congress, she wrote outlining a plan for them to
live apart. She couldn't bear him to leave the farm he loved for her,
but she could never work there; and only if she wrote could he be
freed for 'public work', so her moving away to Kimberley was for
his sake only.

In July 1894 C-S sold his interest in the farm to move to
Kimberley with OS: he 'had to give her the chance ... at almost any
cost to myself. I did not know ... then ... her inability really to work'
(269). He 'decided to give her' the two years she thought it would
take to finish two novels then underway (later published as FMTM
and the short story 'The Buddhist Priest's Wife'), which they

expected to make a lot of money: 'I gave her the opportunity ... the dye was cast ... I gave her the chance she asked for' (271).

They lived in Kimberley until 1898. Their house was bought by OS (she had an inheritance that gave an income, as well as savings from her writing); she was well there and 'had the conditions under which she could have worked' (273). At the end of April 1895 their baby daughter was born but died within hours of birth;[17] both suffered greatly and could never speak to each other about it.

By August 1894 a long contentious speech against Rhodes made by C-S (275) was turned into the pamphlet published under both their names as The political situation, to launch his political career. In September in writing to Mary Brown, OS says that her collection of essays, Thoughts on South Africa, was finished and would be out the following year and that she was hard at work revising her 'big novel', while C-S notes that an essay now in Thoughts on South Africa was written at this time. December 1895 saw the Jameson Raid and bitter divisions in the Schreiner family over Rhodes' complicity in it (277-86). A letter to her mother about this dispute states the sole authorship of The political situation as OS's. Later C-S notes that the Jameson Raid and its aftermath occasioned her 1897 novel-allegory Trooper Peter Halkett of Mashonaland (Trooper Peter).

1896 came and C-S says that the two years she had asked him for had gone but the writing she promised hadn't materialised: 'True, the baby had been born, but before its birth she had been working' (286). He fails to register the many writings that had materialised: 'We were rushing on to ruin ... Yet she seemed quite oblivious' (287). The chapter continues with its account of 1886 to 1907, including the Boer War, and notes that by 1907 they were living apart for most of each year. Leaving farming, C-S articled himself as an attorney, then started a business as an estate agent and auctioneer as well as continuing his political involvements within an increasingly racially oppressive South African state after 1902.

In 1907 C-S transferred his business to De Aar, which remained OS's base until she left for England in 1913. Of this six year period C-S says 'She spent some of her time in writing, but apparently did not do much' (351). However, in March 1911, and two pages in The Life later, C-S notes her journal saying "Heard of my book being out from the papers today" (353); and I now examine what is said about the book in question (1911), Women and Labour (W&L).

OS had worked on W&L for 'some considerable time ... she

worked on it at Hanover' (353) during the Boer War; she revised it
in 1910 and completed it in 1911. Its 1910-composed Introduction,
C-S says, 'is at fault in a good many respects' (354) because she was
supposedly incapable of 'hard facts'. In particular C-S insists that
'there never was such a sex book as the one she mentions' (354). His
view is presented as obviously the truth about the fictitiousness of
this 'sex book'.

In 1886 in a letter to Ellis, OS mentions a 'sex paper' for a male
friend (unnamed but Karl Pearson[18]) which wasn't finished. She later
sent Ellis a copy of its projected contents, which C-S reproduces
(355). He concludes such a book was beyond her: it would have
entailed 'hard, exact, systematic reading and study, and a collection
... of exact scientific facts, a kind of labour she was incapable of'
(356). He doesn't believe that OS worked at this project before
1887, beyond thinking about it, nor afterwards either. He says that
from 1884 details of her work and life were communicated to Ellis,
and from 1894 on she was in even closer contact with C-S himself;
he concludes 'In my opinion it is certain there never was such a
book' (357).

C-S then adds two 'clinchers': OS mentions her other books and
articles in letters and her journal before 1887 but never the 'sex
book'; and there are only five mentions of it (all to Ellis) after the
1887 mentions, including the last in 1911 when she lamented '"the
part of the book on sex-relations"' (357). His 'proof' that the loss
never occurred is as follows: 'It was Olive's inevitable practice, I
believe, to take her manuscripts with her wherever she went' (368);
therefore she would not have left behind such a manuscript in
Johannesburg; a letter from her to him from Hanover in 1900
'seems, in itself, almost to dispose of her contention' (358), for in it
she regretted most the destruction by the soldiers of family memen-
tos and '"my old journals and about twenty dreams that were really
good"' (358). He says that not even these were really destroyed – he
'thinks' he has all of these journals, and the dreams are 'probably'
those he found in her papers, some of which he later published.

His final arguments to demolish her 'contention' are, firstly, that
W&L bears no evidence of 'scientific fact or ... detailed study or even
systematic reading; it is thought' (359); and, secondly, that in 1893
she had written to him that most of the projected book had appeared
in the story 'The Buddhist Priest's Wife'. C-S sums up 'the contention as to the sex book' (359) thus. He has pointed out that people

and events of the imagination were more real to OS than 'hard fact'; she thought about this 'imaginary sex book until ... it assumed objective form' (359); and then the only way she could account for its absence was to say it was destroyed by soldiers during the war.

It is clear from even a cursory reading of The Life that C-S had an almost complete lack of understanding of what 'the writing process' was like. Almost as soon as they married (the morning after, in fact) OS was left alone in the house with nothing to do but write. C-S seems to have thought that 'writing' and 'ostrich farming' were fairly much the same: you just got down to it. OS identified the factors that destroyed her imagination and her ability to write as tension and stress. For an imaginative and 'inspirational' writer, as OS was, being placed in a situation in which she had to write, and knowing that if she didn't it would seem almost deliberate, would surely encourage a high level of both. And a clear indication that she identified the source of the pressure thus is that she so quickly tried to leave the farm/C-S in an 'honourable' way, because of illness and for his sake, not hers. However, although OS moved, C-S followed and replicated the same pressures, albeit on a slightly longer time-scale.

Given these pressures to perform, the 'writing block' that C-S describes is remarkable for OS's literary productiveness rather than its lack. In this period OS was pregnant and experienced a still birth she never really recovered from, suffered a number of miscarriages, wrote The political situation, wrote and revised various of the pieces published in Thoughts On South Africa, produced various other journalistic work, and wrote, revised and completed Trooper Peter as well as worked on the manuscript of FMTM; she also worked on an Introduction to a new edition of Mary Wollstonecraft's A Vindication of the Rights of Women, which was completed but never published.

Clearly, what C-S 'sacrificed' himself for was not merely literary production. It was the financial independence that the two 'big novels' she had promised would have provided. It is possible that he too was aiming at writing and publishing success. It wasn't only publishing outlets that OS secured for C-S (a book on the angora goat), for she encouraged him in the idea of a career as a newspaper leader-writer and seems to have initiated, if not directly obtained, his positions as leader-writer for two newspapers. She also wrote political pamphlets which attracted a good deal of attention (such as 'A letter on the Jew') which he either read for her at meetings or which otherwise underpinned his projected political career. In addition, the J. A. Hobson who asked C-S to be war correspondent for the *Manchester Guardian* and arranged an anti-Boer war speaking tour of England was an admirer of OS; and his famous book's argument (Hobson, 1900) is greatly influenced by her analysis of capitalism in Africa and indeed includes a lengthy interview with her.

At the very least it seems likely that C-S would not have been offered the opportunities he was had he not been OS's husband. Moreover, OS's supposed incapacity for sustained literary work seems in the period 1894 to 1896 actually the product of C-S's imagination, for her actual rate of production was extraordinarily high considering what else was going on in her life. To my mind C-S shows a similar lack of comprehension with regard to the question of the 'sex book'.

First, what OS says was destroyed at Johannesburg was, precisely, "the *part* of the book on sex relations" (357, my emphasis). Not an entire book, then, but a specific part of one; the 'contention' she actually makes is thus rather different from that which C-S says she makes. Second, the 'plan' of the 1881 projected book, a project C-S says would require skills OS was incapable of, is not so different from the actual content of *W&L*. The focus on women in early German tribes and in Europe historically, the summary of the contemporary situation, and the account of how she thought the situation might change, are in both. Indeed, an analysis of marriage (i.e. heterosexuality) and its relationship to prostitution (i.e. men's sexual oppression of women) is in *W&L* as well as the plan, although it centrally figures elsewhere in her work, in FMTM in particular. C-S seems to have seen a sharp, indeed total, divide between 'science' and 'thought', and projected the former onto the planned book *Women* as an impossibility for OS.

Third, there is no good reason to discount what OS said about the 'sex book', to suppose that she 'lied' or 'exaggerated' about its existence, other than what C-S claims about her 'personality'. There is no reason to accept that the journals C-S says he has and the allegories he says he found are the ones OS said were destroyed. There are absolutely no grounds on which either he or we could prove it one way or the other. More than this, there are good reasons, most of them within the text of *The Life* itself, for at the very least suspecting C-S's motives.

Two additional extra-textual factors suggest some doubt is in order concerning C-S's claim that the sex book did not exist. One is that there is a fully documented example of him not knowing about the existence of a completed manuscript of OS's. In spite of what in *The Life* he says are many journal references to it, he didn't know until after her death that OS had given Ellis the manuscript of *Undine* for safekeeping some thirty or more years before. If C-S could remain ignorant of *Undine*, it seems likely that he could have been equally unaware of a part-manuscript on sex relations. The other is that Mary Brown, back in South Africa at the time of OS's death, received a letter from C-S, which unfortunately she seems not to have kept, in which he acknowledged the existence of such a manuscript; and she repeated this to various other women friends of OS.[19] Clearly some scepticism concerning C-S's categorical statements about what manuscripts did and did not exist is called for.

(e) Little remained ... of that bursting elemental force

The remainder of Chapter VI and the bulk of Chapter VII discusses OS's travels within the Cape from 1911 to 1913 and her return to England from December 1913 to August 1920. In this latter period C-S saw her only once, for a month, in England in July/August 1920 immediately before her return to South Africa.

C-S re-emphasises their constancy in letter writing while apart and provides an extract written by him which declares '"I love, revere and reverence you ... as I have never done anyone else"' (373); other letters spell out OS's attitude to death in general and to the recent deaths of a close friend and a brother. Their letters cease, he says, about May 1920 as he was sailing to England having sold his business and retired. 'Urgent business' kept him in South Africa until the end of June, 'a delay ... with tragic consequences' (374), in particular that they only had one month together before OS left England for South Africa.

Arriving in England in mid July 1920, C-S was shocked that OS had changed greatly and 'little remained ... of that bursting elemental force' (374-375). They spent time together every day, going to the theatre or for long rides on buses. She had decided another winter in England was impossible, so she was to return to South Africa with a nephew and his family, and 'I should follow later, after I had rested'

(376). C-S made her travel arrangements and moved her luggage; she commented on how strong he was and he says it must have appeared a 'giant's strength' to her. Then he and various other people saw her off in August 1920.

Staying first with friends and relatives, OS retained her need for independence and solitude and moved into a boarding house in late October, with letters still exchanged between her and C-S. In December he read a press cable in his newspaper saying she was dead, then received a cable from OS's sister-in-law. Letters and cards continued to arrive from her for three weeks, including one in which she enjoys thinking of him in Rome, then Basle and Stuttgart (380). In early January 1921 he received letters with details of her death and burial. She had died naturally and peacefully without any sign of pain while reading in bed. A post-mortem, which she had arranged and part of which is contained in an appendix, showed chronic hardening of arteries in her heart.

Little new is added to the account of 'OS's asthmatic personality' in this last section of The Life, although some facets are reiterated. One is the emphasis on her tempestuous outbursts, firstly in relation to a controversy with the Cape Women's Enfranchisement League, secondly her claimed 'intemperance' in reacting 'wildly' to other people's lack of pacifism during the First World War. There is also an insistence on her 'lack of realism', her 'exaggeration', particularly here with regard to her health; and C-S's 'doubts' as to there being anything wrong with her heart following failure to 'prove' organic heart disease.

Documentation discussed in First and Scott's (1980) biography shows OS's supposedly 'wild' reactions to the Women's Enfranchisement League to have been misrepresented by C-S. OS angrily resigned when the League adopted an apartheid policy regarding women's future enfranchisement. She could not stomach this from women who claimed to be feminist. Similarly, her 'lack of realism' with regard to her heart, in the light of not only her death and post-mortem, but also the similar early deaths of all members of her family except her mother, seems more a justified and realistic fear. As C-S briefly notes, few doctors then could find any tangible and 'objective' proof of hardening arteries, the condition she suffered from.

The 'typical' pattern of unrealistic response C-S earlier claimed described her relationship with Rhodes is described here regarding an Italian heart specialist whose promise of a cure she first believed then later realised was false. What supposedly 'generally happened' is therefore described only in relation to two relationships: one with Rhodes, about whom C-S notes many others reacted similarly; the other a professional relationship in which a 'cure' had been half promised. My view is that this 'typical pattern' is better applied to C-S's own feelings about OS, as exemplified by the text of his biography itself. One important contribution to this view derives from outside The Life.

C-S says that OS and he wrote regularly while she was in England. First and Scott (1980, pp. 315-19) note that the bulk of these letters is intact and that C-S specially archived them. They document OS's knowledge of C-S's long-standing involvement with a woman acquaintance that she thought and feared was romantic. It was this which precipitated her deteriorating health (asthma again) in 1912 and 1913. C-S admitted the 'friendship' but insisted OS's fears and worries were the product of her 'wild imaginings'.[20] His letters made clear his anger with her in 1912/1913, and which erupted again when he planned to come to England: he wrote that he felt like not seeing her again and would reject her totally were the matter to be raised.

I conclude here with C-S's statement that during the war years OS was in a 'very difficult' state of mind concerning her pacifist ideals. Given that he was in South Africa, there was no way that C-S could have first-hand knowledge of this. He relied on accounts from other people, but the only one specifically referred to is from Joan Hodgson, a young woman friend. This gives a rather different picture of OS at this time: a still fascinating woman, vivid and amusing, and with great power of mind and personality. It seems likely, given what Ellis says about OS's intolerance of differences of opinion during the war, that he is the source.

However, a rather different reading of Ellis's views can be produced using additional material (from My Life, also from Ellis' biographer Phyllis Grosskurth (1980), and from First and Scott (1980)). During the 1914-1918 war and with some reluctance, Ellis chose nationalism over pacifism. OS's refusal to compromise constituted her 'undoubtedly difficult' frame of mind. That it was difficult for people to cope with is brought out when Joan Hodgson says she felt 'overwhelmed' by OS's denunciation of war and killing. That it was particularly difficult for erstwhile pacifists like Ellis is certain.

However, C-S denies a genuine moral and political disagreement, and OS's 'difficulty' is presented as a personality failing, not a political difference.

Treating text as ideology: I have been inspired throughout by ...?

I have provided a detailed account of C-S's main arguments and evidences for the 'asthmatic personality' of OS, using as many of his own words as sensibly possible. I have described the linear chronological account these arguments are structured through, and then, at key points in The Life where major personality summations appear, I have evaluated the foregoing evidence and the arguments it supports. My conclusion is that C-S is no more an impartial biographer than he is one inspired 'throughout' by love, admiration and reverence, as he puts it in the Preface. The 'personality' he constructs for OS is an almost entirely negative one, counterbalanced by occasional insistences that she was a genius. On one side of C-S's scales lies OS's 'genius on a spiritual plane', and on the other a catalogue of negative traits: her supposed lack of realism, exaggeration, failure to construct any character other than her own, inability to judge people and to sustain relationships, her nerve storms, neurosis, explosions of energy and intolerance, and her rapid changes in mood and temper. Interestingly, this catalogue is cross-cut by reminiscences of OS by other people as a laughing, mocking, enjoyable person, but which are nowhere assimilated within the 'personality' C-S constructs, so that they remain one-off ad hoc behaviours.

It is clear that C-S held a very definite vision of what OS was like, admired a few aspects of her personality and achievements but came to disapprove greatly of the rest. Such a fervent disapproval of one's spouse, a powerful and internationally famous figure, could have been no easy matter to handle at the personal level or any other. In trying to cope with it in The Life, C-S sets up OS as a 'divine child', a compound of wild elemental nature and childish lack of realism, and over and against this he sets himself as the arbiter of dispassionate fact, realism and moderation.

Such a view of C-S the biographer is sustained through the trust that readers assume in his goodwill, his desire to play fair with his biographical subject. However, there are good reasons why readers should actually suspend trust in C-S. Firstly, evidence from outside The Life supports a more critical reading of C-S's biography. Secondly, it is easy using the same evidence as C-S to construct a very different view of 'Olive Schreiner's personality'. C-S is highly selective in his choice and use of witnesses, interprets the evidence through a highly determinate view of his subject when other more plausible readings of the evidence are apparent, and strains the evidence to unjustifiable conclusions.

C-S describes OS as an unhappy and fragile person. Yet embedded within The Life are passages which suggest something very different. Early in her life as a governess C-S reports OS mocking the solemn portentousness of a male visitor, who was outraged at her failure to take him seriously. Later she looked beyond Gladstone's solemn exterior to laugh at the 'cute old devil' within, and her memories of his sly tigerishness always led her to dissolve in laughter whenever she heard about or saw a tiger. During her 1893 visit to England, OS energetically mimicking C-S's handiness with his fists both mocked his 'physical maleness' (which he seems quite unaware of) and defused an awkward situation by causing a roomful of her feminist friends to collapse in laughter. And Joan Hodgson's memories of OS between 1915 and 1920 emphasise her 'wicked' and laughing enjoyment of the most eloquently denunciatory passage in the Bible.

These events, from OS at fifteen to OS at sixty-five, suggest a woman with an extremely robust, indeed rumbustious, sense of humour, a woman mocking and amused and as ready to laugh at her own ridiculousness as other people's. My intention is not to replace 'fragile OS' with 'robust OS', merely to propose that, firstly, there is evidence in The Life for both, and, secondly, no 'proof' exists to legitimate C-S's view rather than the alternative. Indeed, what 'proof' there might have been – a balanced selection of views from OS's closest friends – is excluded. In The Life these friends, who were women, feminists and socialists, simply fail to exist except, in the case of four (Mary Brown, Eleanor Marx, Constance Lytton and Adele Villiers-Smith), through mentions which ignore them as political women. This example is an apparently trivial one; however, there is continuity between C-S's treatment of the 'trivial' and his treatment of the 'important'.

Until he established himself as a smalltown business man, C-S's life was a series of failures. He became an ostrich farmer, having failed to enter the legal profession. He then tried journalism, but in

spite of OS's help failed as a leader writer. He produced 'serious' and
'scientific' writing which OS arranged for her agent to place, but this
too failed. Then he attempted a political career, which OS actively
facilitated, but although he eventually entered the South African
parliament, here too he failed to make his mark. I write of 'failure'
here because it is clear that C-S construed 'success' in precisely the
ambitious ways that OS warned him about before their marriage.

Many writers of the Victorian period wrote by the yard, often
before breakfast, and earned vast sums by doing so. Typically if not
invariably (notable exceptions being Margaret Oliphant (1899/
1990) and Harriet Martineau (1877/1983)) these were men who
saw literary production in remarkably similar terms to any other
capitalist output. But OS's 'inspirational' mode of literary production
was very different. The act of writing was never a matter of effort of
will for her; it was thus neither a regular 'job of work' nor an easily
controllable source of income. OS's optimistic hopes only occasionally matched her actual output – even though this was often (and in
spite of C-S's laments to the contrary) very high. The consequence
was, in C-S's terms, a lack of tangible and material measures of
success: ergo, her failure.

C-S's 'failures' in material terms, then, mirror his construction of
hers. It may be that he saw them as causally linked: if she had done
better, so too would he. What is certain is that C-S was a man who
took failure, her failure, hard. This makes it more likely that he
might have seen his failures as in some way a product of hers: she
couldn't come up with the promised success, so he was held back by
her failures and inadequacies. In addition, there are various occasions
when, from other sources, it is clear that C-S silenced concrete
evidence about OS's 'worldly', if not financial, success. Perhaps the
most significant of these is her role in providing the prime analytic
objection to the coming English/Boer war just before 1899; also that
her views provided a centrepiece for Hobson's work is never so
much as mentioned. From C-S's account readers gather that Hobson
was interested in him, not in OS. Other silencings involve the
invisibility in The Life of OS's feminist and socialist connections; and
thus C-S's effective denial not only of her marked importance in
international feminist and English radical circles, and her growing
commitment to militant anti-racism in South Africa, but more starkly
that she even had such political commitments.

OS's closest friendships were with women who shared her

political convictions and involvements. However, Mary Brown appears only as 'wife of Dr Brown' rather than as a feminist active as a Poor Law Guardian and in the Cooperative Women's Guild; Eleanor Marx appears merely as 'daughter of Karl', rather than someone who shared a commitment to grassroots feminist and socialist activity; Constance Lytton appears as 'niece of the once governor of the Cape' rather than someone who shared a fervent feminist pacifism; Alice Greene and Betty Moltano appear only as well-born teachers rather than women who shared anti-racist beliefs and a woman-centred way of life; Dora Montefiore, Emma Cons and Edith Lees never so much as appear; and so on.

OS's denied relationships with women were close and successful, for they persisted over time on a basis of mutual support and enjoyment. What is stressed in The Life are outlines of her fundamentally unsuccessful relationships with three men: Ellis, Rhodes, and C-S himself. I think that OS's woman-centredness was one more feature of her 'personality' that C-S found hard to take, so much so that, like her conterminous political life, he rendered it invisible.

C-S's treatment of the 'important', OS's socialist and feminist analytical and organisational importance, thus mirrors his treatment of the apparently trivial. He refuses to recognise the existence of evidence which fails to corroborate his view of OS as a 'divine child': he either omits it from The Life altogether, or treats it as though it does corroborate his view, or reports it while not acknowledging that it contradicts his 'asthmatic personality'. Working within an essentially closed system – which is what C-S's view of OS's personality is – is to work in a self-evidently ideological fashion, and it is useful to further explore such a view of The Life.

Dorothy Smith (1974a) has outlined the 'three tricks' that Karl Marx and Frederick Engels (1968) describe in The German Ideology as the practical and everyday means by which 'ideology' is produced. My version of the 'three tricks' is: (1) separate what is said from who says it and from the actual empirical circumstances in which both what is said and the underlying events took place; (2) arrange these statements, descriptions etc. into an order which links them: that is, produce 'a pattern', preferably causal in nature; (3) then change this pattern or order back 'into a person', so that an actual person is seen as embodying the components of the order, thus proving its 'objective' and 'factual' existence apparently independent of the researcher/analyst.

For Marx and Engels, as for Dorothy Smith (1974b, 1980, 1983, 1984), ideology is by definition a *method*, a practical means of utilising written or visual or verbal accounts and which can be properly conceptualised and understood only in the context of the specific *conditions of its use*. Marx & Engels's three-step method of ideological practice can be discerned within the activities of biographers, of course including what I am doing in this chapter. This is precisely how 'a personality' for their biographical subjects is constructed. My specific example of biographical ideology production, C-S's *The Life*, shows this particularly well. It is replete with examples of the ideological three-step in action, as a relatively 'naive' and unsophisticated example of biographical writing, although any other example would have shown the same thing even if in relatively sophisticated forms (and see here for example Kathryn Dodd's (1990) discussion of similar features in Ray Strachey's *The Cause*). I have chosen to discuss *The Life*, however, because it stands in a particular ideological relationship to later writing on OS.

The Life and The Letters were prepared by C-S himself: they are an authorised 'widower's biography', to stand alongside 'widow's biographies' (and I wonder how many of these, examined more closely, would reveal a similarly ambiguous attitude to their dead spouses). Much of the material C-S collected was later destroyed, and thus what most people interested in OS have had available to them has been *The Life* and *The Letters*. A particular impression of OS's personality is gained from reading them, as two examples show: Virginia Woolf's (1925/1979) review of *The Letters*, and Ruth First & Ann Scott's (1980) biography of OS.

Virginia Woolf, reviewing *The Letters* in 1925, sees OS's letters as a careless 'jumble and muddle of odds and ends, plans and arrangements, bulletins of health and complaints of landladies – all of which are related as if Olive Schreiner were a figure of the highest importance' (180). Woolf draws this together around her understanding of OS's 'fate': the 'discrepancy between what she desired and what she achieved' (181) in her relationships and accomplishments. Woolf then explains OS's misfortune or fate: she achieved early fame and popularity; her husband sacrificed himself for her work 'as he told us last year in his biography' (181; a sting in that: I hope it went home); but all that resulted was the remarkable though flawed *The Story of An African Farm* and 'a few other fragmentary works' (181).

The SAF's brilliance and power is offset by limitations, Woolf feels: OS's interests are local and personal, she probably couldn't enter into experiences different from her own. Woolf sees OS's private life as thwarted and disappointed: she was driven by asthma to perpetual travel, unrest, dissatisfaction and in the end loneliness; she was a self-propelled martyr who sacrificed humour, sweetness and a sense of proportion. However, she remains powerful and uncompromising and her cause of the greatest importance. And Woolf sums up this personality by comparing OS's obsessions and egotism with her convictions and ruthless sincerity and her masterly sanity, which is contrasted with, 'often on the same page', childish outbursts of unreason. Although cross-cut by her appreciation of OS's feminism and personal power, Woolf's view is in essentials derived from C-S's supposedly 'loving and reverential' account.

First and Scott's biography uncovers much new material which substantially undercuts C-S's work. They demonstrate that without doubt he suppressed material and silenced important persons and evidence. Yet, in spite of this, the view of OS's 'personality' they adopt is effectively that adopted in Virginia Woolf's review. In showing the lasting and insidious influence of C-S's hatchet job on OS, I sketch out the main dimensions of their treatment of 'OS's personality' and show its basis in a largely uncritical absorption of C-S's construction.

First and Scott rely on C-S and The Life for much 'fact' concerning OS. One instance is found in the notes to their chapter two (First and Scott, 1980, pp. 344-5), which deals with OS's childhood and period as governess: where no specific references are given, 'information about this period of Olive's life, including quotations ... and others' recollections of her, can be found in Life, Ch. 2 ... and Ch. 3' (First and Scott, 1980, p. 344). They rely on C-S for more than this, for this reference to The Life is immediately followed by 'Where verbal recollection of her as a child is involved, we have relied more on others statements than on hers, since she was given to exaggeration and getting her dates wrong' (First and Scott, 1980, p. 344). This version of 'what OS was like' is of course a central feature of C-S's ideologically constructed account. With all their benefit of hindsight and proofs of C-S's basic untrustworthiness as a biographer, it is surprising that First and Scott utilised his view as the centrepiece in their psychoanalytically-based account of 'OS's asthmatic personality'. It is not possible easily to present First and Scott's account of this 'asthmatic personality' since it permeates the entire book, so I focus on a discussion in the last chapter, 'Broken and Untried?'.

OS's illness, her asthma, is presented as expressive of the conflicts she experienced about power and control: 'The literal duty of the asthmatic was to 'lie still'. If Olive could do this, there might be moments of relief from the contradictions of her situation' (First and Scott, 1980, p. 335). Engagement in life's struggles and periodic retreats into illness/asthma is portrayed as her life's dynamic: she continually swung between one and the other. First and Scott see the asthma as a product of OS's contradictory situation, as a psychosomatic product of mother-child relations arising from conflicts over in/dependence. They 'mention it here as a way of looking at asthma consistent with the main themes of Olive's personal life' (First and Scott, 1980, p. 336). But this is actually a product of C-S's *account* of OS's childhood and later differences with her mother, not incontrovertible evidence about either. As I have suggested, there are ample grounds for proposing that OS's asthma was the product of material conditions she was *currently* experiencing at different points in her life, and in relation to *men*, not her mother.

First and Scott look at OS through Cronwright-coloured spectacles. I conclude by considering why *The Life* is read in this way by sensible and inquiring feminists. In doing so I return to the effects of its Preface on how readers interpret *The Life*.

In the Preface C-S uses OS's reported wishes and intentions to legitimate his biography, also insisting that a biography by anyone else would have been 'incomplete' and 'gravely incorrect'; readers 'read in' the implied contrast, to see his work as complete and correct. He then advances powerful personal claims for his knowledge of OS's supposedly strange and incredible personality, such, he repeatedly insists, that no one else could know it but him. The result is that we take her to be strange, rather than treating this claim as itself rather peculiar. He goes on to re-emphasise the status of *The Life* as 'unusually complete' and correct and ties these claims to his status as an OS-legitimated and trusted biographer, and makes a powerful statement about his 'loving and reverential' feelings about and intentions towards her, both when she was alive and now in the biography. Finally he status-ranks himself in relation to other knowledgeable sources of information about OS, including Havelock Ellis.

The Preface, then, strongly frames and underpins a particular reading of what follows. It provides a framework by which we read *The Life* through an already articulated account of the 'nature' of the biographical subject and also the status, feelings and intentions of her biographer. It adds up to a very powerful case indeed for readers to take C-S and the contents of his book on trust. That so many people have done so for so long, and in the face of a growing feminist critique of the ideological basis of men's sexual political relations with women, is an indication of just how successful it has been.

I conclude by returning to the general argument about biographical writing introduced at the start of this chapter. What I have provided in this chapter is one particular instance of a set of working practices shared by all biographers. 'A biography' involves a set of textual practices which produce a supremely ideological product; and these practices enable 'a life' to be written around a framework of interpretation decided by the biographer and not by the life itself. Essential to these textual practices is the use of the 'ideological three step', for this provides a proficient means of preserving a narrative while enabling rigorous summarising of detail, and thus it underpins a form or structure to the written life and also provides apparently causal links between events and occurrences. I have described the particular biographer discussed as ill-willed and as having tampered with evidence; while most biographers are well-intentioned and scrupulous, the point remains that the basic practices involved – that biographers adopt a particular view of their subject, and they select out material which does not fit this view – are defining features of all biography.

Notes

1 This chapter originally appeared in *Studies in Sexual Politics* 8 (Stanley, 1985a).
2 Of course truisms are not necessarily true, and there are recent examples which eschew any hint of hagiography: Susan Crosland's (1982) biography of Antony Crosland, for example.
3 Olive Schreiner was born in what later became South Africa in 1855 to missionary parents. From a very young age she rebelled against many of the regulations for correct behaviour that bound her life. She came to England in 1883 expecting to train as a doctor; ill-health prevented her, but in 1881 her first book, *The Story of An African Farm*, was published by Chapman & Hall. Eleanor Marx, Havelock Ellis and Edward Carpenter became close friends. An uneasy and unreciprocated relationship with Karl Pearson

foundered on many tensions, not least those of sexual politics (Bland, 1990). Olive Schreiner returned to South Africa in 1889, met and opposed Cecil Rhodes, foretold and opposed the Boer War, almost succeeded in her and others endeavours to prevent an apartheid constitution for the new South Africa following the Boer War. She married Samuel 'Cron' Cronwright. In 1913 she returned to England and remained during the First World War. She returned to South Africa, very ill, in late 1919 and died soon after. A summary of her work and publications appears in Stanley, 1983.

4 See here Stanley, 1985a and Stanley, 1993 forthcoming.

5 With the publication of Richard Rive's (1987) first volume of the edited Olive Schreiner Letters.

6 This and the following section headings in the chapter are quotations from The Life.

7 Havelock Ellis spent time in the Australian outback as a teacher in his teens and trained as a doctor to carry out his plan to scientifically study sex and sexuality. He combined this with numerous writing and editing ventures and was also involved in radical and socialist circles. He married Edith Lees, an active feminist and socialist and later to become Britain's first 'out', publicly open, lesbian – the source of much friction with Ellis. In the 1920s and 1930s Ellis became well-known as the author of the Studies in Sex Psychology and as the first 'sexologist'. I discuss their relationship and evidence concerning Edith Lees' sexual status in Chapter 8.

8 These are: (a) the Preface, which I have already discussed; (b) Chapters I ('Ancestry and Family') and II ('Childhood and Girlhood'), through to the major summary of her 'genius and intellect' that occurs just after the beginning of Chapter III ('The Governess'), on pages 100 and 102 (101 is a map); (c) the bulk of Chapter III, Chapter IV ('In Europe') and most of Chapter V ('Return to South Africa – Marriage'), to the second major summary of OS's personality on pp. 234-41, at age thirty-eight when C-S first met her; (d) the remainder of Chapter V and the bulk of Chapter VI ('Married Life') to the third major summation of OS's personality that occurs around the question of the 'sex book' in pp. 353-9; and, finally, (e) the remaining pages of Chapter VI through Chapter VII ('Last Years And Death' to the end of The Life proper. There are various appendices. I have omitted for space reasons a discussion of these even though they are important in rounding off the preferred reading of The Life set up in the Preface.

9 She habitually did so and had her wages lowered as a consequence.

10 It seems much more connected with C-S's reactions to OS's later dealings with Cecil Rhodes, the imperialist entrepreneur, following her return from England to the Cape in 1889. I discuss this later in the chapter.

11 Mary Brown was a politically active Liberal feminist with many radical connections during her years in Burnley, in the north of England. These included her work as one of the first women Poor Law Guardians and in the Cooperative Women's Guild. It was through her that OS was introduced to northern Guild circles.

12 As a reader of the Olive Schreiner letters in the Carpenter Archive in Sheffield City Public Library and in the Humanities Research Center in Austin, Texas, I suggest a more simple explanation than C-S's. At the start of letters her writing is relatively readable because done carefully, but it soon turns into a careless scrawled writing that is huge but often indecipherable.

13 These reminiscences are included, more or less verbatim, in his posthumously published autobiography My Life (Ellis 1940).

14 Edward Carpenter left clerical orders for University extension teaching and middle class radical and socialist circles in London. He then moved to live among working class socialists in Sheffield. His writing, particularly that on 'homogenic love', changed many people's lives. He and OS were mutual confidants (1886 and 1887 were years of 'great suffering' for him too), as well as regularly corresponding, including about political issues and their own and each other's writing. Another close friend of Carpenter's was Edith Lees; he shared OS's, Stella Browne's and other feminists' anger concerning Ellis'

treatment of Lees before her death from diabetes, as well as maintaining his distance from C-S after OS's death.

15 Although not mentioned in The Life, in fact it was Ellis who labelled OS's symptoms as asthma and treated her for it, including by prescribing various then popular drugs and remedies. In My Life Ellis implies OS was drug dependent while failing to make as much of his assiduous dosing of his own ailments.

16 Ellis' biographer, Phyllis Grosskurth (1980), far too readily accepts Ellis' construction of not only these specific events but also the question of the 'neurotic' because lesbian personality of Edith Lees. Certainly OS and Stella Browne among other feminist friends of Lees were very concerned about Ellis' behaviour in the period leading up to Lees' death from diabetes (e.g. Carpenter Archive 358.19), as indeed was Carpenter, who accordingly absented himself from the funeral of one of his closest friends.

17 There were also a large number of miscarriages, mainly after this, which C-S does not mention.

18 Karl Pearson was a then socialist university lecturer colleague of OS in the Men and Women's Club (Bland, 1990), a kind of seminar to discuss gender politics and analysis. OS was non-reciprocally attracted to him, an attraction she denied was either romantic or sexual, but which certainly devastated her life. A natural scientist turned statistician, Pearson later became a leading supporter of eugenicism and a fervent imperialist.

19 Some details of this are contained in First and Scott (1980).

20 However, C-S married this younger woman after OS's death, becoming a father in his fifties.

8

Feminism and friendship

Biography and friendship

Here as in the previous two chapters I discuss my activities as a writer, rather than as a reader, of biography. As I explained in Chapter 1, I became a writer of biography because as a reader I felt placed in a 'take it or leave it' position by the biographies I read, rather than my active readership being enabled. In this chapter I look at three case studies, each of them pieces of work I undertook because I wanted answers to questions which the books I read neither answered nor encouraged me to ask. These questions are concerned with patterns of friendship between women of the past.[1]

The 'spotlight' approach to 'modern biography' emphasises the uniqueness of a particular subject, seen in individualised terms rather than as a social self lodged within a network of others. It casts these other people known and liked or disliked throughout the subject's life into the shadows; and doing so has interpretative importance for the way we understand 'a life', not only as textually related but also as interactionally understood. It essentialises the self, rather than focussing on the role of social processes in producing – and changing – what 'a self' consists of. And it enshrines an entirely de-politicised notion of 'greatness', presenting this as a characteristic of individuals rather than than the product of political processes and con-structions.

However, this is not the only approach possible. One alternative is to be concerned with the interplay of a group of lives in a particular social milieu; another is to explore the interplay of biography and autobiography in particular histories; and both have proved attractive to feminists. For instance, Kim Chernin's (1985) and Carolyn Steedman's (1986) feminist auto/biographies focus on changing ideas about the past and intra-family dynamics and their impact on these authors. In feminist biography Barbara Caine's (1986) work is concerned with the relationships of the Potter sisters; Sybil Oldfield's (1984), Tierl Thompson's (1987) and Johanna Alberti's (1990) emphasis is on the changing dynamics of two-partner friendships;

and Philippa Levine's (1990) is on tracing the overlaying of friendship and family relationships of Victorian feminists. This approach
combines the detailed specificity of biography with a social and
indeed sociological view of individuals lives connnected with others,
and also with a broad knowledge of the social, economic and
political context in which those lives were led. Here structure and
process, and individuals and collectivities, are treated as symbiotically related, and biography seen as intellectually adequate only if it
comes to grips with both aspects of each supposed binary.

I begin with a critical outline of the assumptions and consequences of the 'spotlight' approach, and also of a particular feminist
conceptualisation of women's friendships from the late-eighteenth to
the early-twentieth century − that of 'romantic friendship'. Then I
discuss interpretive issues concerning friendship in three case studies
from my research. The first concerns the friendship group of some
militant women in the Edwardian Women's Social and Political
Union associated with Emily Wilding Davison, in particular issues
involved in understanding the close friendship between Emily
Davison and Mary Leigh. The second concerns claims made about the
'romantic friendships' of Edith Lees, married to Havelock Ellis,
looked at through various of her letters to Edward Carpenter. And the
third concerns the related claim that the 'mannish' lesbian is a
stereotype invented by sexologists such as Ellis, investigated in
relation to correspondence sent by a number of women to Edward
Carpenter.

Feminism and friendship

Margaret Forster's excellent biography of Elizabeth Barrett Browning
(1988) positions her subject within the context of family: initially
within the framework of her father and siblings; later within the
closer, more fulfilling and supportive relationship with Robert
Browning and their son Penn. 'The Brownings in Italy' appear as
Robert going out to bring back social gossip and stimulation,
Elizabeth in her sitting room waiting and writing and timorously
receiving the occasional bold visitor.

It is a convincing picture, one that doubtless closely fits the
archive and other sources used by her biographer. And yet from
other more renegade sources (Stanley, 1985a) a rather different

picture can be assembled. These other sources consist of the diaries, letters and other textual products of Victorian feminism; and from these it is apparent that Elizabeth Barrett Browning in Italy was a key reference point for a group of expatriate largely English-speaking women. This group included Fanny Kemble, Harriet Hosmer and Charlotte Cushman the actors, Mary Somerville the mathematician and astronomer, Natalie Micas the inventor, Rosa Bonheur the painter, Matilda Hays who worked on the English Women's Journal, Mary Lloyd the sculptor, Frances Power Cobbe the journalist and social reformer, and others. Theirs was no admiration from afar, but the social association of like-minded women who considered Elizabeth Barrett Browning an interesting equal.

Noting this different picture is not to be critical of Margaret Foster's research, for no biographer can be totally conversant with every single textual reference to their subject. Rather, it is to emphasise that all biographical research involves making choices about what counts as 'knowledge' about the subject, what people have such knowledge, and where to look for both. These are epistemological choices, which result in a particular construction of the subject and their social world. It is not possible to avoid making such choices. My preferred – anti-spotlight, feminist, constructionist – approach equally excludes some things from consideration as well as highlighting others; however, I find focussing on networks and relationships better fits my concern with the social.

The spotlight approach obscures and makes insignificant what was important in the daily lives of those who become the subject of biography: their relationships with others, how they were seen and treated by them, how they responded to these others. Stripping this fabric of relationships down to a select few 'significant' (as seen by the biographer, perhaps as seen by the subject) others has implications for the view of 'the self' that modern biography inscribes. It promotes a particular ontological view, one which treats the subject as a hub at the centre of a wheel with few spokes, the epicentre of their world. Behind these choices lies the biographer's assessment of who they deem to be important and who not – and inevitably such assessments derive from more than an 'objective' reading of their importance to the subject's life. Convention, for instance, about who can be 'seen' and what it is possible to write has produced the failure to 'see' Ellen Tierney in most biographies of Charles Dickens, and the recent almost feverish concern sparked off by Peter Ackroyd's biography of Dickens (1990) and Claire Tomalin's of Tierney (1990) to pin down the extent of their involvement and whether she gave birth to a child fathered by him.

There are also choices about how the subject is to be textually constituted. The role of metaphor, irony and synecdoche, of different kinds of narrative, of different kinds of 'voice', is important in auto/biographical texts. In many biographies metaphorical means of representation have proved especially appealing, for they offer a memorable shorthand way of conveying the essence of how the biographer sees – or rather how they choose on paper to represent, which is not necessarily the same thing – their subject. And in part such choices stem from, and/or produce, particular views of the reading audience: how this is assumed to be composed will affect not only writing style, but also what material will be included, what excluded.

Even when the importance of friendship links and patterns is conceded, choices in themselves epistemologically consequential for the production of biography remain. Lillian Faderman (1979) conceptualises close friendships between women until the early twentieth century as romantic ones involving passionate emotional commitment expressed openly. Faderman argues, using a wide range of secondary sources, that these friendships were neither seen as 'unnatural' nor as sexual, even though their romantic character was recognised and accepted. Faderman's approach recognises two important things: that there are large temporal differences in how friendship is defined and treated (i.e. its meaning is socially constructed), and that in past times women's friendships were seen as a central social relationship; while the focus in modern biography is usually on marriage or other kinds of heterosexual sexual relationships and is a reflection of current definitions and understandings, not necessarily those of the times and places of biography's subjects.

Despite its undoubted strengths, Faderman's approach romanticises the past by constructing a lost age of innocence: a time before patriarchal oppressiveness in the work of sexologists invented 'the lesbian' as a sexualised mannish stereotype and imposed it on passionate friendships between women in order to condemn them. Her focus on romantic friendships between women fails to notice that romantic friendships between men were at least as common, a prototype being Alfred Tennyson's romance with and life-long mourning for Arthur Hallam. If sexologists can be seen as having invented the 'mannish' lesbian stereotype (and I later argue that they did not), they have to be seen as equally responsible for inventing the sexualisation of the 'effeminate' homosexual male stereotype and thus of persecuting men as well as women.

Romantic friendships in Faderman's terms are not sexual relationships; and in an examination of the historical case study of Jane Pirie and Marianne Woods (Faderman, 1983) she argues her grounds for this. However, there are problems with Faderman's approach. It proceeds from the assumption that 'sexual' means the same things now that it meant in the late-eighteenth century, early, mid and late-nineteenth century. It makes a distinction between 'the sexual' as genital acts of various kinds and the non-sexual, thereby defining much erotic behaviour as non-sexual. It defines as 'lesbian' only a very narrow set of genital sexual relationships. And it ignores the understandings of the protagonists of romantic relationships in favour of a researcher-imposed set of understandings and meanings.

A paradigmatic example of Faderman's approach involves the 'Ladies of Llangollen', Sarah Ponsonby and Eleanor Butler (Mavor, 1971), who ran away from Ireland in 1778 and then lived together a life of 'sweet contentment' in rural retreat from the corruptions of urban social life. Faderman argues that everybody knew they were romantic friends, everybody approved, nobody thought it was a sexual relationship, nobody shunned them because they thought the relationship was 'unnatural'. There are, however, good reasons for suggesting that the facts were otherwise: that indefatigable diarist Hester Thrale Piozzi[2] refers to the ladies and their friends as 'damned sapphists' and writes that this is why various literary women will not visit them overnight unless accompanied by men; while the de-coded diary of one of their friends, Anne Lister (Whitbread, 1988), contains details of her explicitly sexual conquests of women and clearly opens up the possibility that other members of her circle were as genitally aware as she.

However, whatever its problems Faderman's work at least thinks about women's historical friendships outside of present-day biographical convention, a convention which assumes that in adulthood the ties of women's friendships give way to the presumed-to-be more important ones of marriage and family. What is needed is a broader view of friendship than Faderman's, which rejects the assumptions of the convention but does so in favour of a detailed investigative approach rather than a reliance on secondary sources and theoretical deductivism. It needs to include at least the following.

'Friendship' can encompass different kinds of ties and bonds between people. Relatedly, the significance and extent of friendships will differ for different people, and different meanings will be attached to these friendships not only by their protagonists but also in relation to the particular time-period and social context they take place within. The friendship patterns of even one person are highly complex and variegated and are socially and temporally located.

Friendship links are positive and negative (not just positive or negative); they change over time; and they are interconnected with each other. Friendships are not necessarily nor uniformly about 'love' but can encompass dislike as well as like, respect instead of love, influence instead of sympathy.

The 'significance' of a relationship is very difficult to determine post hoc and with the kinds of materials that biographers usually work with. Personal testimony, moreover, may not help and indeed may hinder a biographer's understanding (as with Hilary Spurling's (1974, 1984) biography of Ivy Compton-Burnett discussed in Spurling, 1988). However, insofar as such assessments can be made, they have to be founded upon detailed research inductively argued from. The first step is to establish what social relationships existed in a particular subject's life; readers can do this at least in part from published biographies by tracing out those the biographer mentions, although of course writers of biography can do this much more completely should they see the importance of doing so.[3]

While recognising the influences on them, it is crucial to treat biographical subjects as agents of their lives and not as puppets whose thoughts and actions were determined, whether by social structures, or by ideological prescriptions of how women and men were supposed to be, or indeed by others within their social and political circles. It would be ironic indeed if a feminist approach to friendship, by wanting to recognise women's oppression in the past as well as the present, should treat these friendships as determined by patriarchy. In the section of the chapter, 'Dear Edward', I discuss these issues by considering material from the Carpenter Archive which addresses Faderman's claim that Havelock Ellis morbidified not only lesbianism in general but the romantic friendships of his wife Edith Lees in particular; and then in 'Dear Edward Carpenter' I discuss the related claim that he and other sexologists invented the 'mannish' lesbian stereotype which was then imposed on women's romantic and/or erotic relationships.

However, working with large amounts of secondary material, as readers of biography necessarily do, produces a temporally flat view of friendship, whereas a key feature is its dynamic quality: friendships change. In the following section of the chapter I discuss aspects of the friendship network of one particular group of feminists, including Emily Wilding Davison, from approximately 1908 to 1914/1918.

From comrade Davison

Between 1986 and 1988 I worked with Ann Morley[4] on a biography of Emily Wilding Davison (Stanley, 1988b), the suffragette who died as a consequence of action she took at the 1913 Derby. In disentangling feminist myth from anti-feminist rhetoric, and establishing something of the contemporary meaning of Emily Davison's death and her preceding feminist activities, one of the main concerns was to establish her closest friendships. These friends were present at her funeral procession in London and then Morpeth in the north of England, and their presence was contemporaneously seen as an acknowledgement of their central importance in her life, although they were not named in funeral reports.

None of these women was well-known except within feminist circles. They, and Emily Davison herself, were women of action; and they left no personal archives of papers except for a few relatively impersonal ones,[5] unlike for example feminist writers such as Evelyn Sharp who left extensive personal as well as political archives.[6] Their energies went into feminist causes and struggles and insofar as they wrote did so in instrumental ways and in passing, in notes, on postcards and brief letters.

There were said to be six of these closest friends of Emily Wilding Davison. We established the firm identities of four: Rose Lamartine Yates, Edith Mansell-Moullin, Eleanor Penn-Gaskell and Mary Leigh; we also discounted two other contenders, Vera Holme and Elsie Howey (Stanley, 1988b, pp. 96-146). And, after the biography was published, we finally concluded that the other two were Mabel Capper and Charlotte Marsh (Stanley, 1988b, pp. 72-117).

For each of these women, feminism entailed a political commitment through and through, a commitment which infused all their other relationships, subordinating these to the cause of feminism. For Emily herself, and also for Charlotte Marsh and Mary Leigh, their primary and indeed their only emotional commitments were to other feminist women. Their feminism was a complex phenomenon, blending socialism, animal rights, vegetarianism, pacifism, support for Irish unity and opposition to British colonialism. It was a feminism of practice, practice which infused all aspects of their lives. However, they were not 'cultured' in the sense of being involved with feminist literature, art and music. Rather theirs was a feminism of action in the public sphere and, overarching everything else, one expressed through a growing and widespread women's community embedded in a myriad of local groups, organisations and friendship networks.

Beyond establishing that these women were indeed friends of Emily Wilding Davison, there are interpretive problems and dilemmas in saying anything about the qualities of their relationships.[7] Partly because of the absence of alternative archival sources, and partly because of the nature of these friendships, there are complex interpretive issues involved in making any kind of pronouncement about their meaning to the protagonists, not least because contemporary custom and practice often combined formalism of address with an often highly florid style of expression – and did so in relation to a wide variety of different kinds of relationships from acquaintances through to close friends and relatives. I go on to illustrate some of these complexities in relation to the close friendship between Emily Davison and Mary Leigh, because it highlights the interpretative difficulties in ways that touch directly on both the friendship debate and also the wider question of the form that biography should take.

Mary Leigh was a Manchester woman, Mary Brown by birth; she came from a working class background and became a teacher; she married a builder called Leigh who thereafter disappeared from the scene. By 1908 she was already prominent in WSPU circles, a woman renowned for her acts of militancy and who, although disliked by them for her independence of mind and action, could not be cast off by the WSPU leadership. There were some hundreds of Manchester-born Mary Browns in the likely years of her birth, at least as many Mary Leighs nationally in the likely years of her death in the middle 1960s, so even the dates of her birth and death remain unknown. But not so some of the salient facts of her feminist career, for Mary Leigh was a fearless and determined woman much of whose feminist activity took place in a very public sphere.

Mary Leigh spent her time in the WSPU, from the time of the 1907 split with the Women's Freedom League (WFL),[8] in opposition to its leadership. A socialist and democrat through and through, she nonetheless preferred to stay in the WSPU because she thought that the WFL women 'went over too much to the men'. She was a national figure not in any way controllable by leaders: her own woman, unpredictable, a force to be reckoned with. A series of militant events from 1910 on led Mary Leigh to achieve even more kudos in the WSPU, but also to her effective abandonment by the leadership once in prison in 1912 and facing an attempt to declare her a lunatic and thus able to be detained indefinitely 'at his majesty's pleasure'.

Later Mary Leigh was a founding member of the Emily Wilding Davison Fellowship following Emily's death; and the Fellowship not only instituted close links with the WFL, but also set up a series of public speaking tours by radical feminist women, many of whom spoke in favour of pacifism, against British colonialism, for Irish unity, against the 1914-1918 war, against the British presence in India. She was involved in the pacifist rump of the WSPU, the 'Suffragettes of the WSPU', during the war; before it in the East London Federation of the Suffragettes led by Sylvia Pankhurst; and after it in the Communist Party and later in the Campaign for Nuclear Disarmament (CND) and in activities for pensioners' rights.

As well as being involved in the Fellowship, Mary Leigh tended Emily Wilding Davison's grave until her own death in the 1960s and led an annual pilgrimage there. She was a fiercely courageous, loyal, dynamic, radical and much admired woman. Emily Davison invented many of the acts of militancy that later became synonymous with the WSPU; each time she did so it was in response to a perceived leadership betrayal of Mary Leigh which Emily Davison wanted to bring to public attention.[9] Mary Leigh was similarly attached to Emily Davison, carrying the flag that Emily had carried at the 1913 Derby on CND marches and promoting the causes that Emily supported through the Fellowship. She was clearly emotionally and politically very close to Emily Davison, but reading the nature of this closeness is difficult indeed.

One of the main pieces of evidence about the emotional dimensions of their relationship is a copy of the abridged poems of Walt Whitman now in the Emily Wilding Davison collection in the

Fawcett Library[10] inscribed 'from Comrade Davison to Comrade Leigh' and dated 29 December 1912. Many lines and passages are marked: the inscription is headed 'the dear love of comrades', while other marked passages include 'I hear it is charged against me that I seek to destroy institutions' and 'I dreamed a city of friends'. These markings point up both the love of friends and comrades and the more overtly political elements of Whitman's poem, those dealing with the destruction of old institutions, the founding of new ones on the basis of comradeship.

However, this gift, intended to go from Emily Davison to Mary Leigh, remains in Emily Davison's papers, which are also those of the planned 'Women's Record House' museum/archive of the 1930s. In December 1912 Mary Leigh was in prison in England for acts of militancy, and Emily Davison was also briefly in prison in Aberdeen. Was the gift ever given? The markings and underlinings are more those of the reader of such a gift than of the person who gave it, but the underlinings, unlike the writing, cannot be attributed. However, if the gift was given to her then it is not likely that Mary Leigh, a woman who was known to guard her personal privacy absolutely, would later give it away. And even if she did, the question still arises as to how it ended up in these papers, for whatever else it is highly unlikely that Mary Leigh would give such a very personal gift to the Women's Record House for public exhibition.

Beyond the problem of establishing whether the gift was given or not, further issues arise in interpreting its meaning for Emily Davison and, if it was given, for Mary Leigh also. Whitman's long prose poem Leaves of Grass (1860), from which this abridgement was made, was well-known in England, particularly in radical circles. It lent itself to interpretations which stressed its socialist message, its idealism, its crossing of class boundaries, and its promotion of comrade love both of the spirit and also of the flesh. While Whitman was later concerned to minimise this, many gay men and lesbian women of the time read it as a promotion of physical love between people of the same sex (cf. Eve Kosofsky Sedgwick (1985) and Elaine Showalter (1991)). In particular Whitman's poem became associated with Edward Carpenter's promotion of it and his own English paeon to comradeship Towards Democracy (1883). For many, 'comradeship' and the 'dear love of comrades' had become a coded way of talking and writing about 'same-sex love', sexual love, and this was furthered by Carpenter's references to 'homogenic' comradeship in his essay

Homogenic love and its place in a free society (1894) and the later and more
influential collected essays in the second edition of *Love's Coming Of Age*
(1906) and in *The Intermediate Sex* (1908).

'The dear love of comrades', then, for many people had particular
resonances associated with the early homosexual rights movement
and a more open public presence of gay women and men in
England. The question thus becomes whether Emily Davison could
have been unaware of these resonances, moving as she did in
feminist circles and on the fringes of socialist circles which were
well-aware of Carpenter's own homosexuality and his work in
textually defending and promoting same-sex sexual love. My conviction is that Emily Davison could not have been unaware of it; she
was too well read and too well-connected, and also too closely
involved with women who, like herself, showed never the slightest
interest in men and a great deal of interest in other women. Certainly
one such feminist woman corresponded with Edward Carpenter, and
I later discuss her letter to him which traces the path by which KO[11]
came to define and name her feelings for other women as involving
sexual desire. I think that Emily Davison travelled the same path, as
did many other feminist women of her day, and that Mary Leigh did
too. I also think it likely that by late 1912 and early 1913 the two
women had moved closer to expressing these feelings to each other,
and of this the gift of the Whitman poems is a marker.

However, it is more complicated than this. One of the chief
mourners at Emily Davison's funeral in Morpeth, who arranged for a
marble stone commemorating 'A veritable princess of spirituality.
From a loving Aberdeen friend' to be placed on her grave, was not
Mary Leigh but Edith Morrison (Stanley, 1988b, pp. 134-46), even
though it was Mary Leigh who later tended the grave and arranged
the annual pilgrimage to it. Establishing Edith Morrison's connections with Emily Davison was even more difficult; nevertheless at
every point it became clear that it was Mary Leigh that Emily Davison
worked with, defined herself politically in relation to; and it was
Mary Leigh who never forgot Emily Davison during the fifty or so
years from 1913 to her own death. But I still wonder about the
friendship with Edith Morrison.

These are my speculations about the relationship between Emily
Davison and Mary Leigh based on *thoughts* and *feelings*; and I know of
no more concrete evidence than I have referred to here which
corroborates these theories. There is the evidence of the unwavering

political commitment that existed between them; and there is the Whitman poems and its marked passages. But no firm conclusion about the relationship between Emily Davison and Mary Leigh can be drawn. Theirs could have been a political relationship of great respect and commitment but with no personal emotions involved; it could have been a romantic friendship writ large through passionate feminist commitment; it could have been, or have been in the process of becoming, a passionate sexual relationship; indeed, it could have been all of these at different times between 1908 and Emily's death in 1913. However, and as Dale McNab learned the hard way, whichever it was is not available to us now to speak to and write about, even supposing that we have the ability to comprehend the meaning and naming given to such relationships by women then. Certainly naming this relationship and those of others of their friends as 'lesbian' in the terms in which present-day lesbian feminism understands this is just as unhelpful as denying that such relationships had passionate emotional and in many cases sexual dimensions to them.

I have no answers to these interpretive issues, indeed I think they are actually irresolvable given the nature of the historical record that exists concerning these and many other women. However, the issues are fundamental and need to be addressed and debated by both writers and readers of biography from a variety of viewpoints. My experience as the biographer of Emily Davison and her relationship with Mary Leigh overwhelmingly suggests that looking at one particular historical friendship over a period of time does not resolve interpretive problematics: it does, however, raise and highlight them in clear and challenging ways, both for the biographer and also hopefully for readers. I now go on to discuss other aspects of the claims made about romantic friendships, in particular the role of sexologists and especially Havelock Ellis in 'sexualising' and 'morbidifying' these in creating a 'mannish' lesbian stereotype.

Dear Edward

From the letters that survive in the Edward Carpenter Archive,[12] Carpenter's three main women correspondents were Kate Salt,[13] Olive Schreiner and Edith Lees Ellis, but with smaller numbers of letters being received from a large number of feminist women such as Isabella Ford, Annie Besant, Charlotte Despard, Stella Browne, Constance Lytton, Dora Montefiore and others. Edith Lees, married to Havelock Ellis, has been seen as a woman whose non-sexual romantic friendships with women were 'morbidified' by Ellis: effectively, that he created her as a lesbian when in fact she was not. Thus Lillian Faderman argues that her case-history in Ellis' *Sexual Inversion*[14] (1897) suggests that Edith Lees experienced romantic friendships with women rather than erotic or sexual feelings for them.

Faderman's general argument is that romantic friendships were 'love relationships in every sense except perhaps the sexual' (Faderman, 1979, p. 16) but were condoned and indeed accepted except where one of the partners cross-dressed, thus violating men's presumptive property rights over women. What changed this was the activity of late nineteenth and early twentieth century sexologists who defined such love as a medical problem. Faderman suggests that Sarah Ponsonby and Eleanor Butler, the 'Ladies of Llangollen', given their generally conservative views, would not want 'genital expression' in the absence of a man demanding marital rights – 'they were probably happy to be oblivious to their genitals' (Faderman, 1979, p. 123). And she mistakenly suggests that the generally 'homophobic' Hester Thrale Piozzi did not see them as lesbians. Faderman then argues that sexologists, Krafft-Ebing and Ellis in particular, codified and promulgated the punitive ideas of von Westphal (pp. 239-53), which focussed on transvestite women. Relatedly, in her discussions of the growth and importance of sexology, Margaret Jackson (1984) accepts Faderman's estimation of the role and centrality of sexologists in creating 'the lesbian', and her analysis focusses on the role of Havelock Ellis in particular. Esther Newton's (1984) discussion of the 'mythic mannish lesbian' similarly insists that women's romantic friendships were a quasi-legitimate supplement to marriage and sees Krafft-Ebing and Ellis as the protagonists in the invention of 'the lesbian'.

Ellis's role, Faderman suggests, was to promote Krafft-Ebing's morbidification of love between women, presenting it as a degeneracy, and she sees Ellis's book as 'one of the most successful treatises on homosexuality written in English' (Faderman, 1979, p. 241). Ellis distinguishes between the 'true invert' and the 'spurious imitation'; and Faderman – again mistakenly, as I discuss later – sees the term 'invert' as a perjorative technical term invented and used by the sexologists; and she comments that:

one wonders how many romantic friends, who had felt themselves to be perfectly normal before, suddenly saw themselves as sick, even though their behaviour had in no way changed, as a result of the sexologists' formulations. (Faderman, 1979, p. 244)

It is at this point that she footnotes comments on Edith Lees. Lees, Faderman claims, was a victim of Ellis's theories:

From his own account, Ellis apparently convinced her that she was a congenital invert, while she believed herself to be only a romantic friend to other women... He thus encouraged her to see herself as an invert and to regard her subsequent love relations with women as a manifestation of her inversion. (p. 454)

It is interesting that Ellis, portrayed as the author of a sexual political 'fall' as consequential for women as that from Eden, is believed without question by Faderman. His hint that he created Edith Lees' sexual interest in women is taken at face value, perhaps because it is one of the few pieces of evidence that Faderman has for demonstrating that Ellis' ideas had any influence on how women thought of their love and/or desire for other women, whatever influence they may have had on the writing of other sexologists. Faderman does not ask whether Ellis might have had other motives for claiming such influence, nor does she consider whether contrary evidence about Lees' feelings might exist.

On the first point, Ellis' motives, it is clear from Ellis' (1940) biography *My Life* that considerable tensions existed in his and Edith Lees' relationship and that he invested a good deal of trouble in textually locating these as her problem and not his. In examining whether Ellis 'morbidified' Edith Lees' feelings for women, Faderman's acceptance of his statement should therefore be suspended and instead the circumstances of his claim investigated. And on the second point, whether contrary evidence about Edith Lees' feelings exists, the short answer is that yes, it does, in the form of two letters in particular written to her close friend and confidant Edward Carpenter.[15]

These two letters are undated, although they appear in an archive sequence which suggests they were written in about 1915, probably because of Edith Lees' reference in the first to a lecture on Hinton, for a posthumously published book on Hinton appeared after her death in 1916. However, it is at least equally likely that they were

written considerably before this. Lees started lecturing on Hinton
many years before 1915 and in the first letter it is clear that
Carpenter's sister Alice still does not know, although she suspects,
that her brother is homosexual; Edith Lees' first letter notes that: 'she
has a fear for your reputation & hers & the religion through you. She
said she felt sure I knew you were that & it wd hurt your message &
mine etc etc'. Given Carpenter's publications, by 1915 Alice Carpenter could have had no doubt about her brother's homosexuality for a
number of years.[16]

In the first of these letters Edith Lees writes about her questioning
by Alice Carpenter:

'this *of course* between us – my inversion is the 'talk' in that higher thought.
How it has got out heaven knows or whether they only think it or know it
I don't quite realise but when I went to your sister the other day with
trembling lips & hands she questioned me about what she had heard'
('higher thought' is a sarcastic reference to Carpenter's sister Alice's piety)

She goes on, 'your sister wrote me a long letter after in which she
called me 'a fine, loving teacher' etc – but but – you know'.

Lees' main response to Alice Carpenter's questioning was to add a
statement (the precise content of which she does not specify) to a
public lecture she gave that week (this could have been her lecture
on 'Eugenics and abnormality', although she also lectured on 'Oscar
Wilde: A problem in eugenics'). Certainly during Lees' 1914 lecture
tour of America she had already considerably startled many audiences by speaking of her own 'inversion', so this is certainly before
1914. The letter concludes by Lees writing that 'I'm so thankful for
these last ten years of lying low'.

The second of the two letters is written in reply to Carpenter's
response to her first. Among a number of other matters, she says that
'I've had a vision – as clear & inspiring as ever St Paul had & it's just
altered everything for me'; she also discusses how she thought the
gossip got out, and her feelings for the woman, now dead, she had
been overwhelmingly in love with.[17]

Interpreting these two letters is a difficult matter, not least because
they do not directly pronounce on the claims made on her behalf by
Ellis and by Faderman. However, it is clear that Edith Lees herself
definitely thinks that she is an 'invert', was startled to be questioned
but responded through public statement about her 'inversion', and is
grateful for ten years of 'lying low'. Edith Lees wrote to Carpenter

because they shared 'inversion' and Alice's questioning concerned them both. She responded to Alice's 'accusation' not only by writing that 'if it is true it wd be sheer purity & sweetness to me and so for *me* the best the world cd have for me' but also by publicly speaking about her sexuality. I very decidedly prefer to accept what Edith Lees says about herself than what Ellis claims his role in her lesbianism and Faderman's acceptance of this.

Dear Edward Carpenter

In addition to the Edith Lees material, there are some letters from women in the Carpenter Archive[18] written to Carpenter after publication of the second edition of *Love's Coming Of Age* in 1906 and *The Intermediate Sex* in 1908. There are many other letters from gay men in the Archive; it is therefore likely that Carpenter received many more than these four from women, but that only these have survived. These letters throw an additional light on the question of the 'invention' of the sexualised and 'mannish' lesbian through sexologists' morbidification of love between women.

On 21 July 1913 AT[19] wrote Carpenter a detailed letter about her 'condition'. Against the backdrop of the women's movement and the possibility of women gaining financial and thus familial independence, AT outlines her first memories of wanting to wear boy's clothes and doing so in secret, her involvement in outdoor sports, her attempts to end her 'unnatural life' in marriage but with engagement accentuating her feelings for women, her thwarted wish for a career, and her duty fixed at caring for her mother during her last years. The women who attract AT are gentle and 'feminine' and have 'that wonderful maternal instinct'; and she expresses all her relations with women as 'masculine' and feels 'a deference for them as women'. She loved and lost one woman, then in her late thirties met 'the woman of my dreams', who reciprocated her great love even though because of family commitments they could not live together. However, six years later, and a month before the letter was written, this woman became engaged following her family's sudden loss of income. AT sadly states her 'agony of suffering' and her 'unspeakable loss' of the woman she considered her wife and the 'mother of my children'.

On 25 October 1915 KO wrote to Carpenter that her recent

reading of The Intermediate Sex had made it dawn on her 'that I myself belong to that class', it 'made everything fall into place'. KO outlines her 'horrible loneliness' and need to meet other like-minded women: she is a feminist and in touch with many other feminist women, and 'the average woman does not easily attract me'. KO writes that a letter to a radical newspaper[20] about her spinsterhood and rejection of marriage brought sixteen replies and with one of these women she has become friends; indeed, although this woman is 'absolutely normal' she gave KO The Intermediate Sex. KO is also in correspondence with two women who are physically lovers and longs to meet 'my other half' (from Plato's Symposium). KO says she felt no physical desire at all until she was twenty-eight (two years before), but she also felt 'a strong desire to kiss and fondle' one woman she was in love with, apparently seeing 'kissing and fondling' and 'desire' as different.

On 19 August 1921 EC wrote to Carpenter, having consulted her friend Charles Lazenby (he calls her 'the boy') who in turn consulted Havelock Ellis who suggested a letter to Carpenter. In a business-like way she outlines her idea 'in my mind for some time of getting together a group of Uranian women to form the nucleus of a club' and asks him for the names and addresses of any women he thinks 'would be glad of companionship'. EC notes that having lived in London she must perpetually come across like-minded women and that she needs their companionship: she knows only too well the loneliness of her present situation. She is a 'pagan' and believes in the complete beauty and cleanness of sex; and she portrays herself as 'not of the masculine type', being 'fairly evenly mixed male and female'. The Intermediate Sex, however, was a revelation to her: 'it was like being given sight'. She thanks Carpenter for what he has done to change society; and she now wants 'to do something however small to help with that work', for the more public attention to the question, the more suppression there will be.

The last of these four letters was written on 16 March 1925 by BR, who, although 'physically a girl', chooses to call herself by a man's name. BR now teaches 'slum boys' in Derby, but at college two years before (she is now twenty-one) she met a girl she was attracted to but thought wouldn't be interested in her. The girl later showed BR a letter of rejection from the girl who had been her lover for three years. Now BR and her friend have become lovers and will live together soon; and BR says that 'in almost every respect (she) is quite

different from me – small, dainty & feminine'. BR and her lover met
and remained in contact with six boys who are lovers 'like that' who
they talked to about their own situation.

None of these women mention the ideas or the work of Havelock
Ellis or any other 'sexologist', only that of Carpenter. Carpenter
himself discounts the 'inversion' theory of Ulrichs and Hirschfield;
his writing does however outline and discuss it. Ellis appears
tangentially in EC's letter, but not as a source of ideas about
'Uranianism'. For each of these women it is reading Carpenter's
work that acts 'like being given sight', 'a revelation', 'making
everything fall into place; and for KO in particular, although for the
others in a different way, this enables her to give a name to and thus
gain a new understanding of her long-standing feelings.

Three of these women, KO, EC and BR, are relatively open, albeit
in different ways, about their 'inversion': BR by having a lover at
twenty-one and being in contact with a group of gay men, EC by
wanting to start a club for 'Uranian' women and to do her bit to
change public ideas about 'inversion', KO through feminism and the
ability to be fairly open about her feelings and analyses with women
who share her political stance. Only the older AT, in her forties at the
time of writing and of a more 'genteel' class background, appears to
locate her feelings within the framework of romantic friendship
rather than of sexual as well as 'spiritual' responses to women.
Nevertheless AT wrote to Carpenter, author of a book about homosexuality and widely known to be homosexual himself, and presumably would not have done so had she not construed her own
responses to women in similar terms – indeed, the way her letter is
written makes this incontestable. Interestingly, KO is the only one of
these women who appears not to have had some kind of conceptual
appreciation of her feelings before reading Carpenter's work – she
literally could not 'name' herself and her feelings; and only as she
came to do so through debate with other feminists does she learn to
experience desire itself.

At least two of these women, AT and BR, position themselves as
not like 'normal' – i.e. 'feminine' – women and correspondingly
identify themselves as 'masculine', while EC sees herself as 'evenly
mixed male and female'. Carpenter's conceptualisation of
'homogenic love', 'comrade love', 'inversion', 'uranianism' by people of the 'intermediate sex' (all terms used by him, sometimes
critically) follows even where (as with 'inversion') it discounts the

earlier pioneering work of Karl Heinrick Ulricks in the 1860s.
Magnus Hirschfield and the Scientific Humanitarian Committee from
1897 on promoted Ulrick's theory of a 'third sex', of a literal
inversion of one sex's mind with the other sex's body: the Committee's Yearbook, published from 1899 to 1923, was 'for Intermediate
Sexual Types'.

It was the work of gay men as scientists of homosexuality,
supported by many other gay men and women, that promoted the
idea of 'inversion' and its accompanying 'mannish' lesbian and
'effeminate' gay male stereotypes. Inversion offered a framework of
understanding for many people whose experience of themselves
accorded with it; but even for those who did not it offered a
powerful rhetoric to compel tolerance if not acceptance. Sexologists
such as Krafft-Ebing (in fact a supporter of the German early
homosexual rights movement) and Havelock Ellis (who counted a
number of openly gay men among his closest friends) followed gay
custom and practice, not the other way about. Thus AT, BR and EC
position themselves both in relation to experiential feelings and
responses and in relation to existing gay-derived conceptualisations
of the 'homosexual condition'. Only KO, working within a feminist
framework that in practice if not so clearly in theory challenged
conventional ideas of 'feminine' and 'masculine', outlines her feelings without reference to 'inversion' and 'intermediacy'. It is
therefore ironic that she does so through a debate which Sheila
Jeffreys (1985) sees as indicative of heterosexual oppressiveness
within feminism of the time.[21]

Each of these four women experienced themselves as 'different' in
their attraction to women. Each of them experienced their difference
'pre-textually', in the sense that Carpenter's work seems to have been
the first writing on the subject they had come across, and thus its
powerful impact for them. For the women who experienced their
feelings for women as 'masculine', this derives from seeing themselves as different in a context in which the only difference possible
from 'feminine' was 'masculine'. However, it is worth nothing that
the source of their 'masculine' feelings was their everyday life and
struggles to understand their place within it, not the imposition of
theoretical ideas by patriarchal male sexologists.

Not surprisingly, these letters do not address in a direct way the
terms of the 'romantic friendship v. friendship' debate as it has been
constructed by present-day feminist writers. However, they do

suggest very clearly for these four women that the experience and expression of their feelings and desires differs between them; that the idea of 'inversion' made sense because it named and described pre-existing feelings about themselves and other women; and that apart from Carpenter's work, no other writing about 'inversion' or 'Uranianism' is mentioned by them. Condemning sexology out of hand, as Faderman and Jackson appear to do, ignores the origins in gay writings of most of the key ideas and terms used within it; such condemnation also sees sexology as deterministic of how lesbian women understood their lives and experiences, and is at best simplistic and at worst dismisses what such women themselves said about their situations.

Pursuing friendship: recovering women's history

Once friendship is admitted to be an important aspect of biographical investigation, unresolved issues remain concerning how this investigation should be carried out as well as the significance that should be accorded to its textual product. In particular, there are methodologically important considerations here, not least because the nature of surviving sources is usually such that only some aspects of some friendships at particular points in time but not others can be recovered. One danger is that what is now visible will be accorded a significance it did not have for the participants. But to keep a perspective on this, this is a major consideration in whatever kind of biographical research is carried out and is certainly not unique to an emphasis on patterns of friendship.

Moreover, even when one person or one set of friendships is focussed on, unless these are of people who were writers or who otherwise committed much of their lives to paper, there are still problems in establishing the nature and extent of personal relationships in the absence of such testimony. And the difficulties do not disappear even where there is a large volume of written material, the diaries of Hannah Cullwick and Arthur Munby, and the diaries and letters of Harold Nicholson and Vita Sackville-West, being cases in point, for these were used to create as well as to record the social worlds these people lived within; and this is of course one of the functions of all textual representations, no matter how factual they may seem.

There is certainly a need to conceptualise women's patterns of friendship in biography, as well as to record these. However, as I have shown, there are epistemological and other problems with the main current feminist conceptualisation of friendship. This not only sees friendship between women before the advent of sexology as a kind of paradise before a fall brought about by evil men, and accords far more power and influence to these men than they actually had, it also imposes on the past what are present-day definitions and understandings of friendship, love, sexuality. There are also factual problems with this approach in relation to various of the examples it uses: there was an understanding that the 'Ladies of Llangollen' were sapphists among at least some of their friends and acquaintances, and some of their women friends were involved in genital sexual relations with each other; Edith Lees most certainly did see herself as an 'invert', and later in her life publicly lectured about her situation; and 'mannishness' did already exist in particular women's behaviours and identifications in the absence of a demonstrable influence on them of sexologists' writings about lesbianism.

Much of the feminist debate about romantic friendships of the past is concerned with recovering lesbian history from its present near-invisibility (e.g. Lesbian History Group, 1989). This is an aim I wholeheartedly support; but it is also one which can lead to temporal chauvinism of a kind which blandly assumes that relationships and behaviours have a meaning which has remained constant over the last 200 years. This is certainly insufficient; however, understanding these relationships in the terms they were understood by their protagonists is an impossibility: we now can never understand the past as it was understood by those who lived it. What is needed is a middle way, one which does not impose a theoretical structure on the lives and experiences of historical people whose lives we become interested in, but which also recognises that love between women could take many shapes and meanings, one of which was an erotic genital sexual involvement.

Teasing out these complexities can best be done through bio-graphical means, looking closely at particular lives and how these are intertwined with others in patterns of friendship. It is biography which enjoins historical change and social structure within the dynamics of particular lives, and indeed in a sense it is only biography which can make available to us the detailed processes of historical change. But even so, pinning down with any certainty even the changing outward behaviour dynamics of a relationship, as I have shown with Emily Wilding Davison and her friend Mary Leigh, is not only not easy but can often prove impossible. Moving beyond this into the more complex realms of the feelings friends had for each other and the behavioural expression (or not) of these brings with it even greater interpretive challenges.

The case studies discussed in this chapter – Emily Davison's friendship with Mary Leigh, Edith Lees' 'inversion', and the letters about their sexuality and relationships with women written to Carpenter by AT, KO, EC and BR – show that a focus on friendship can be of great analytic interest. Through the lens of friendship all the varied relationships women of the past had with each other can be looked at and their meanings – for the protagonists and also for present-day readers – pondered. Writers of biography have always had available to them such patterns of friendship in their lives of their subjects; however, the conventional form that biography has been written in has denied this information to readers, and its absence needs to be redressed in feminist auto/biography. Feminist ideas have rejected the contemporary existence of 'stars', instead stressing the collective production of ideas, art, music, literature, and in doing so pre-dated postmodernist theories about the 'death of the author'. It is a paradox that most feminist biography retains the 'spotlight' approach to its subjects; and in this chapter I have tried to show some of the benefits of an alternative, for both readers and writers of biography.

Notes

1 The first thing I wrote because of this is the title essay in 'Feminism and Friendship' (Stanley, 1985a), which traces out Olive Schreiner's patterns of feminist friendship. It starts with six women she knew – Eleanor Marx, Emma Cons, Edith Lees, Constance Lytton, Dora Montefiore and Virginia Woolf – and traces out their own feminist connections, going back in time to the early-nineteenth century and forward to the end of the 1930s. In doing this I reinscribe 'friendship', not as conventionally seen in terms of love and positive commitment (like the friendships I deal with in this chapter), but rather as a relationship which encompasses a wide range of different kinds of emotions, involvements, activities and so forth.

2 Hester Thrale Piozzi's manuscript diarists are in the John Rylands University of Manchester Library.

3 And see here the title essay in Stanley, 1985a.

4 While Ann was a full participant in the research for this biography, she preferred not to be involved in its writing.

5 Emily Wilding Davison's papers are now in the Fawcett Library; and indeed they are mis-named as such, being largely one part of the planned Women's Record House archives, the other part of which forms the collection of women's suffrage/feminist papers now lodged in the Museum of London. The Women's Record House was planned by Rose Lamartine Yates, one of Emily Davison's closest friends, to be the most important archive source about feminism of her time. It was however bombed during the early days of the Second World War and was thereafter lodged in a number of different locations before one part ended in the Museum of London. Another part ended in the Fawcett Library after the war; while its final part remained in Lamartine Yates family hands until recently donated to the Fawcett Library.

6 Evelyn Sharp's papers are now to be found in the Bodleain library in Oxford.

7 For example, one such document is a note dated 28 May 1913 from Katherine Gillett-Gatty asking Emily Wilding Davison to tea (Emily Wilding Davison Papers item number A.3/3). Gillett-Gatty at this time was secretary of the National Amalgamated Union of Shop Assistants, Warehousemen and Clerks, a member of the Ealing WSPU, and in despair at the sexism of her union's Executive Committee. Is this invitation to be seen as a private act of friendship or a public political act? the answer surely is that it is both, because for these women the public and the private were closely linked and both totally infused with political commitment.

8 This was between the Pankhurst-led oligarchy which gained control of the WSPU and the more democractic and socialist women who thereafter formed the Women's Freedom League in opposition to the WSPU leadership.

9 The main evidence here is Emily Davison's draft letters and articles, contained in a number of notebooks in the Emily Wilding Davison Papers in the Fawcett Library (eg. A.4/2, A.4/4/1), as well as a number of newspaper accounts of her speeches in court. Her habitual response was to make a long speech in court following arrest for militant action; invariably she did só in the context of state action taken against Mary Leigh where the WSPU leadership failed to act. It was thus a means of bringing both to public attention.

10 Item A3/1/2 in the Emily Wilding Davison Papers.

11 KO's letter to Carpenter is printed, using the pseudonym 'Frances Wilder', as part of Claus (1977). Ruth Claus erroneously claims that KO's letter is unique in the Carpenter archive; as I discuss later in the chapter, there are (at least) three others from women who wrote to him because of Carpenter's books on 'homogenic love'; and many others from Edith Lees and from Kate Salt, the sexuality of both being in dispute among present-day writers. Kate Salt's sexual feelings, for example, have been subject to widely differing assessments by present-day researchers such as Sheila Rowbotham (1977), Jan Marsh (1986) and Ruth Brandon (1990).

12 Located in the Archives Department of Sheffield Public Library.

13 Kate Salt was born Kate Joynes. Her brother Jim and Henry Salt were both masters at Eton, during which time they and Kate became converts to socialism. Later all three became involved in the Fellowship of the New Life, a socialist group, through which they met Carpenter. The marriage of Kate Joynes and Henry Salt has been described as a celibate one (Marsh, 1986; Brandon, 1990) and Kate herself as a lesbian (including by George Bernard Shaw, an acquaintance). However, in spite of this – and like Sheila Rowbotham (1977) – I have found reading and interpreting Kate Salt's letters to Edward Carpenter a good deal more complex than this suggests, for they show her to have been hopelessly in love with Carpenter himself.

14 In spite of Faderman's assumption, there is no definite evidence that this case history is indeed that of Edith Lees; the grounds for the claim are circumstantial only.

15 These are in the Carpenter Archive and are, in the order in which I discuss them, Carpenter Archive letters numbers 358.15 and 358.16.

16 Carpenter's pamphlet Homogenic love... was published in the socialist press in 1894. A

collection of essays, *Love's Coming of Age*, one of which was entitled 'The intermediate sex',
was to have been published as Carpenter's response to the Oscar Wilde trial of 1895;
pressures from the publisher forced the removal of this particular essay from the 1896
edition. The excised essay was, however, published in the 1906 second edition, and
then, with a group of related essays on gay themes, it appeared in 1908 as *The Intermediate
Sex*. By 1909 Carpenter was under open attack as a gay propogandist as witnessed by
O'Brien's pamphlet of that year 'Socialism and Infamy. The Homogenic or Comrade
Love Exposed'. After 1883 Carpenter's relative openness about his sexuality and his
increasing fame made him and his work a rallying point for other gay women and men,
particularly so after 1908.

17 Ellis refers to this woman as 'Lily' and suggests it occurred early in their marriage.
However, the question arises as to Ellis' reliability, particularly as he fails to mention
except in pseudonyms any of Lees' friends, so that corroborating or otherwise his claims
is almost impossible, not least because most of Edith Lees' papers and all her diaries
appear to have been destroyed after her death.

18 Carpenter Archive letters numbers 386.218, 386.262, 386.355 and 386.409 respec-
tively in the order in which I discuss them.

19 I have used initials only for these four correspondents, as they wrote to Carpenter
personal letters clearly not intended for other eyes.

20 This appeared in *The Freewoman* and was part of a controversy concerning 'the spinster'
and her sexual and other status that appeared in its pages.

21 It was within this debate that KO contributed the letter which put her in touch with
the two feminist women who were lovers that her later letter to Carpenter mentions.

Part III: On feminist auto/biography

9

Is there a feminist auto/biography?[1]

Feminism, difference, essentialism

There are a number of general themes which the previous chapters of this book have addressed mainly indirectly, even though they are fundamental to my reasons for writing it. This last chapter directly confronts these general themes and ties them into ideas and debates concerned with feminist auto/biography.

The chapter begins with the postmodernist[2] precept potentially (think about it) most consequential for feminist work on auto/ biography, indeed for the proposal that a distinct feminist way of writing auto/biography does or could exist. This concerns 'difference', women's actual or claimed difference from men, the related question of whether these claims necessarily entail essentialism, and the accompanying insistence that feminism should become 'indifferent' to gender. In common with most other feminist responses to such arguments (and see Morris, 1988 for a response similar to my own), I am aware of the determined albeit denied masculinism of such apparently ungendered proposals. In this chapter I argue that there has always been a (de)constructionist basis for the feminist concern with gender; and I outline some ways in which a feminist writers' and readers' interest in auto/biographical writing opens up many kinds of difference previously denied, dismissed or denigrated.

The chapter concludes by asking – and answering – the question of whether there is a feminist auto/biography. It argues that a distinctly feminist approach to writing and reading biography and autobiography is or could be productive of a feminist genre different in form as well as in content from the mainstream of auto/ biography. This answer to the question is implicit in discussion and argument elsewhere in the book, but here its grounds are explicated in a more focussed way.

On difference and 'the self'

In recent years feminism, particularly academic feminism, has become highly sensitive to arguments about 'difference'. These arguments have become central to present-day western feminism, and they derive from opposite directions and encapsulate different, indeed contradictory, notions of difference.

What is still the major version of 'difference' within feminism points up difference within the category -- and experience – of 'women'; and it derives from the increasingly influential voices of black feminists speaking to the white centrism and chauvinism of supposedly 'universal' feminist theorising. Black feminists have thus impressed upon white what lesbian feminists have been unable to impress upon heterosexual, disabled unable to impress upon able-bodied, working class unable to impress upon middle class, older unable to impress upon younger: that there are feminismS speaking to the multiple experiences and understandings of women's varied although overlapping conditions and oppressions. Its accompanying argument has been that the *de facto* power structure of (both academic and movement) feminism, in which an elite group speaks and theorises for the rest of us, must be assailed and dismantled. This version of difference, then, speaks to and encodes the multiple differences of condition and experience glossed and/or denied by categorical statements concerning 'women'.

The other version of 'difference' within feminism, still minor but rapidly growing in influence academically, concerns women's putative difference from men. Because feminism argues, indeed is founded upon, the view that women *are* different from men,[3] some postmodernist critics see it as by definition encapsulating an outmoded essentialism and a naïve humanism that foregrounds a realist notion of the self. This criticism goes on to insist that feminism should become 'indifferent' to gender, seeing anything else as outmoded at best, at worst intellectually contemptible (cf. Derrida, 1980, 1982, 1987). By doing so in effect it insists upon the end of feminism, or rather its reduction to textual strategies that can be utilised by anyone. In the wake of such criticisms some feminist postmodernists deny the material socially constructed realities of gender. Here feminism is reduced to the niceties of textual voice, leading Biddy Martin (1988), for example, to conjecture that *Roland Barthes by Roland Barthes* (1975b) may be a more 'lesbian' text than the coming out stories written by lesbian women discussed in Chapter 4 because it utilises 'subversive' textual strategies, sees identity as fluid, and rejects the 'normalising' impulse of most autobiographies. In contrast, I read this book as part of a project of constructing Barthes-as-theoretical-guru, a very alive, dominant and imperialist author, which at the least says something about the contingencies of reading practices.

These two difference arguments push feminism in contrary directions. One – recognition of difference between women – moves feminism in the direction of a fragmentation of voice, a decentering of theoretical authority, a positive polyphony of voices and conditions speaking to the local specificity of women's oppressions and conditions. The other – the rejection of any material grounds for women's difference from men – ironically moves feminism in the direction of theoretical certainty and centrality, a single voice arguing for the virtues of ungendered feminism consisting of textual strategies that men can engage in as fully as women. But of course – an inconvenient point – there can be nor is there any indifference to gender at this point in time: one either insists upon the political importance of women's gender, so making visible men's, or one lets men's highly gendered views, arguments and theories pass as ungendered, generic.

A feminist interest in auto/biography provides an analytic as well as substantive purchase on both of these difference arguments and by doing so perhaps enables us to surmount their apparent mutual exclusiveness. A concern with the details of particular lives – even if these are read or written in highly representational terms – points up difference in the first sense. It stops in their dubious tracks 'women this' and 'women that' categorical statements by showing the importance of time, place, gender, community, education, religious and political conviction, sexual preference, race and ethnicity, class, and of the indomitable uniqueness of people who share social structural similarities. An interest in the textual representation of particular lives emphasises the highly problematic nature of realist views of auto/biography, emphasising the necessarily selective nature of memory, of evidence, of what is included and excluded, and also the equally necessary role of the conventions of narrative form and the concomitant infusion of auto/biographical products with fictive devices of various kinds. A concern with auto/biography shows that 'self' is a fabrication, not necessarily a lie but certainly a highly complex truth: a fictive truth reliant on cultural convention concerning what 'a life' consists of and how its story can be told both in speech and, somewhat differently, in writing. But this does not mean that such writings have no points of connection with the material realities of everyday life: it rather emphasises how complex this relationship is and that neither realism nor a total rejection of it will do.

There is another 'difference' here, the factor that enables the mutual exclusiveness of these two difference arguments to be surmounted. This is the difference of feminism itself: the difference of feminists from other women, of feminists from female as well as male non-feminists, the difference of feminist thinking and analysis. Feminism is predicated upon a constructionist and indeed deconstructionist view of gender that a priori rejects essentialism, and was doing so long before postmodernism was even a twinkle in any male theoretician's eye. For as long as there has been feminism it has been devoted to the dismantling of essentialist views of sex and the insistence on the social construction of gender. And as each and every feminist, regardless of age, sex, colour, ethnicity, sexuality, class or anything else, knows from the inside, the acceptance of feminist ideas brings with it the dismantling of 'self' and its artful reconstruction on other lines. Whatever else, feminism grows up on anti-realist, anti-essentialist foundations – which is not to say that some feminists may not have realist, foundationalist ways of working, but rather that these, paradoxically and almost wilfully, come out of de/constructionist experiences and analyses. Regardless of what feminist grand theories may suggest, feminist experience is of different and disagreeing interpretations of the world, founded upon the often profoundly different material and experiential positions of differently socially located groups of women. Feminism is actually feminismS, internally highly differentiated in experiential and analytical terms, and encompassing both unities and multiple divisions.

Feminism, then, has a hand on the reins of both difference arguments. The means of harnessing both lie in recognising and analytically engaging with the specificity of lives and the problematics of how these are represented – that is, with the auto/biographical, for it encompasses both kinds of difference. Lives as they are lived surmount the differences between the two. They may be expressed (but by whom, we should ask) as almost bina oppositions, but in practice there is – in life – much comr

ON FEMINIST AUTO/BIOGRAPHY

ground. The auto/biographical, transformed by feminist ideas and analyses, can encompass such complexities, dealing with both process and product, fiction and fact, selves and others, ideological representation and its deconstruction. This is not to treat the auto/biographical as an unproblematic panacea, a kind of paracetemol for analytic ills, but rather as producing a focus and a set of tools which can be differentially used by writers and readers, each intent upon their own aims and purposes. These complexities, I have argued, are expressed in the narration of *a life* and the ways in which its realist facticities are embedded therein: awareness of the ontological complexities of self is not reserved for analysts, but is equally to be found within apparently referential autobiographies once readers take the 'bio' in auto/biography, the narration of a life, seriously at a theoretical and analytical level. But there is also a good deal more to 'self' than feminist theoretical writings seemingly recognise, and I can best explain this contention auto/biographically.

During the summer of 1990 my mother had a devastating 'cardio-vascular arrest' or stroke which she was not expected to survive but did, in the sense that she did not actually die. She thereafter became right-side paralysed and blind in one eye, with no ability to speak because of the enormous amount of brain-damage she sustained. This brain-damage, among other consequences, destroyed her ability to understand language conceptually: only the specifically visual enables her to understand what other people try to tell her. As well as many other things, she has thereby become a great ontological puzzle to me.

In 1984 following my father's death after six years of less severe strokes than my mother had, my mother and I started a process of tape-recording in a project called 'Our Mother's Voices'. As well as the healing and recovering that these discussions occasioned for us personally, I shared this process with three other working class by birth feminist sociologists, all of us unhappy with the representations of women's class produced by feminist researchers and theorists, all of us wanting our mothers to speak about their lives, to become centred selves.

With my mother, I explored at her direction our family history (on both sides, hers and my father's), working class life in Portsmouth, its patterns of migration into and sometimes back out of the [cit]y, ethnic complexities, and Portsmouth as a *habitus* in the inter-war [peri]od. During the course of some fifty hours of taped talk, she said in September 1984 in a conversation about her parents and siblings and their deaths that 'I don't exist anymore'. In March 1985, telling me about Portsmouth in the 1930s, she said that 'it's all gone, the world I lived in, Portsmouth doesn't exist anymore, it's all roads and flats now, not a real place anymore'. In October 1986 when we were talking about family holidays shared with two of her sisters, their husbands and children, and the subsequent deaths of all those of her generation, she said to me that 'they're all gone, so have I really'. And on the same topic, in December 1989 she said 'there's no point in my being alive, well, I'm not really, I'm just waiting'.

I read these remarks of my mother's, made when she was fully 'a self' as we culturally understand this, as indicating that she held a view of her self as one shared in common with an age cohort centering on her family and friends, a decidedly non-unitary anti-individualist self, a collective self and one which had 'gone' and was just 'waiting' after that collectivity had through death departed from her life.

From being a self who was no self, my mother has moved via her mid-1990 stroke and demolition of the apparatus of self – language, interaction – to something very different. Since my mother's stroke my diary, typically a 'work and weather' diary, has changed considerably and includes much reflection on my mother's situation. This 'situation' has included my spending the best part of four months on a daily basis with her in the hospital she was based in, thereafter on a fortnightly, three days at a time, basis. On 3 October 1990 I wrote:

Nothing I've said above (about Mum's presence on a particular hospital ward) has depicted, nor anything I could possibly convey in words could depict, how changed she is and in what ways I perceive this happening. CVA brain damage for Mum like for Dad doesn't make them 'mad' or 'not people' as I am a person. They rather react more on internal assessments, thoughts & so on, not the ways we learn as interactionally inappropriate. Yes that's it I suppose, it's really something about being an entirely solitary self, a Warty Bliggins[4] who knows that all the world centres on him and his toadstool. For Mum 'intersubjectivity' in Schutzian terms doesn't really take place: I enter her domain on her terms and her terms alone.

Then on 20 October 1990 I commented that:

In Stanton's terms the referentiality of the I is despised, passé. I wonder how she would fare on a daily basis with Mum, nine weeks on this ward? Mum now has an 'I' of steely strength, an absolute, and an imposition on a' who engage with her.... (some examples follow, including of her infantalising consultants on ward rounds by chuckling them under their chins, playing with their lips and hair and kissing them)... This self insists each minute on its identity, its reality, its needs & demands, pleasures & pains, & those of others do not exist at all. It also recognises 'the past' but excises it, like her refusal to hear of Dad, of Whisky (her cat), of Julie's (her granddaughter's) children, & her wanting me to take all the photographs away. This absolute I is aware (is it? how to tell the difference between aware and not?) of its gaps & fractures & displacements.... 'bio' exerts its primacy over & against these fractures & splits that Mum seems at some level to know exist but refuses to allow into this domain of her self as she now creates and controls it.

I draw some simple but important conclusions from my mother's tragedy. Understanding and theorising 'the self' is no easy matter. If theoretical accounts do not fit actual biographical selves and the material realities of their lives, then there is something wrong with the theory, not the lives. Auto/biographies, both written and spoken, are intertextual, but within this there is the primacy of everyday life and its concrete material events, persons, conversations. 'Bio', the narration of the material events of everyday life, is the crucial element in theorising and understanding both 'auto' and 'graph', albeit, regarding written (but not spoken) auto/biography, that the only way readers have of relating to this is through 'graph', is through the writing. At some point, surely, we have to accept that material reality does exist, that it impinges upon us all the time, that texts are not the only thing.[5] After all, the Gulf War that was under way when I first drafted this chapter, and the failed Stalinist coup in the USSR which occurred as I finished this book are not just textual representations constructed by the media: they involve real people being frightened, disturbed and killed as well as, indomitably, endeavouring to carry on their everyday lives. Equally my mother lives and suffers and has been transformed from someone with a socially constructed self, fully aware of its ontological symbiosis with other selves, to her present residual totally unitary and individualised self.

Women, feminism, auto/biography

Feminist publishing houses and imprints have increasingly featured biography and autobiography in their lists. However, the relationship between feminism and these auto/biographies of a mixed bag of women is a complex and interesting one; and it raises questions concerning whether a distinct *women's* autobiography exists and/or whether a distinct *feminist* auto/biography exists.

In relation to women's autobiographies, Estelle Jelinek's and Mary Mason's argument that women write autobiography differently from men has, not unexpectedly, found favour among many feminists. But as I argued earlier, this position ignores, silences, or otherwise denies the existence of the many 'transtextual' autobiographies that exist: it has been seduced by a political rhetoric which is actually frequently belied by women's *and* men's autobiographical textual practice.

The question of a distinct genre of women's autobiography is related to but not synonymous with the question of whether a distinct *feminist* auto/biography exists. Certainly there are biographies and autobiographies written by feminists, such as Cathy Porter's biography of Alexandra Kollontai (1980), Jill Liddington's of Selina Cooper (1984) and Judith Okely's of Simone de Beauvoir (1986); and autobiographies by Liz Wilson (1982), Ann Oakley (1984) and Carolyn Steedman (1986). However, is the fact that a text is feminist *authored* or about a feminist *subject* sufficient to define it as feminist auto/biography? Is the *form* or *structure* of what is written as feminist auto/biography, not just the subject who forms the bones of its *content*, actually different from any other auto/biography? My response is that it is, or rather could be, different.

The autobiographies just mentioned self-consciously and self-confidently mix genres and conventions. Within them fact and fiction, fantasy and reality, biography and autobiography, self and others, individuals and networks, not only co-exist but intermingle in ways that encourage, not merely permit, active readership. The boundaries between conventional dichotomies are traversed here and shown to be far less impermeable than generally supposed. These feminist autobiographies challenge the boundaries of conventional autobiographical form, indeed play with some of its conventions such as the 'autobiographical pact' of confessional truth-telling, a narrative that moves uni-directionally from birth/beginning to maturity/resolution/end, and the insistence on a unitary self.

This feminist challenge to autobiographical form and thus to genre convention has a history which encompasses Kate Millet's *Flying* (1974) and *Sita* (1977) as well as (largely horrified) critical reactions to them (and see here Kolodny, 1980). Millet's experimental autobiographies depart from form by treating autobiography as part diary, part free form writing, part 'stream of consciousness' depiction in narrative form. It is clear that many reviewers and critics found its unconventionality deeply offensive, for by writing in this way Millet's textual life encompasses many aspects of actual life typically omitted, excised, from 'the life' that is autobiography. This includes not only the 'trivia' many critics commented upon but also the embarrassing inclusion of the agonising – and soon boring – development and conclusion of Millet's sexual and emotional dependence on Sita. Not only this, but Millet's form of writing abandons a temporal narrative sequencing, or rather this is multiply cross-cut with other writing forms.

However, more recent feminist autobiographers such as Steedman and Chernin have taken a different route away from the conventions of autobiography, not least because of their decentering of self. Millet centres self in order to foreground its fragmentation, while these feminist autobiographers position self as an interactional process as well as product.

The feminist biographies referred to are very different from these innovative and experimental developments in feminist autobiography. Reconstructing feminism from them, a reader would conclude that apart from the interest in female and/or feminist subjects, feminist biography is in many respects conventional and indistinguishable from the best products of the mainstream,[6] following the conventions of genre rather than challenging them.

Virginia Woolf, it has been variously and contradictorily noted, wrote no autobiography, wrote diaries and letters that exist in lieu of an autobiography, wrote autobiography in various of her works of fiction, wrote autobiography in the memoirs published in Moments of Being (1978a), and produced her true autobiography in A Room Of Her Own (1929) and Three Guineas (1938). Howsoever 'autobiography' is defined, it is clear that claims can be made for the existence of an autobiographical corpus in Woolf's writings existing largely outside of the conventional form that autobiography takes, and haunting much of her 'other' writing. Her claims as a biographer are more definite, more focussed, but perhaps more revolutionary. There is the anti-realist Orlando (1928), which I discuss later. There is Flush (1933), a fictional biography of Elizabeth Barrett Browning's spaniel that contains much illuminating factual material about the poet herself – a biography of her 'from below'. And then there is *Roger Fry: A Biography* (1940).

Reading Woolf's letters and diaries over the period of the preparation, writing and publication of *Roger Fry*, it is clear she experienced boundaries and confinements unlike with any others of her books. At points in exasperation she curses 'the letters' and 'the facts', feeling constrained to work within limits set by 'the evidence' and 'the proprieties', and thus unable to craft new limits which would take her closer to the truth about her subject as she experienced it.

Biography poses problems for the construction of a specifically feminist form in a way that autobiography does not. These problems relate closely to the boundaries set by 'the facts', the external collectable challengeable facts. I certainly found Fay Weldon's (1985) fictional depiction of a particular point in Rebecca West's life more convincing than the highly factual biographies that exist; and Virginia Woolf's (1985) fictional creation of the feminist historian Rosamund Merridew and the diaries of Mistress Joan Martyn more illuminating than factual histories of the period in question. However, typically there is felt to be a readerly unwillingness to stretch biographical convention thus far: once 'fiction' and 'fantasy' enter, then biography as 'the truth' about a self is assumed to depart along with positivist ideas about research and writing.

It appears, then, that biographical form is much less easy to subvert, to extend, to play with, than autobiographical form because it is founded upon and makes central use of positivist foundationalist and realist assumptions and rhetorical stances.[7] But as well as a mainstream and a set of conventions, biography also contains an avant-garde and iconoclasms.

Three interesting departures from biographic convention are: non- or even anti-spotlight approaches, such as St Clair's (1989) work on the Godwins and the Shelleys, and Dennis Brown's (1990) on the symbiosis of friendship and intertextuality in the relationships of James Joyce, Ezra Pound, Tom Eliot and Wyndham Lewis; meta-biographies that include the biographer and the process of researching biography such as Symons' work on Corvo (1934); and anti-realist biographies that subvert or flout foundationalist principles and practices. The absence of an example of this third departure from convention here is deliberate, for the one almost invariably mentioned (e.g. in Nadel, 1984) is Virginia Woolf's *Orlando*, and I go on to discuss innovative feminist biographies using *Orlando* as one of my own examples. There is of course a fourth departure, of fictitious biographies; that is, writings which are published as biographies and intended to be read as such, but which are later discovered to be fakes, fictions dressed to deceive rather than entertain. I disregard these because internally they contain all of the defining accoutrements of the conventional mainstream, whereas my interest is in departures in form or structure which are innovative of the genre.[8] Feminist examples of each of these departures exist; and my argument is that a distinct feminist auto/biographical form will trade on such innovations and take them further.

The baseline of a distinct feminist auto/biography is the rejection of a reductionist spotlight attention to a single unique subject. This is not to suggests that women's or feminists' lives are innately different from those of men in this regard: no 'difference' argument is proposed or intended here. It is however to propose that one of the defining principles of feminist biography – and whether its subject/s is/are women or men[9] – should be an attention to social location and contextualisation and in particular to subjects' position within, not apart from, their social networks.

Johanna Alberti's *Beyond Suffrage* (1989) discusses feminism between 1918 and 1939 by taking a collection of women subjects whose political principles, aspirations and practices she embeds within their feminist and related networks; while in a related discussion (1990) she teases out the complexities expressed in a long-term exchange of letters between Elizabeth Haldane and her niece Naomi Mitchison. Socialising the lives of biography's subjects should be a principled political choice. Whether it provides 'better' or 'truer' information is not the point, which is rather that socialising subjects' lives, action, work, importance, effectiveness or indeed failure is epistemologically important. The content of what counts as 'knowledge' in feminist and cultural political terms needs to be shifted; the act of socialising biography de-centres the subject; and, relatedly, it shows both subjects to share much with their peers and also that *everyone* is in some sense unique.

Founded upon this social rather than individualist approach, a distinct feminist biography textually recognises that its facts and arguments are *contingent*. That is, it recognises that biographical as any other writing is produced from a particular viewpoint, that of the busily inscribing author. Authors are 'dead' only in the sense that subjects are – we are none of us unique great minds, all of us are social beings whose ideas derive, acknowledged or not, from particular socio-political milieux. Postmodernist and all other authors are at work constructing authoritative voices, the facts, the correct conclusions, but typically doing so in a rhetoric which denies the conditions of its own production and also of its consequentiality for readers.

Biographies that turn their faces away from the implied and intended power relationship between writers and readers, which open up the production processes of biography to critical inquiry from readers, especially appeal to me. I have read far too many closed biographic texts to feel otherwise. This is most certainly not to deny that 'open' texts are also *constructions* that select as much as any other kind of text, albeit in rhetorically different ways. It is however to propose that these 'different ways' are important, for they facilitate or at the least do not hinder active readership for those readers who want it, thereby creating a (possible) dialogue by providing alternative evidences and points of view: speech is a creative medium, and once it exists in however truncated a form, readers will never return to muteness, can potentially autonomously overturn the Delphic qualities of authorship. One recent addition to a contingent and accountable feminist biography is Germaine Greer's *Daddy we hardly knew you* (1989). This traces out the starts and shifts and even more unexpected conclusions of the author's search for 'the truth' about her distant and unknown father, ending in the awareness that there was no truth but rather a series of mystifications within mystifications that had no – or a number of – sites of origin. What this points up (thus explaining why it has remained a minority form within biography's mainstream as within feminist biography's mainstream) is that knowledge is indeed contingent, depends upon, derives from, a particular and socially located viewpoint. This approach may not constitute 'the death of the author' in postmodernist terms, but it does put her in her proper place, as one particular, albeit privileged, voice among other voices.

This second departure of a socially-focussed but also a contingent and thus disputable authorial voice marks a fundamental shift within feminist biographical writing, for it proffers the grounds for rejecting foundationalist principles within biography as within other 'scientific' positivist writing: once there are defensible viewpoints, the notion of a single social reality known and retrieved by experts is assailable, assailed, defeated. The most revolutionary departure from biography's mainstream is thus writing which explicitly and in a number of ways (not just that of the contingency of authorial voice) departs from realist principles and practices. The most thorough-going example of this is Virginia Woolf's *Orlando* (1928).

At its most superficial level *Orlando* offers an assault upon gender, the social construction or interpretation of the *appearance* of femininity and masculinity. In Orlando's/Vita Sackville-West's changes, 'gender' is transformed across the ages: gender is convention and is subject to actually startling shifts, for the once masculine becomes feminine. At a deeper level Orlando/Vita changes *sex*, not merely gender, changes at a more profound level, for the arrogant Elizabethan codpieced blood is fundamentally different from Marmaduke's semi-tamed wife. The fixed and unassailable (sex, biology, essentialism) as well as the assailable (gender, society, constructionism) are assailed. But there is more to Orlando than this, for those most profound of certainties, the temporal, are challenged by him. Age gives way to age and con-vention to convention; there is a chronology but what is unexpected is that this does not matter. At points Orlando's concentration wanders, is distracted or sleeping, and what happens 'in reality' in particular historical periods is nothing much or things that are irrelevant to the reality in Orlando's mind; those things we know as socio-economic and political change but which are unimportant for the shifts and changes that are Orlando. So much for periodisation.

There is another equally seditious element to *Orlando*. Orlando, the actor-out of roles, is despised as well as truly and unshakably loved: clear eyes, admiring but also contemptuous, look on Orlando and see and judge, the eyes of the author. And Virginia Woolf in *Between The Acts* (1941) continues this scrutiny, now turned upon herself in the guise of Miss La Trobe, the organiser of the social play of life whose bed has been deserted by her actress lover. But this ruthless clear-sightedness also gives heart's desires, gives what cannot 'realistically' exist – the possession of Knole and the white feather of genius for Sackville-West, the birth of children for Woolf (Sackville-West, 1932). 'Reality' is again assaulted.

Anti-realism disrupts chronology and periodisation; disputes gen-der and fixes 'sex' as character, in character flaws and not essential-ism; combines love with contempt; multiply disrupts 'reality'; and turns aside the eyes of the seen, not the seer. Anti-realism in this biography confounds the certainties of the reader, pulls away all that can be pulled from under our collective readerly feet. We end with one certainty: that lives are not simple.

Three crucial elements within feminist auto/biography, then, are anti-spotlight, contingent and anti-realist stances. A distinctly feminist auto/biography will include a fourth element. From the ideas and analyses of feminist sociology, feminist auto/biography includes an *a priori* insistence that auto/biography should be treated as composed by textually-located ideological practices – including of course auto/biography produced by feminists – and analytically engaged with as such.

These four elements are the key features of a 'method' and a 'form' for producing feminist auto/biography and are influenced by feminist epistemology and social science. On their own these departures are of course not unique to a feminist approach; but, taken together, may be seen to define it. Can men then write feminist auto/biography? Feminism is not merely a 'perspective' or viewpoint on the world, not even an epistemology or a theory of knowledge about it; feminism constitutes an *ontology*, a different way of being in the world which is rooted in the facts of oppression.[10] In the same way that that I would argue that whites, no matter how well meaning nor how politically right-on, cannot share a black ontology and its resultant epistemology, so too I argue that men cannot share a feminist ontology nor its resultant epistemology.[11] Consequently men cannot write feminist auto/biography in the sense that I understand it, for the contingencies of men's lives are different from those of feminism and feminists, although what these contingencies are in precise terms remains to be explored, analysed and theorised in relation to the processes of writing lives.

However, it could be argued that auto/biography is by definition about an individual self, and that if feminist auto/biography departs from this then it is no longer 'auto/biography' but something different in kind: an entirely different genre. It is certainly usual to see auto/biography as about single selves; and the general run of auto/biographies do indeed as I have suggested enshrine the 'spotlight' approach. However, it is equally true that there are already feminist auto/biographies that depart to one degree or another from this convention. Moreover, conventions are merely orthodoxies, the statement of particular ideological positions, and should be rigorously scrutinised and deconstructed by feminism in relation to auto/biography as all other aspects of life.

Also some readers may feel that it isn't possible to be concerned with an auto/biographical self without trading on essentialist and/or reductionist ideas about a 'real self'. And it is certainly true that one of the main forms auto/biographies have taken is tracing out the unfettering of a 'real' inner self (as for example in feminist factional form in Marilyn French's *The Women's Room* (1977)); and more recently Freudian and Lacanian ideas about the subject have greatly influenced those who write about auto/biography. However, this is a by no means *necessary* emphasis, and equally illustrious alternative constructions of 'self' can be found – in earlier chapters, for example, I outlined Virginia Woolf's approach to 'moments of being' and Rosemary Manning's construction of self around a 'corridor of mirrors'. There is no necessity to define auto/biography in terms of essentialism unless one accepts the more extreme precepts of biographical convention – and as I have just argued, these orthodoxies need challenging and changing, not accepting and lamenting their dominance.

In addition, some readers may think that proposing a feminist auto/biography which is reflexively concerned with its own labour process is merely narcissistic. But surely it would be paradoxical if a concern with process, with opening up biographical processes for scrutiny by readers, should be so labelled. After all, the aim here is to enable more people than just one, the auto/biographer, to analytically engage with the auto/biographical investigative approach. For instance, Carolyn Steedman's *Landscape For A Good Woman* (1986) points up the severe limitations of most feminist biography for those of us who are not middle class (and I would add, not white or heterosexual), and emphasises how interwoven her autobiography is with her construction of her mother's biography; it also illuminatingly shows the reader that understanding these links involves a process within which her changing thinking was located. Similarly Audre Lorde's *Zami* (1983) suggests that we see whiteness as a limiting convention, a confinement within superficial realisms, with its attention to the mythological truths and transformations of black lesbian women's lives. Autobiographical writing such as this, which I find immensely open in its crossing and re-crossing of all generic boundaries, concerned as it is with rejecting a narrow version of 'self' and arguing for its social construction within a network of others, must surely become central to a feminist auto/biography, for it re-makes the genre in exciting and challenging feminist ways.

Biographies and autobiographies are as popular as they are because they tell an interesting story and usually tell it accessibly and enjoyably; because they apparently let readers into lives different from our own; and because they can provde feminist heroes to stand alongside the more usual subjects of auto/biography. These sources of interest need to be recognised and accepted as legitimate in feminist terms, not treated as a supposedly naïve response to auto/biography. Nonetheless, we need to develop the means for a more active readerly engagement with such writings, one which does not take them on trust as sources of fact and information, but rather recognises their role in the construction of particular views of the 'self' they present.

Equally important as the question of how feminists should read auto/biography is the question of whether and in what ways there are distinctly feminist ways of writing them, and the associated question of the interconnections between reading and writing. I have suggested that a distinct feminist autobiography is in the process of construction, characterised by its self-conscious and increasingly self-confident traversing of conventional boundaries between different genres of writing. I have also argued that a distinct feminist biography is less well developed because innovations in form are less easily accomplished here than in autobiography; and thus such innovations will centre a social focus, a contingent and engaged authorial voice, a thorough-going anti-realism, and a focus upon textual practice, innovations which will encourage active reading.

My answer to the question of whether there is a feminist auto/biography is therefore less 'yes, there is' than 'well, there might be'. Whether these possibilities come to fruition as actualities depends upon how willing – not how able – feminist auto/biographers and writers about auto/biography are to put into practice feminist principles and precepts, and how concerned readers are to demand that they do.

A finale

Colette taps her teeth and frowns. She points and smiles, the facial outlines of her younger self leaping fleetingly to the surface. She says something, her Burgundian accent defeating understanding – 'You mean...?'. But she turns her head away, bored. She stares out of the window. Suddenly she turns back, picks up her pen and writes. She is alone once more – 'and I am not making my portrait here, only my model'.

Notes

1 Part of this chapter was given as a plenary address on '"Difference" and autobiography' at a conference on 'Women's Lives, Women's Times' at the University of York in January 1991. I am grateful to Treva Broughton and Linda Anderson, its organisers, for the opportunity to speak at the conference. An earlier version of the section on 'Is there a feminist auto/biography' was published in the *Gender & History* 2:1 special issue on autobiography (1990).

2 In this chapter I make a number of statements about 'postmodernism'. In doing so I am not arguing that all postmodernist writers accept the views I assign to it, but rather suggesting that these views are dominant strains within postmodernist discourse, which of course also encompasses variant strains.

3 Alternative versions of feminism see the basis of this difference originating in 'nature' or biology or psychology, in 'culture' and social construction, and in politics and the material products of oppression. My own allegiance is to the latter.

4 Warty Bliggins appears in Don Marquis's wonderful collections of poems featuring Archie the verse-writing cockroach, Mehitabel the cat who is a reincarnation of Cleopatra, and other characters; Warty is a toad who is convinced that his toadstool is the centre of the entire universe.

5 One response to my conference paper discussing this, and in which I read the above extracts from my diary, was the conjecture that there are no grounds for supposing that these events were 'real', had actually happened (and see also *Network* (newsletter of feminists in literature) May 1991, no.26). A bad case of Baudrillard.

6 There are always exceptions, and a particularly interesting one here is Carolyn Steedman's (1990) biography of Margaret McMillan.

7 This is not to say that it *cannot* be subverted (and see here Alison Hennegan 1988), merely that this is more difficult.

8 'False' *autobiographies* are more usual than false biographies; and they depart from one of the crucial elements of the 'autobiographical pact' as seen by Lejeune, for they are not written in 'good faith' and there is no synonymity between the protagonist and the name on the title page. But of course establishing this is a difficult matter, particularly for readers rather than for researchers. There are also important issues here in danger of being missed in a formalist response, concerning how to distinguish between the false fictions of these pseudo-autobiographers and the true fictions of real ones such as Mary McCarthy.

9 I can think of no good reason why feminist biography should not include biographies of men, as my work on Peter Sutcliffe suggests.

10 I consider in more detail the role of men in relation to feminist research more widely in Stanley, 1990a.

11 I am not suggesting that these differences have any essentialist basis nor that they will always exist: when women's oppression and black oppression no longer exist, then men, women, white and black people, may share a common ontology and epistemology.

References and bibliography

Aaron, Daniel (ed.) (1978), *Studies in Biography*, Harvard University Press, Massachusetts

Abbs, Peter (1974), *Autobiography in Education*, Gryphon Press, London

Abbs, Peter (1983), 'Introduction', in Gosse, Edmund (1907/1983), *Father and Son*, Penguin, Harmondsworth, pp. 9-31

Abel, Elizabeth, Hirsch, Marianne & Langland, Elizabeth (eds) (1983), *The Voyage In: Fictions of Female Development*, University Press of New England, Hanover

Ackland, Valentine (1985), *For Sylvia: An Honest Account*, Chatto & Windus, London

Ackroyd, Peter (1990), *Charles Dickens*, Sinclair-Stevenson, London

Ackroyd, Peter (1985), *Hawksmoor*, Penguin, Harmondsworth

Ackroyd, Peter (1987), *Chatterton*, Abacus, London

Alberti, Johanna (1989), *Beyond Suffrage*, Macmillan, London

Alberti, Johanna (1990), 'Inside out: Elizabeth Haldane as a women's suffrage survivor in the 1920s and 1930s', *Women's Studies International Forum*, 13 pp.117-26

Alegria, Claribel (1983), *They Won't Take Me Alive* (translated by Amanda Hopkinson), The Women's Press, London

Alexander, Ziggi (1990), 'Let it lie upon the table: the status of black women's biography in Britain', *Gender & History*, 2 pp. 23-3

Alexander, Ziggi and Dewjee, Audrey (eds) (1984), *Wonderful Adventures of Mrs Seacole in Many Lands*, Falling Wall Press, Bristol

Alpers, Antony (1982), *The Life of Katherine Mansfield*, Oxford University Press

Altman Dennis et al. (1989), *Which Homosexuality? essays from the international scientific conference on lesbian and gay studies*, Gay Men's Press, London

Anderson, Linda (1986), 'At the threshold of the self: women and autobiography' in (ed.), Moira Monteith, *Women's Writing: A Challenge To Theory*, Harvester Press, Brighton, pp. 54-71

Andrews, William (1986), *Sisters of the Spirit: Three Black Women's Autobiographies of the Nineteenth Century*, Indiana University Press, Bloomington

Angelou, Maya (1969), *I Know Why The Caged Bird Sings*, Virago Press, London

Angelou, Maya (1974), *Gather Together in My Name*, Virago Press, London

Angelou, Maya (1976), *Singin' and Swingin' and Gettin' Merry Like Christmas*, Virago Press, London

Angelou, Maya (1981), *The Heart of a Woman*, Virago Press, London

Angelou, Maya (1986), *All God's Children Need Travelling Shoes*, Virago Press, London

Anony, Ms (1984), 'Mr Normal meets the beast, or how "The Yorkshire

Ripper" became Peter Sutcliffe', *Women's Studies International Forum*, 7 pp. 19-23

A People's Autobiography of Hackney (1977a), *Working Lives: Hackney Volume One: 1900-1945*, Centerprise, London

A People's Autobiography of Hackney (1977b), *Working Lives: Hackney Volume Two: 1945-77*, Centerprise, London

Archer, Robyn & Simmonds, Diana (1986), *A Star Is Torn*, Virago Press, London

Barnes, Julian (1984), *Flaubert's Parrot*, Picador, London

Barnes, Ron (1976), *Coronation Cups and Jam Jars*, Centreprise, London

Barthes, Roland (1975a), 'An introduction to the structural analysis of narrative', *New Literary History*, 6 pp. 237-72

Barthes, Roland (1975b), *Roland Barthes by Roland Barthes*, Macmillan, London

Barthes, Roland (1977), 'The death of the author', in *Image, Music, Text*, Flamingo, London, pp. 142-8

Barthes, Roland (1980), *Camera Lucida*, Flamingo, London

Bashkirtseff, Marie (1928), *Journal*, New York: Dutton

Baudrillard, Jacques (1979), *Seduction*, Verso, London

Baudrillard, Jacques (1988a), *America*, Verso, London

Baudrillard, Jacques (1988b), *Selected Writings*, Stanford University Press, Massachusetts

Bauman, Zigmaunt (1988), 'Is there a postmodern sociology?' *Theory, Culture & Society*, 5 pp. 217-37

Beaton, Cecil (1973), *The Strenuous Years: Diaries 1948-1955*, Wiedenfeld & Nicolson, London

Beaton, Cecil (1979), *Self Portrait with Friends: The Selected Diaries of Cecil Beaton 1926-1974*, Wiedenfeld & Nicolson, London

Becker, Howard (1974), 'Photography and sociology', *Studies in the Anthropology of Visual Communication*, 5 pp. 3-26

Becker, Howard (1979), 'Do photographs tell the truth?' in (eds), T. Cook and C. Reichardt, *Qualitative and Quantitative Methods in Evaluation Research*, Sage Publications, pp. 93-127

de Beauvoir, Simone (1959), *Memoirs of a Dutiful Daughter*, Penguin, Harmondsworth

de Beauvoir, Simone (1960), *The Prime of Life*, Penguin, Harmondsworth

de Beauvoir, Simone (1963), *Force of Circumstance*, Penguin, Harmondsworth

de Beauvoir, Simone (1964), *A Very Easy Death*, Penguin, Harmondsworth

de Beauvoir, Simone (1972), *All Said And Done*, Penguin, Harmondsworth

de Beauvoir, Simone (1981), *Adieux – Farewell To Sartre*, Penguin, Harmondsworth

Bell, Quentin (1972a), *Virginia Woolf: 1882-1912*, Paladin, St Albans

Bell, Quentin (1972b), *Virginia Woolf: 1912-1941*, Paladin, St Albans

Bendix, Reinhart (1977), *Max Weber: An Intellectual Portrait*, California University Press, Berkeley

Bennett, Paula (1990), *Emily Dickinson Woman Poet*, Harvester Press, Brighton

Benstock, Shari (ed.) (1988a), The Private Self: Theory and Practice of Women's Autobiographical Writings, Routledge, London

Benstock, Shari (1988b), 'Theories of autobiography' in (ed.) Shari Benstock (1988a), The Private Self: Theory and Practice of Women's Autobiographical Writings, Routledge, London, pp. 7-9

Benstock, Shari (1989), 'Paris lesbianism and the politics of reaction, 1900-1940' in (eds), Martin Duberman, George Chauncey Jnr and Martha Vicinus, Hidden From History: Reclaiming The Gay and Lesbian Past, Penguin, Harmondsworth, pp. 332-46

Berger, John (1972), Ways of Seeing, Penguin, Harmondsworth

Bertaux, Daniel (ed.) (1981), Biography and Society: The Life History Approach in the Social Sciences, Sage, Beverley Hills

Bhutto, Benazir (1988), Daughter of the East, Hamish Hamilton, London

Blackburn, Regina, 'In search of the black female self: African-American women's autobiographies and ethnicity' in (ed.), Estelle Jelinek, Women's Autobiography, Indiana University Press, Bloomington, pp. 133-48

Bland, Lucy (1984), 'The case of the Yorkshire Ripper: mad, bad, beast or male?' in Phil Scraton and Paul Gordon (eds), Causes For Concern, Penguin, Harmondsworth, pp. 184-209

Bland, Lucy (1990), 'Rational sex or spiritual love? The Men and Women's Club of the 1880s', Women's Studies International Forum, 13 pp. 33-48

Blodgett, Harriet (1988), Centuries of Female Days: Englishwomen's Private Diaries, Rutgers University Press

Blyton, Enid (nd), The Story of My Life, Pitkins, London

Bogdan, Robert (ed.) (1974), Being Different: The Autobiography of Jane Fry, John Wiley, London

Boswell, James (1934), Life of Johnson, Clarendon Press, Oxford

Boswell, John (1989), 'Revolutions, universals and sexual categories' in (eds), Martin Duberman, George Chauncey Jnr and Martha Vicinus, Hidden From History: Reclaiming The Gay and Lesbian Past, Penguin, Harmondsworth, pp. 17-36

Boulos, Baron (1984), 'The Yorkshire Ripper: a case study of the "Sutcliffe Papers"', Manchester Occasional Papers in Sociology, 11, Department of Sociology, University of Manchester

Bowen Stella (1941), Drawn From Life, Virago Press, London

Brandon, Ruth (1990), The New Women and The Old Men: Love, Sex and The Woman Question, Secker & Warburg, London

Bree, Germaine (1976), 'The fictions of autobiography', Nineteenth Century French Studies, 4 pp. 438-49

Bree, Germaine (1988), 'Foreword' in Bella Brodzki and Celeste Schenck (eds) (1988), Life/Lines: Theorising Women's Autobiography, Cornell University Press, Ithaca, pp. ix-xii

Breslin, James (1980), 'Gertrude Stein and the problems of autobiography' in (ed.), Estelle Jelinek, Women's Autobiography, Indiana University Press, Bloomington, pp. 149-62

Brittain Vera (1933), Testament of Youth, Gollancz, London
Brittain, Vera (1957), Testament of Experience, Gollancz, London
Brittain, Vera (1981), Chronicle of Youth: Vera Brittain's War Diary 1913-1917, Gollancz, London
Brittain, Vera (1986), Chronicle of Friendship: Vera Brittain's Diary of the 1930s 1932-1939, Gollancz, London
Brittain, Vera (1989), Diary 1939-1945 (ed. A. Bishop and Y. Bennett), Gollancz, London
Brock, Peggy (ed.) (1989), Women Rites and Sites: Aboriginal Women's Cultural Knowledge, Allen & Unwin, London
Brodzki, Bella and Schenck, Celeste (eds) (1988), Life/Lines: Theorising Women's Autobiography, Cornell University Press, Ithaca
Bromley, Roger (1988), Lost Narratives, Routledge, London
Bromwich, David (1984), 'The uses of biography', Yale Review, 73 pp. 161-76
Brophy, Brigid (1973), Prancing Novelist: A Defence of Fiction in the Form of a Critical Biography in Praise of Ronald Firbank, Macmillan, London
Brown, Dennis (1990), Intertextual Dynamics Within the Literary Group, Macmillan, London
Browning, Elizabeth Barrett (1856/1978), Aurora Leigh and other poems (ed. Cora Caplan), The Women's Press, London
Brunsdon, Charlotte (ed.) (1986), Films For Women, British Film Institute, London
Bruss, Elizabeth (1976), Autobiographical Acts, John Hopkins University Press, Baltimore
'Bryher' (1962), The Heart of Artemis: A Writer's Memoirs, Collins, London
Burgin, Victor (ed.) (1982), Thinking Photography, Macmillan, London
Burke, Kenneth (1955), A Grammar of Motives, Prentice-Hall, New York
Burn, Gordon (1984), '...somebody's husband, somebody's son.': The story of Peter Sutcliffe, Heinemann, London
Burney, Fanny (1778/1968), Evelina, Oxford University Press, London
Burney, Fanny (1976-1986), The Journals and Letters of Fanny Burney (Madame d'Arblay), 1791-1840 (edited by Joyce Hemlow and others), 12 vols, Clarendon Press, Oxford
Byatt, Antonia (1990), Possession, A Romance, Chatto & Windus, London
Caine, Barbara (1986), Destined To Be Wives: The Sisters of Beatrice Webb, Clarendon Press, Oxford
Caplan, Jay (1985), Framed Narratives: Diderot's Genealogy of the Beholder, Manchester University Press, Manchester.
Carpenter, Edward (1883), Towards Democracy, Allen & Unwin, London
Carpenter, Edward (1894), Homogenic love and its place in a free society, Manchester Labour Press Society Ltd, Manchester
Carpenter, Edward (1896 1st edition, 1906 2nd edition), Love's Coming of Age, Allen & Unwin, London
Carpenter, Edward (1908), The Intermediate Sex, Allen & Unwin, London

Carpenter, Edward (1916), *My Days and Dreams*, Allen & Unwin, London
Castle, Barbara (1980), *The Castle Diaries 1974-1976*, Wiedenfeld & Nicholson, London
Chamberlain, Mary (ed.) (1988), *Writing Lives: Conversations between women writers*, Virago Press, London
Chevigny, Bell Gale (1983), 'Daughters writing: towards a theory of women's biography', *Feminist Studies*, 9 pp. 79-102
Chernin, Kim (1985), *In My Mother's House: A Daughter's Story*, Virago Press, London
Chitty, Susan (1974), *The Monk and the Beast: A Life of Charles Kingsley*, Hodder & Stoughton, London
Christie, Agatha (1977), *An Autobiography*, Fontana, London
Clarke, Norma (1990), *Ambitious Heights: Writing, Friendship, Love, The Jewsbury Sisters, Felicia Homans and Jane Carlyle*, Routledge, London
Claus, Ruth (1977), 'Confronting homosexuality: a letter from Frances Wilder', *Signs*, 2 pp. 928-33
Clausen, Jan (1988), *The Prosperine Papers*, The Women's Press, London
Cliff, Michelle (1980), *Claiming an identity they taught me to despise*, Persephone Press, Watertown, Massachusetts
Clifford, James (ed.) (1962), *Biography as an Art*, Oxford University Press
Clifford, James (1978), 'Hanging up looking glasses at odd corners' in Daniel Aaron (ed.), *Studies in Biography*, Harvard University Press, Massachusetts, pp. 41-56
Clifford, James and Marcus, George (eds) (1986), *Writing Culture: The Poetics and Politics of Ethnography*, University of California Press, Berkeley
Cline, Sally (1984), 'The case of Beatrice: an analysis of the word "lesbian" and the power of language to control women' in Olivia Butler (ed.), 'Feminist Experience In Feminist Research', *Studies in Sexual Politics 2*, Sociology Department, University of Manchester, pp. 5-32
Cobbe, Frances Power (1904), *Life of Frances Power Cobbe As Told By Herself*, Swan Sonnerschein, London
Cockshut, A. (1984), *The Art of Autobiography*, Yale University Press, New Haven
Colette (1922 and 1929/1968), 'Sido' and 'My Mother's House', Harmondsworth: Penguin
Colette (1932/1968), *The Pure and the Impure*, Penguin, Harmondsworth
Colette (1936 and 1913/1957), 'My Apprenticeships' and 'Music Hall Sidelights', Penguin, Harmondsworth
Colette (1961), *Break of Day*, The Women's Press, London
Collingwood, Robin George (1939), *An Autobiography*, Penguin, Harmondsworth
Conway, Martin (1990), *Autobiographical Memory*, Open University Press, Milton Keynes
Coveny, Lal, Jackson, Margaret, Jeffreys, Sheila, Kaye, Leslie and Mahoney, Pat (1984), *The Sexuality Papers*, Explorations in Feminism, Hutchinson, London

Coward, Noël (1982), The Noel Coward Diaries, Methuen, London
Coward, Noël (1986), Autobiography, Methuen, London
Coward, Rosalind (1984), Female Desire, Paladin, London
Craney-Francis, Anne (1990), Feminist Fiction, Polity Press, Cambridge
Cronwright-Schriener, Samuel (1924a), The Life of Olive Schreiner, Haskell House, New York
Cronwright-Schriener, Samuel (ed.) (1924b), The Letters of Olive Schreiner, Fisher Unwin, London
Crosland, Susan (1982), Tony Crosland, Cape, London
Cross, John Walter (1885), George Eliot's Life as Related in Her Letters and Journals, Blackwood, Edinburgh
Criuckshank, Margaret (ed.) (1985, 2nd edition), The Lesbian Path, Grey Fox Press, San Francisco
Culler, Jonathan (1983), On Deconstruction, Routledge & Kegan Paul, London
Culley, Margo (1985), A Day At A Time: The Diary Literature of American Women from 1764 To The Present, The Feminist Press, New York
Davidoff, Leonore (1979), 'Class and gender in Victorian England: the diaries of Arthur J. Munby and Hannah Cullwick', Feminist Studies, 5 pp. 87-141
Davis, Gwenn and Joyce, Beverly (eds) (1989), Personal Writings By Women to 1900: A Bibliography of American and British Writers, Mansell, London
Demetrakopoulos, Stephanie (1980), 'The metaphysics of matrilinearism in women's autobiography: Studies of Mead's Blackberry Winter, Hellman's Pentimento, Angelou's I Know Why The Caged Bird Sings and Kingston's The Woman Warrior', in (ed.), Estelle Jelinek, Women's Autobiography: Essays in Criticism, Indiana University Press, Bloomington, pp. 180-205
Denzin, Norman (1989), Interpretive Biography, Sage International Qualitative Methods Series 17, Sage Publications, Newbury Park
Derrida, Jacques (1980), 'The law of genre', Critical Inquiry, 7 pp. 55-82
Derrida, Jacques (1982), 'Choreographies: an interview with Christie McDonald', Diacritics, 12 pp. 66-76
Derrida, Jacques (1987), 'Women in the behive: a seminar with Jacques Derrida' in (eds), Alice Jardine and Paul Smith, Men In Feminism, Methuen, New York, pp. 189-203
Desalvo, Louise (1989), Virginia Woolf and the Impact of Child Sexual Abuse on Her Life and Work, The Women's Press, London
Dodd, Kathryn (1990), 'Cultural politics and women's historical writing', Women's Studies International Forum, 13 pp. 126-36
Dodd, Philip (1985), 'Criticism and the autobiographical tradition', Prose Studies, 8 pp. 1-13
Dowling, William (1978), 'Boswell and the problem of biography' in (ed.), Daniel Aaron, Studies in Biography, Harvard University Press, Massachusetts, pp. 73-93
Eakin, Paul (1985), Fictions in Autobiography, Princeton University Press
Edkins, Carol (1980), in (ed.), Estelle Jelinek, Women's Autobiography: Essays in Criticism, Indiana University Press, Bloomington, pp. 39-52

Edwards, Ruth Dudley (1976), Patrick Pearse: The Triumph of Failure, Gollancz, London

Edwards, Ruth Dudley (1988), 'Confessions of an Irish revisionist' in (eds), Eric Homberger and John Charmley, The Troubled Face of Biography, Macmillan, London, pp. 63-74

Elbaz, Robert (1987), The Changing Nature of the Self: A Critical Study of the Autobiographical Discourse, University of Iowa Press, Iowa

Ellis, Havelock (1897), Sexual Inversion, Wilson & Macmillan, London (reprinted in 1915 as Volume II, Studies in Sex Psychology, F. A. Davis, Philadelphia)

Ellis, Havelock (1940), My Life, Heinemann, London

Ellmann, Richard (1959/1982), James Joyce, Oxford University Press, Oxford

Ellman, Richard (1973), Golden Codgers: Biographical Speculations, Oxford University Press, London

Ellmann, Richard (1979), Yeats, The Man and The Masks, Penguin, Harmondsworth

Ellman, Richard (1987), Oscar Wilde, Penguin, Harmondsworth

Else, Anne (1985), 'From little monkey to neurotic invalid: limitation, selection and assumption in Antony Alper's "Life of Katherine Mansfield"', Women's Studies International Forum, 8 pp. 497-505

Empson, William (1984), Using Biography, Chatto & Windus, London

Erikson, Eric (1958), Young Man Luther, Norton, New York

Evans, Mary (1985), Simone de Beauvoir: A Feminist Mandarin, Tavistock, London

Faderman, Lillian (nd, but 1979), Surpassing the love of men, Junction Books, London

Faderman, Lillian (1983), Scotch Verdict: Miss Pirie and Miss Woods v. Dame Cumming Gordon, Quill, New York

Farran, Denise, Scott, Sue and Stanley, Liz (1985), 'Writing Feminist Biography', Studies In Sexual Politics, 13/14, Department of Sociology, University of Manchester

Farran, Denise (1990), 'Analysing a photograph of Marilyn Monroe' in (ed.), Liz Stanley, Feminist Praxis: Research, Theory and Epistemology in Feminist Research, Routledge, London, pp. 262-73

Fielding, Sarah (1749/1968), The Governess, Or, Little Female Academy (ed. J. Grey), Oxford University Press, Oxford

Finn, Frankie (1984), Out On The Plain, The Women's Press, London

First, Ruth and Scott, Ann (1980), Olive Schreiner, André Deutch, London

Fitzgerald, F. Scott (1936), 'The crack-up' in The Crack-Up with other pieces and stories, Penguin, Harmondsworth, pp. 39-56

Flax, Jane (1987), 'Postmodernism and gender relations in feminist theory', Signs 12 pp. 621-43

Foster, John (1844), Walter Savage Landor, A Biography, Chapman & Hall, London

Foster, John (1872-74), The Life of Charles Dickens, J. M. Dent, London

Foster, John (1875), The Life of Jonathan Swift, John Murray, London

Foster, Margaret (1988), Elizabeth Barrett Browning, a Biography, Chatto & Windus, London

Foster, Margaret (1990), Lady's Maid, Chatto & Windus, London

Foucault, Michel (1977), 'What is an author?' in Language, Counter-Memory, Practice (edited and translated by Donald Bouchard), Basil Blackwell, Oxford, pp. 113-38

Fox-Genovese, Elizabeth (1988), 'My statue, my self: autobiographical writings by Afro-American women' in (ed.), Shari Benstock, The Private Self: Theory and Practice of Women's Autobiographical Writings, Routledge, London, pp. 63-89

Frank, Anne (1947), The diary of Anne Frank, Pan Books, London

Freccero, John (1986), 'Autobiography and narrative', in (eds), Thomas Heller, Morton Sosna and David Wellbery, Reconstructing Individualism, Stanford University Press, Stanford, pp. 16-29

French, Marilyn (1977), The Women's Room, Sphere, London

Freud, Sigmund (1947), Leonardo Da Vinci (translated by A. A. Brill), Random House, New York

Friedan, Betty (1963), The Feminine Mystique, Penguin, Harmondsworth

Freidman, Susan Stanford (1988), 'Women's autobiographical selves: theory and practice' in (ed.), Shari Benstock, The Private Self: Theory and Practice of Women's Autobiographical Writings, Routledge, London, pp. 34-62

Froude, James Anthony (1882), Thomas Carlyle: A history of the first forty years of his life, 1795-1835, Longmans, Green & Co, London

Froude, James Anthony (1884), Thomas Carlyle: A history of his life in London, 1834-1881, Longmans, Green & Co, London

Frow, John (1990), 'Intertextuality and ontology' in (eds), Michael Worton and Judith Still, Intertextuality: theories and practices, Manchester University Press, Manchester, pp. 45-55

Furnas, J (1982), Fanny Kemble, The Dial Press, New York

Fuss, Diana (1989), Essentially Speaking: Feminism, Nature & Difference, Routledge, New York

Gamman, Lorraine and Margaret Marshment (eds) (1988), The Female Gaze The Women's Press, London

Gaskell, Elizabeth (1966), Letters (edited by J. Chapple and A. Pollard), Manchester University Press, Manchester

Gatehouse (1985), Just Lately I Realise, Gatehouse, Manchester

Geertz, Clifford (1988), Works and Lives: The Anthropologist as Author, Polity Press, Oxford

Gender & History (1990), 2:1 special issue on autobiography edited by Lucy Bland and Angela John

Giddens, Anthony (1991), Modernity and Self-Identity: Self and Society in the Late Modern Age, Polity Press, Cambridge

Gilbert, Olive (1850/1968), Narrative of Sojourner Truth, A Northern Slave, Arno Press, New York

Gilbert, Sandra and Gubar, Susan (1988), No Man's Land: The Place of the Woman

Writer in the 20th Century, Volume 1: The War of the Words, Yale University Press, New Haven

Gilbert, Sandra and Gubar, Susan (1989), No Man's Land: The Place of the Woman *Writer in the 20th Century, Volume 2: Sex Changes*, Yale University Press, New Haven

Gilmore, Michael (1978), 'Eulogy as symbolic biography' in (ed.), Daniel Aaron, *Studies in Biography*, Harvard University Press, Massachusetts, pp. 131-57

Glendinning, Victoria (1983), Vita: *Life of Vita Sackville-West*, Penguin, Harmondsworth

Glendinning, Victoria (1988a), Rebecca West: *A Life*, Macmillan, London

Glendinning, Victoria (1988b), 'Lies and silences' in (eds), Eric Homberger and John Charmley, *The Troubled Face of Biography*, Macmillan, London, pp. 49-63

Goffman, Erving (1976), *Gender Advertisements*, Macmillan, London

Gordon Lyndall (1984), *Virginia Woolf: A Writer's Life*, Oxford University Press, Oxford

Gosse, Edmund (1907/1983), *Father and Son*, Penguin, Harmondsworth

Graham, Elspeth, Hinds, Hilary, Hobby, Elaine and Wilcox, Helen (eds) (1989), *Her Own Life: Autobiographical Writings by Seventeenth Century English-women*, Routledge, London

Graves, Robert (1936a), *I, Claudius*, Penguin, Harmondsworth

Graves, Robert (1936b), *Claudius The God*, Penguin, Harmondsworth

Greer, Germaine (1989), *Daddy, we hardly knew you*, Penguin, Harmondsworth

Grenfell, Joyce (1988), *Darling Ma: letters to her mother 1932-1944* , Hodder & Stoughton, London

Grenfell, Joyce (1989), *The Time of My Life: her wartime journals*, Hodder & Stoughton, London

Gristwood, Sarah (1988), *Recording Angels: The Secret World of Women's Diaries*, Harrap, London

Grosskurth, Phyllis (1980), *Havelock Ellis: A Biography*, Quartet, London

Grosskurth, Phyllis (1984) (ed.), *The Memoirs of John Addington Symonds*, Random House, New York

Gunn, Janet Varner (1982), *Autobiography: Toward a Poetics of Experience*, University of Philadelphia Press, Philadelphia

Gusdorf, Georges (1980), 'Conditions and limits of autobiography' in (ed.), James Olney *Autobiography: Essays Theoretical and critical*, Princeton University Press, Princeton, pp. 28-48

Haight, Gordon (1968), *George Eliot, A Biography*, Clarendon Press, Oxford

Hall, J. Dowd (1987), 'Second thoughts on writing a feminist biography', *Feminist Studies* 13, pp.19-37

Hall Carpenter Archives/Lesbian Oral History Group (eds) (1989), *Inventing Ourselves: Lesbian Life Stories*, Routledge, London

Hall Carpenter Archives (1989), *Walking After Midnight*, Routledge, London

Hall, Doris (1985), Growing Up In Ditchling, Queenspark Book no.16, Queens Park Books, Brighton

Halperin, David (1989), 'Sex before sexuality: pederasty, politics, and power in classical Athens', in (eds), Martin Duberman, George Chauncey Jnr and Martha Vicinus, Hidden From History: Reclaiming The Gay and Lesbian Past, Penguin, Harmondsworth, pp. 37-53

Hankiss, Agnes (1981), 'Ontologies of the self' in (ed.), Daniel Bertaux, Biography and Society, Sage Publications, Beverley Hills, pp. 203-9

Hanscombe, Gillian and Smyers Virginia (1987), Writing For Their Lives: The Modernist Women 1910-1940, The Women's Press, London

Heilbrun, Carolyn (1988a), Writing A Woman's Life, The Women's Press, London

Heilbrun, Carolyn (1988b), 'Non-autobiographies of "privileged" women: England and America' in (eds), Bella Brodzki and Celeste Schenck, Life/Lines: Theorising Women's Autobiography, Cornell University Press, Ithaca, pp. 62-76

Hellman, Lilian (1969), An Unfinished Woman, Quartet, London

Hellman, Lilian (1974), Pentimento, Quartet, London

Henke, Suzette (1986), 'Incidents in the life of a slave girl: autobiography as reconstruction', Feminist Issues, 6, pp.33-9

Hennegan, Alison (1988), 'On becoming a lesbian reader', in (ed.), Susannah Radstone, Sweet Dreams: Sexuality, Gender and Popular Culture, Lawrence & Wishart, London

Heywood, Eliza (1751), The History of Miss Betsy Thoughtless, T. Gardner, London

Highsmith, Patricia (1984), 'Fallen Women', London Review of Books, 21 June – 4 July, pp. 20-2

Hobsmith, Janet (1975), Everybody Who Was Anybody: A Biography of Gertrude Stein, Arena, London

Hobson, John Atkinson (1900), The War in South Africa: Its Causes and Effects, Nisbet, London

Hobson, John Atkinson (1902), Imperialism: A Study, Nisbet, London

Hollway, Wendy (1981), '"I just wanted to kill a woman" Why? The Ripper and male sexuality', Feminist Review, 9 pp. 33-41

Holmes Richard (1982), Coleridge, Oxford University Press, Oxford

Holroyd, Michael (1968), Lytton Strachey, A Critical Biography, Penguin, Harmondsworth

Holroyd, Michael (1971), Lytton Strachey and the Bloomsbury Group: His Work, Their Influence, Penguin, Harmondsworth

Holroyd, Michael (1974-75), Augustus John (2 vols.), Heinemann, London

Holroyd, Michael (1988), Bernard Shaw Volume 1: 1856-1898, Chatto & Windus, London

Holroyd, Michael (1990), Bernard Shaw Volume 2: 1898-1918 Chatto & Windus, London

Holroyd, Michael (1991), Bernard Shaw Volume 3: 1918-1950, Chatto & Windus, London

Homberger, Eric, and Charmley, John (eds) (1988), The Troubled Face of Biography, Macmillan, London

Hong Kingston, Maxine (1977), The Woman Warrior: Memoirs of a Girlhood Among Ghosts, Picador, London

Hong Kingston, Maxine (1981), China Men, Picador, London

Hudson, Derek (1972), Munby: Man of Two Worlds, John Murray, London

Huff, Cynthia (1985), British Women's Diaries, AMS Press, New York

Humez, Jean (1984), '"My spirit eye": some functions of spiritual and visionary experience in the lives of five black women preachers, 1810-1880' in (eds), Barbara Harris and JoAnn McNamara, Women and the Structure of Society, Duke University Press, Durham, pp. 129-43

Humm, Maggie (1991), Border Traffic: Strategies of Contemporary Women Writers, Manchester University Press, Manchester

Hurston, Zora Neale (1942), Dust Tracks On A Road, Virago Press, London

Iles, Teresa (ed.) (1992), All Sides of the Subject: Women and Biography, Pergamon Press, New York

Jackson, Margaret (1984), 'Sex research and the construction of sexuality: a tool of male supremacy?', Women's Studies International Forum 7, pp. 43-52

Jacobs, Harriet (Linda Brent) (1861/1973), Incidents in the Life of a Slave Girl, Written By Herself, Harcourt, Brace, Javanovich, New York

James, Henry,(1956), Henry James: Autobiography (edited by Frederick Dupee), New York, Criterion Books

Jay, Paul (1984), Being In The Text, Cornell University Press, Ithaca

Jefferson, Ann (1990), 'Autobiography as intertext: Barthes, Sarrante, Robbe-Grillet', in (eds), Michael Worton and Judith Still, Intertextuality: theories and practices, Manchester University Press, Manchester, pp. 108-29

Jeffreys, Sheila (1982), 'Free from all uninvited touch of man: women's campaigns around sexuality 1880-1914', Women's Studies International Forum 5, pp. 629-46

Jeffreys, Sheila (1985), The Spinster and Her Enemies: Feminism and Sexuality 1880-1930, Pandora Press, London

Jelinek, Estelle (ed.) (1980), Women's Autobiography: Essays in Criticism, Indiana University Press, Bloomington

Jelinek, Estelle (1980), 'Women's autobiography and the male tradition' in (ed.), Estelle Jelinek, Women's Autobiography: Essays in Criticism, Indiana University Press, Bloomington, pp. 1-20

Jelinek, Estelle (1986), The Tradition of Women's Autobiography: from Antiquity to Present, Twayne Publishers, Boston

John, Angela (1980), By the Sweat of their Brow, Routledge & Kegan Paul, London

Juhasz, Suzanne (1980), 'Toward a theory of form in feminist autobiography: Kate Millet's Flying and Sita; Maxine Hong Kingston's The Woman Warrior', in (ed.), Estelle Jelinek, Women's Autobiography: Essays in Criticism, Indiana University Press, Bloomington, pp. 221-37

Kaplan, E. Ann (ed.) (1988), Postmodernism and its Discontents, Verso, London

Kaplan, Justin (1978), 'The real life' in (ed.), Daniel Aaron, *Studies in Biography*, Harvard University Press, Massachusetts, pp. 1-8

Kapp, Yvonne (1972), *Eleanor Marx: Family Life 1855-1883*, Virago, London

Kapp, Yvonne (1976), *Eleanor Marx: The Crowded Years 1884-1898*, Virago, London

Keays, Sarah (1986), *A Question of Judgement*, Quintessential Press, London

Keller, Helen (1905/1954), *The Story of My Life*, Doubleday, New York

Kemble, Frances, Anne (1835), *Journal of Frances Anne Butler* (2 vols) Carey, Lea & Blanchard, Philadelphia

Kemble, Frances Anne (1863), *Journal of a Residence on a Georgian Plantation in 1838-1839*, Harper & Bros, New York

Kemble, Fanny (1990), *The America Journals of Fanny Kemble* (edited by Elizabeth Mavor), Wiedenfeld & Nicolson, London

Keneally, Thomas (1982), *Schindler's Ark*, Hodder & Stoughton, London

Kessing, Roger (1978), *Elota's Story: The Life and Times of a Kwaio Big Man*, Holt, Rinehart, Winston, New York

Kessing, Roger (1985), 'Kwaio women speak: the micropolitics of autobiography in a Salamon Island society', *American Anthropologist* 87, pp. 27-39

Kessing, Roger (1987), 'Ta'a geni: Women's perspectives on Kwaio society' in (ed.), Marilyn Strathern, *Dealing With Gender*, Harvard University Press, pp. 1-32

King, Coretta Scott (1969), *My Life With Martin Luther King Jr*, Hodder & Stoughton, London

Kingsley, Frances E. (1877), *Charles Kingsley: His Letters and Memories of His Life Edited by His Wife*, Henry King & Co, London

Kingsmill, Hugh (1949), *The Progress of a Biographer*, Methuen, London

Kohli, Martin (1981), 'Biography: account, text, method' in (ed.), Daniel Bertaux, *Biography and Society*, Sage Publications, Beverley Hills, pp. 61-75

Kolodny, Annette (1980), 'The lady's not for spurning: Kate Millett and the critics' in (ed.), Estelle Jelinek, *Women's Autobiography: Essays in Criticism*, Indiana University Press, Bloomington, pp. 238-60

Kosofsky Sedgwick, Eve (1985), *Between Men: English Literature and Male Homosocial Desire*, Columbia University Press, New York

Kuhn, Annette (1982), *Women's Pictures: Feminism and Cinema*, Routledge & Kegan Paul, London

Kuhn, Annette (1985), *The Power of the Image: Essays on Representation and Sexuality*, Routledge & Kegan Paul, London

Kuzwayo, Ellen (1985), *Call Me Woman*, The Women's Press, London

Lanchester, Elsa (1983), *Elsa Lanchester, Herself*, St. Martin's, New York

Last, Nella (1981), *Nella Last's War*, Falling Wall Press, Bristol

Leaska, Mitchell A., and Louise deSalvo (eds) (1984), *The Letters of Vita Sackville-West to Virginia Woolf*, Macmillan, London

Lee, John (1984), 'Innocent victims and evil doers', *Women's Studies International Forum* 7, pp. 69-73

Lejeune, Philippe (1975), *Le Pacte Autobiographique*, Le Seuil, Paris
Lejeune, Philippe (1977), 'Autobiography in the third person', *New Literary History*, 9, pp. 27-50
Lejuene, Philippe (1989), *On Autobiography*, University of Minnesota Press, Minneapolis
Lensink, Judy Nolte (1987), 'Expanding the boundaries of criticism: the diary as female autobiography', *Women's Studies* 14, pp. 39-53
Lesbian History Group (1989), *Not a Passing Phase: Reclaiming Lesbians in History 1840-1985*, The Women's Press, London
Levine, Philippa (1990), 'Love, friendship and feminism in later nineteenth century England', *Women's Studies International Forum* 13, pp. 63-78
Liddington, Jill (1984), *The life and times of a respectable rebel: Selina Cooper 1864-1946*, Virago Press, London
Lionnet, Françoise (1989), *Autobiographical Voices: Race, Gender, Self-Portraiture*, Cornell University Press, Ithaca
Lively, Penelope (1987), *Moon Tiger*, Penguin, Harmondsworth
Lockhart, John Gibson (1837-1838), *Memoirs of the Life of Sir Walter Scott* (7 vols), Cadell, Edinburgh
Lorde, Audre (1980), *The Cancer Journals*, Sheba Feminist Publishers, London
Lorde, Audre (1983), *Zami: A New Spelling of My Name*, Sheba Feminist Publishers, London
Lovell, Terry (1980), *Pictures of Reality: Aesthetics, Politics and Pleasure*, British Film Institute, London
Lukes, Steven (1975), *Emile Durkheim: His Life and Work*, Harmondsworth: Penguin
Lurie, Alison (1988), *The Truth About Lorin Jones*, Abacus, London
Lury, Celia (1982), 'Ethnography of an ethnography', *Manchester Occasional Papers in Sociology*, 9, Department of Sociology, University of Manchester
Lyotard, Jean (1984), *The Postmodern Condition*, Manchester University Press, Manchester
Lyotard, Jean (1989), *The Lyotard Reader* (ed A. Benjamin), Blackwell, Oxford
Lytton, Constance (1914), *Prisons and Prisoners*, Heinemann, London
McCann, Graham (1988), *Marilyn Monroe*, Polity Press, Cambridge
McCarthy, Mary (1957), *Memories of a Catholic Girlhood*, Penguin, Harmondsworth
Maclaine, Shirley (1970), *'Don't Fall Off The Mountain'*, Bantam Books, New York
Maclaine, Shirley (1975), *You Can Get There From Here*, Corgi Books, London
McHoul, Alec (1983), *Telling How Texts Talk*, Routledge, London
McKay, Nellie (1989), 'Nineteenth century black women's spiritual autobiographies' in (ed.), Personal Naratives Group, *Interpreting Women's Lives: Feminist Theory and Personal Narratives*, Indiana University Press, Bloomington, pp. 139-54
McLellan, David (1973), *Karl Marx: His Life and Thought*, Paladin, London
McLellan, David (1989), *Simone Weil, Utopian Pessimist*, Macmillan, London

McPherson, Dolly (1991), Order out of chaos: the autobiographical works of Maya Angelou, Virago Press, London

Makeba, Miriam (1987), Makeba: My Story, Bloomsbury, London

Mallon, Thomas (1984), A Book Of One's Own, Picador, London

Man, Paul de (1986), The Resistance To Theory, Manchester University Press, Manchester

Manning, Rosemary (1971), A Time And A Time, Marion Boyars, London (originally published under the pseudonym of Sarah Davys)

Manning, Rosemary (1987), A Corridor of Mirrors, The Women's Press, London

Manton, Jo (1976), Mary Carpenter and the Children of the Streets, Heinemann, London

March, Caeia (1988), The Hide and Seek Files, The Women's Press, London

Marcus, George and Fischer, Michael (1986), Anthropology as Cultural Critique, University of Chicago Press, Chicago

Marcus, Jane (1978), 'Transatlantic sisterhood', Signs, 3 pp. 744-55

Marcus, Jane (1988), 'Invincible mediocrity: the private selves of public women', in (ed.), Shari Benstock, The Private Self: Theory and Practice of Women's Autobiographical Writings, London: Routledge, pp. 114-46

Marsh, Jan (1986), Jane and May Morris: A Biographical Story 1839-1938, Pandora Press, London

Martin, Biddy (1988), 'Lesbian identity and autobiographical difference/s' in (eds), Bella Brodzki and Celeste Schenck, Life/Lines: Theorising Women's Autobiography, Cornell University Press, Ithaca, pp. 77-103

Martineau, Harriet (1877/1983), Autobiography (2 vols), Virago Press, London

Marx, Karl and Engels, Frederick (1968), The German Ideology, Progress, Moscow

Mason, Mary (1980), 'The other voice: autobiographies of women writers' in (ed.), James Olney, Autobiography: Essays Theoretical and Critical, Princeton University Press, pp. 207-35; and (1988) in (eds), Bella Brodzki and Celeste Schenck, Life/Lines: Theorising Women's Autobiography, Cornell University Press, Ithaca, pp. 19-44

Mason, Mary and Greed, Carol Hurd (eds) (1979), Journeys: Autobiographical Writings by Women, G. K. Hall, Boston

Masson, J. M. (1984), The Assault on Truth: Freud's Supression of the Seduction Hypothesis, Penguin, Harmondsworth

Masters, Brian (1985), Killing for Company: The Case of Dennis Nilsen, Coronet, London

Mavor, Elizabeth (1971), The Ladies of Llangollen, Penguin, Harmondsworth

Mead, Margaret (1972), Blackberry Winter, Angus & Robertson, London

Meir, Golda (1975), My Life, G. P. Putnam's Sons, New York

Mendelson, Edward (1978), 'Authorized biography and its discontents' in (ed.) Daniel Aaron, Studies in Biography, Harvard University Press, Massachusetts, pp. 9-26

Meyers, Jeffrey (ed.) (1985), The Craft of Literary Biography, Macmillan, London

Middleton, David and Edwards, Derek (eds) (1990), *Collective Remembering*, Sage Publications, London

Milburn, Mrs (1979), *Mrs Milburn's Diaries: An Englishwoman's Day-To-Day Reflections 1939-1945*, Harrap, London

Miller, Isobel (1969), *Patience and Sarah*, Rupert Hart-Davis, London

Miller, Nancy (1988), 'Writing fictions: women's autobiography in France' in (eds), Bella Brodzki and Celeste Schenck, *Life/Lines: Theorising Women's Autobiography*, Cornell University Press, Ithaca pp. 45-61

Millett, Kate (1974), *Flying*, Ballantine Books, New York

Millett, Kate (1977), *Sita*, Virago Press, London

Minnich, Elizabeth Kramarch (1985), 'Friendships between women: the act of feminist biography', *Feminist Studies*, 11 pp. 287-306

Mitchell, David (1977), *Queen Christabel: A Biography of Christabel Pankhurst*, Macdonald & James, London

Moi, Toril (1985), *Sexual/Textual Politics*, Methuen, London

Morgan, David (1982), 'Friendship work and cultural work: the case of Bloomsbury', *Media, Culture and Society*, 4 pp. 19-32

Morgan, David (1990), 'Masculinity, autobiography and history', *Gender & History*, 2 pp. 34-9

Morgan, Keith (1989), *Labour People*, Oxford Paperbacks, Oxford

Morris, Meaghan (1988), *The Pirate's Fiancee: Feminism, Reading, Postmodernism*, Verso, London

Mulford, Wendy (1988), *This Narrow Place: Sylvia Townsend Warner and Valentine Ackland*, Pandora Press, London

Nadel, Ira Bruce (1984), *Biography: Fiction, Fact and Form*, Macmillan, London

Navratilova, Martina (1985), *Being Myself*, Grafton Books, London

Newton, Esther (1984), 'The mythic mannish lesbian: Radclyffe Hall and the New Woman', *Signs*, 9 pp. 557-75

Nicholson, Harold (1966), *Diaries and Letters 1930-1939*, Collins, London

Nicholson, Harold (1967), *Diaries and Letters 1939-1945*, Collins, London

Nicholson, Harold (1968), *Diaries and Letters 1945-1962*, Collins, London

Nicholson, Nigel (1973), *Portrait of a Marriage* (including *Vita Sackville-West's* autobiographical memoir), Weidenfeld & Nicolson, London

Nin, Anaïs (1966, 1967, 1969, 1971), *The Journals of Anaïs Nin 1931-1934, 1934-1939, 1939-1944, 1944-1947* (4 vols), Quartet Books, London

Oakley, Ann (1979), *From Here To Maternity*, Penguin, Harmondsworth

Oakley, Ann (1984), *Taking It Like A Woman*, Flamingo Books, London

Okely, Judith (1986), *Simone de Beauvoir*, Virago, London

Oldfield, Sybil (1984), *Spinsters of This Parish*, Virago Press, London

Oliphant, Margaret (1899/1990), *The Autobiography: the complete text*, Oxford University Press, Oxford

Olney, James (1972), *Metaphors of Self: The Meaning of Autobiography*, Princeton University Press, New Jersey

Olney, James (ed.) (1980), *Autobiography: Essays Theoretical and Critical*, Princeton University Press, New Jersey

Olney, James (1980), 'Some versions of memory/some versions of bios: the ontology of autobiography' in (ed.) James Olney, *Autobiography: Essays Theoretical and Critical*, Princeton University Press, New Jersey, pp. 236-67

Orton, Joe (1986), *The Orton Diaries* (edited by John Lahr), Methuen, London

Painter, Nell Irvine (1990), 'Sojourner Truth in life and memory: writing the biography of an American exotic', *Gender & History*, 2 pp. 3-16

Pascal, Roy (1960), *Design and Truth in Autobiography*, Harvard University Press, Cambridge

Pankhurst, Sylvia (1931), *The Suffragette Movement*, Virago Press, London

Penelope, Julia and Wolfe, Susan (eds) (1980/1989), *The Original Coming Out Stories*, Crossing Press, California

Personal Narratives Group (ed.) (1989a), *Interpreting Women's Lives: Feminist Theory and Personal Narratives*, Indiana University Press, Bloomington

Personal Narratives Group (ed.) (1989b), 'Conditions not of her own making' in (eds) Personal Narratives Group, *Interpreting Women's Lives: Feminist Theory and Personal Narratives*, Indiana University Press, Bloomington, pp. 19-23

Peterson, Linda (1986), *Victorian Autobiography: The Tradition of Self Interpretation*, Yale University Press, New Haven

Petrie, Dennis (ed.) (1981), *Ultimately Fiction, Design in Modern American Literary Biography*, Purdue University Press, West Lafayette, Indiana

Plummer, Ken (1983), *Documents of Life*, Allen & Unwin, London

Pollert, Anna (1981), *Girls, Wives, Factory Lives*, Macmillan, London

Porter, Cathy (1980), *Alexandra Kollontai*, Virago Press, London

Porter, Kevin and Weeks, Jeffrey (eds) (1990), *Between The Acts: Lives of Homosexual Men 1885-1967*, Routledge, London

Prévin, Dory (1976), *Midnight Baby: An Autobiography*, Elm Tree Books, London

Prévin, Dory (1980), *Bogtrotter: an autobiography with lyrics*, Wiedenfeld & Nicolson, London

Prose Studies 8 (1985), Special issue on 'Modern selves: essays on modern British and American autobiography'

Raynaud, Claudine (1988), '"A nutmeg nestled inside its covering of mace": Audre Lorde's *Zami*', in (eds), Bella Brodzki and Celeste Schenck, *Life/Lines: Theorising Women's Autobiography*, Cornell University Press, Ithaca pp. 221-42

Reagon, Bernice Johnson (1982), 'My Black mothers and sisters or on beginning a cultural autobiography', *Feminist Studies*, 8 pp. 81-95

Reuhl, Sonia (1982), 'Review of Lillian Faderman's *Surpassing the love of men*', *History Workshop Journal*, 14 pp. 157-60

Rich, Adrienne (1979), *On Lies, Secrets & Silence*, Virago Press, London

Richardson, Dorothy (1979), *Pilgrimage* (4 vols), Virago Press, London

Riley, Denise (1988), '*Am I That Name?*' *Feminism and the category of women in history*, Macmillan, London

Rive, Richard (1987), *Olive Schreiner Letters, Volume I 1871-1899*, Oxford University Press, Oxford

Robbe-Grillet, Alain (1984), Le Miroir qui revient, Minuit, Paris

Roos, J. P. (1989), 'Life vs. story vs. society: a methodological Bermuda triangle?', Vienna Seminar on Methods for the Study of Changes in Forms of Life, Lidingo, Vienna

Rose, Phyllis (1978), Woman of Letters: A Life of Virginia Woolf, Pandora Press, London

Rose, Phyllis (1982), Parallel Lives, Penguin, Harmondsworth

Rose, Phyllis (1985), Writing Of Women, Wesleyan University Press, Connecticut

Rousseau, Jean-Jacques (1782/1953), Confessions (trans. by J. M. Cohen), Penguin, Harmondsworth

Rowbotham, Sheila (1977), 'Edward Carpenter' in Sheila Rowbotham and Jeff Weeks, Socialism and the New Life, Pluto Press, London, pp. 27-138

Rupp, Leila (1989), '"Imagine my surprise": women's relationships in mid-twentieth century America', in (eds) Martin Duberman, George Chauncey Jnr and Martha Vicinus, Hidden From History: Reclaiming The Gay and Lesbian Past, Penguin, Harmondsworth, pp. 395-410

Russell, Dora (1975), The Tamarisk Tree: My Quest for Liberty and Love, Virago Press, London

St Clair, William (1989), The Godwins and the Shelleys, Faber & Faber, London

Said, Edward (1983), The World, The Text and The Critic, Harvard University Press

Sackville-West, Vita (1932), Family History, The Hogarth Press, London

Sanders, Valerie (1989), The Private Lives of Victorian Women, Harvester, Hemel Hempstead

Sarton, May (1988), After The Stroke, The Women's Press, London

Sartre, Jean-Paul (1964), The Words, Penguin, Harmondsworth

Sartre, Jean-Paul (1971), The Family Idiot: Gustave Flaubert (3 vols) University of Chicago Press, Chicago

Schor, Naomi (1987), Reading In Detail: Aesthetics and the Feminine, Methuen, London

Schreiner, Olive (1883/1982), The Story of an African Farm, Penguin, Harmondsworth

Schreiner, Olive (1890/1982), Dreams, Wildwood House, London

Schreiner, Olive (1893/1977), Dream Life and Real Life, Academy, Chicago

Schreiner, Olive (1896), The political situation, Unwin, London

Schreiner, Olive (1897/1974), Trooper Peter Halket of Mashonaland, Donker, South Africa

Schreiner, Olive (1899), An English South African's View of the Situation, Hodder & Stoughton, London

Schreiner, Olive (1906/1924b), 'A letter on the Jew', Liberman, South Africa, 1906; Appendix F (ed.) Samuel Cronwright Schreiner, The Letters of Olive Schreiner, Haskell House, New York

Schreiner, Olive (1911/1979), Women and Labour, Virago, London

Schreiner, Olive (1923/1976), Thoughts on South Africa, Africana Book Society, South Africa

Schreiner, Olive (1923), Stories, Dreams and Allegories, Unwin, London

Schreiner, Olive (1926/1982), From Man To Man, Virago, London

Schreiner, Olive (1929), Undine, Benn, South Africa

Scott, Bonnie Kime (ed.) (1990), The Gender of Modernism: A Critical Anthology, Indiana University Press, Bloomington

Shaw, Clifford (1930/1966), The Jack Roller: A Delinquent Boy's Own Story, University of Chicago Press, Chicago

Sheridan, Frances (1761/1987), Memoirs of Miss Sidney Biddulph, Pandora Press, London

Shostak, Marjorie (1981), Nisa: The Life and Times of a !Kung Woman, Harvard University Press

Showalter, Elaine (1991), Sexual Anarchy: Gender and Culture at the Fin de Siècle, Bloomsbury, London

Siegel, Jerrold (1978), Marx's Fate, The Shape of a Life, Princeton University Press, Princeton

Simons, Judy (1990), Diaries and Journals of Literary Women from Fanny Burney to Virginia Woolf, Macmillan, London

Sistren Theatre Collective (1986), Lionheart Gal: Lives of Women in Jamaica, The Women's Press, London

Skidelsky, Robert (1980), John Maynard Keynes, Macmillan, London

Skidelsky, Robert (1988), 'Only connect: biography and truth', in (eds), Eric Homberger and John Charmley, The Troubled Face of Biography, Macmillan, London, pp. 1-16

Smith, Dorothy (1974a), 'Theorising as ideology', in (ed.), Roy Turner, Ethnomethodology, Penguin, Harmondsworth, pp. 41-4

Smith, Dorothy (1974b), 'The social construction of documentary reality', Sociological Inquiry, 44 pp. 257-68

Smith, Dorothy (1980), No one commits suicide: textual analysis of ideological practice, unpublished mimeo, Ontario Institute for Studies in Education

Smith, Dorothy (1983), 'The active text', unpublished mimeo, Ontario Institute for Studies in Education

Smith, Dorothy (1987), The Everyday World As Problematic: A Feminist Sociology, Open University Press

Smith, Dorothy (1990), Texts, Facts and Femininity: Exploring the Relations of Ruling, Routledge, London

Smith, Lee (1989), Oral History, Picador, London

Smith, Sidonie (1987), A Poetics of Women's Autobiography: Marginality and the Fictions of Self-Representation, Indiana University Press, Bloomington

Smith-Rosenberg, Carroll (1975), 'The female world of love and ritual: relations between women in nineteenth century America', Signs, 1 pp. 1-29

Smith-Rosenberg, Carroll (1989), 'Discourses of sexuality and subjectivity: the New Woman 1870-1936', in (eds), Martin Duberman, George Chauncey Jnr and Martha Vicinus, Hidden From History: Reclaiming The Gay and Lesbian Past, Penguin, Harmondsworth, pp. 264-80

Smyth, Ethel (1919), *Impressions That Remained*, Longmans Green, London
Smyth, Ethel (1924), *Streaks of Life*, Longmans Green, London
Smyth, Ethel (1928), *A Final Burning of Boats*, Longmans Green, London
Smyth, Ethel (1934), *Female Pipings in Eden*, Peter Davies, London
Smyth, Ethel (1936), *As Time Went On*, Longmans Green, London
Smyth, Ethel (1940), *What Happened Next*, Longmans Green, London
Sommer, Doris (1988), '"Not just a personal story": women's testimonios and the plural self', in (eds), Bella Brodzki and Celeste Schenk, *Life/Lines: Theorising Women's Autobiography*, Cornell University Press, Ithaca, pp. 107-30
Sontag, Susan (1977), *On Photography*, Penguin, Harmondsworth
Soper, Kate (1990), *Troubled Pleasures: Writings on Politics, Gender and Hedonism*, Verso, London
Spacks, Patricia Meyer (1980), 'Selves in hiding', in (ed.), Estelle Jelinek, *Women's Autobiography*, Indiana University Press, Bloomington, pp. 112-32
Spence, Jo (1986), *Putting Myself In The Picture: a political personal and photographic autobiography*, Camden Press, London
Spence, Jo and Holland, Patricia (1991), *Family Snaps: The Meaning of Domestic Photography*, Virago Press, London
Spender, Dale (ed.) (1983a), *Feminist Theorists*, The Women's Press, London
Spender, Dale (1983b), *There's always been a women's movement this century*, Pandora Press, London
Spender, Dale (1984), *Time and Tide*, Pandora Press, London
Spender, Dale (ed.) (1987), 'Personal Chronicles: Women's Autobiographical Writings', *Women's Studies International Forum*, 10: 1 (special issue)
Spengemann, William (1980), *The Forms of Autobiography*, Yale University Press, New Haven
Springer, Michael (1980), *Autobiography: Essays Theoretical and Critical*, Princeton University Press, Princeton
Sprinkler, Michael (1980), 'Fictions of the self: the end of autobiography', in (ed.), James Olney, *Autobiography: Essays Theoretical and Critical*, Princeton University Press, Princeton, 321-42
Spurling, Hilary (1974), *Ivy When Young: The early life of I. Compton Burnett 1884-1919*, Allison & Busby, London
Spurling, Hilary (1984), *Secrets of a Woman's Heart: The later life of I. Compton Burnett 1920-1969*, Penguin, Harmondsworth
Spurling, Hilary (1988), 'Neither morbid nor ordinary' in (ed.), Eric Homberger and John Charmley, *The Troubled Face of Biography*, Macmillan, London, pp. 113-22
St Clair, William (1989), *The Godwins and the Shelleys: the Biography of a Family*, Faber & Faber, London
Stam, Robert (1988), 'Mikhail Bakhtin and left cultural critique', in (ed.), E. Ann Kaplan, *Postmodernism and its Discontents*, Verso, London, pp. 116-45
Stanley, Liz (1983), 'Olive Schreiner: new women, free women, all women', in (ed.), Dale Spender, *Feminist Theorists*, The Women's Press, London pp. 229-43

Stanley, Liz (ed.) (1984a), The Diaries of Hannah Cullwick, Virago, London, and Rutgers University Press

Stanley, Liz (1984b), Accounting for the fall of Peter Sutcliffe and the rise of the so-called "Yorkshire Ripper"', Manchester Occasional Paper, 15, Department of Sociology, University of Manchester

Stanley, Liz (1985a), 'Feminism and Friendship: Two Essays on Olive Schreiner', Studies in Sexual Politics, 8, Department of Sociology, University of Manchester

Stanley, Liz (1985b), 'Our Mother's Voices', Third International Interdisciplinary Congress on Women, Dublin

Stanley, Liz (1986), 'Some thoughts on editing the diaries of Hannah Cullwick' in (ed.), Feminist Research Seminar, 'Feminist Research Processes', Studies in Sexual Politics, 16, Department of Sociology, University of Manchester, pp. 88-99

Stanley, Liz (1987), 'Biography as microscope or kaleidoscope? the case of 'power' in Hannah Cullwick's relationship with Arthur Munby', Women's Studies International Forum, 10.1: 19-31

Stanley, Liz (1988a), 'Behind the scenes during the creation of a Social Services Department statistic', Research, Policy, Planning, 5 pp. 22-7

Stanley, Liz (1988b), The Life and Death of Emily Wilding Davison, The Women's Press, London

Stanley, Liz (ed.) (1988c), 'The Writing I, The Seeing Eye: Papers From Two 'Writing Feminist Biography' Conferences', Studies in Sexual Politics, 26/27

Stanley, Liz (ed.) (1990a), Feminist Praxis: Research, Theory and Epistemology in Feminist Sociology, Routledge, London

Stanley, Liz (1990b), 'Rescuing 'women' in history from feminist deconstructionism' Women's Studies International Forum, 13, pp. 151-7

Stanley, Liz (1990c), 'Moments of writing: is there a feminist auto/ biography?', Gender & History, 2 pp. 58-67

Stanley, Liz (1990d), '"A referral was made": behind the scenes during the creation of a Social Services Department elderly statistic' in (ed.), Liz Stanley, Feminist Praxis: Research, Theory and Epistemology in Feminist Sociology, Routledge, London, 1990e, pp. 113-22

Stanley, Liz (1990e), 'Feminism and the discontents of postmodernism': unpublished paper given to Sociology Department, University of Jyvaskyla, Finland

Stanley, Liz (1993, forthcoming), Olive Schreiner: Woman of Ideas, 'Women of Ideas' Series, Sage Publications, London

Stanton, Domna (ed.) (1984), The Female Autograph: Theory and Practice of Autobiography from the 10th to the 20th Century, University of Chicago Press, Chicago

Steedman, Carolyn (1986), Landscape For A Good Woman, Virago Press, London

Steedman, Carolyn (1990), Childhood, Culture and Class in Britain: Margaret McMillan, 1860-1931, Virago Press, London

Stein, Gertrude (1933), The Autobiography of Alice B. Toklas, Penguin, Harmondsworth

Stein, Gertrude (1938/1985), Everybody's Autobiography, Virago Press, London

Steinem, Gloria (with George Barris) (1986), Marilyn, Henry Holt, New York

Steward, Sue and Garratt, Cheryl (1984), Signed sealed and delivered: true life stories of women in pop, Pluto Press, London

Strachey, Lytton (1918), Eminent Victorians, Chatto & Windus, London

Strachey, Lytton (1922), Queen Victoria, Chatto & Windus, London

Strachey, Lytton (1928), Elizabeth and Essex, Chatto & Windus, London

Strachey, Ray (1928), The Cause, Virago, London

Strachey, Ray (1931), Millicent Garrett Fawcett, John Murray, London

Strouse, Jean (1978), 'Semi-private lives' in (ed.), Daniel Aaron, Studies in Biography, Harvard University Press, Massachusetts, pp. 113-29

Sutcliffe, Sonia (1984), 'Review of Gordon Burn's "… somebody's husband, somebody's son"', The Guardian 19 May

Swindells, Julia (1989), 'Liberating the subject? autobiography and "women's history": a reading of The Diaries of Hannah Cullwick' in (eds), Personal Narratives Group, Interpreting Women's Lives: Feminist Theory and Personal Narratives Indiana University Press, Bloomington, pp. 24-38

Symons, Albert James Alroy (1934), The Quest for Corvo: An Experiment in Biography, Cassell, London

Szondi, Peter (1986), On Textual Understanding And Other Essays, Manchester University Press, Manchester

Taylor, Ina (1989), George Eliot: Woman of Contradictions, Weidenfeld & Nicolson, London

Teilhard de Chardin, Pierre (1962), Letters From A Traveller 1923-1953, Collins, London

Teilhard de Chardin, Pierre (1968), Letters From Hastings 1908-1912, Herder, New York

Teilhard de Chardin, Pierre (1969), Letters To Leontine Zanta, Collins, London

Teilhard de Chardin, Pierre (1970), Letters To Two Friends 1926-1952, Rapp & Whiting, London

Thomas, D. M. (1981), The White Hotel, Penguin, Harmondsworth

Thomas, W. I. and Znaniecki, Florian (1918-1920/1958), The Polish Peasant in Europe and America, Dover Publications, New York (1st edition, 5 volumes)

Thompson, Tierl (ed.) (1987), Dear Girl: The diaries and letters of two working women 1897-1917, The Women's Press, London

Todorov, Tzvetan (1977/1981), Introduction to Poetics (trans R. Howard), Harvester Press, Brighton

Todorov, Tzvetan (1984), Mikhail Bakhtin: The Dialogical Principle, Manchester University Press, Manchester

Tomalin, Claire (1990), The Invisible Woman: The Story of Nelly Tiernan and Charles Dickens, Vicking Press, London

Trefusis, Violet (1952), Don't Look Round: Her Reminiscences, Hutchinson, London

Vance, Carol (1989), 'Social construction theory: problems in the history of sexuality' in Dennis Altman et al. (1989), Which Homosexuality? essays from the international scientific conference on lesbian and gay studies, Gay Men's Press, London, pp. 13-34

Vicinus, Martha (1989a), 'Distance and desire: English boarding school friendships, 1870-1920', in (eds), Martin Duberman, George Chauncey Jnr and Martha Vicinus, Hidden From History: Reclaiming The Gay and Lesbian Past, Penguin, Harmondsworth, pp. 212-29

Vicinus, Martha (1989b), '"They wonder to which sex I belong": The historical roots of the modern lesbian identity', in Dennis Altman et al. (1989), Which Homosexuality? essays from the international scientific conference on lesbian and gay studies, Gay Men's Press, London, pp. 171-98

Wagner, Helmut (1983), Alfred Schutz: An Intellectual Biography, University of Chicago Press, Chicago

Wallace, Michele (1990), Invisibility Blues: From Pop to Theory, Verso, London

Ward Jouve, Nicole (1983), Un homme nomme Zapolski, Des femmes, Paris

Ward Jouve, Nicole (1986), 'The Streetcleaner' The Yorkshire Ripper Case on Trial, Marion Boyars, London

Ward Jouve, Nicole (1987), Colette, Harvester Press, Brighton

Ward Jouve, Nicole (1991), White Woman Speaks With Forked Tongue: criticism as Autobiography, Routledge, London

Washington, Mary Helen (1987), Invented Lives: Narratives of Black Women 1860-1960, Doubleday/Anchor, New York

Webb, Beatrice (1982-1985), The Diary of Beatrice Webb (4 vols) (edited by Norman and Jeanne MacKenzie), Virago Press, London

Webster, Frank (1980), The New Photography, John Calder, London

Webster, Wendy (1990), Not A Man To Match Her: The Making of a Prime Minister, The Women's Press, London

Weeks, Jeff (1977), 'Havelock Ellis', in Sheila Rowbotham and Jeff Weeks, Socialism and the New Life, Pluto Press, London, pp. 141-85

Weldon, Fay (1985), Rebecca West, Penguin, Harmondsworth

Westwood, Sally. (1984), All day, every day, Pluto, London

Whitbread, Helena (ed.) (1988), The Diaries of Ann Lister 1791-1840, Virago Press, London

White, Hayden (1978), Tropics of Discourse: Essays in Cultural Criticism, John Hopkins University Press, Baltimore

White, Hayden (1980), 'The value of narrativity in the representation of reality', Critical Inquiry 7 pp. 5-27

Whitman, Walt (1860, 3rd edition, 1955 reprint), Leaves of Grass (ed. F. Bowers), University of Chicago Press, Chicago

Wieringa, Saskia (1989), 'An anthropological critique of constructionism: berdaches and butches' in Dennis Altman et al., Which Homosexuality? essays from the international scientific conference on lesbian and gay studies, Gay Men's Press, London, pp. 215-38

Williamson, Judith (1978), Decoding Advertisements, Marion Boyars, London

Willis, Paul (1977), *Learning To Labour*, Gower, Farnborough

Wilson, Elizabeth (1982), *Mirror Writing*, Virago Press, London

Wilson, Harriet (1983), *Our Nig: Or, Stretches from the Life of a Free Black*, Vintage, New York

Winkler, Barbara Scott (1980), 'Victorian daughters: the lives and feminism of Charlotte Perkins Gilman and Olive Schreiner', *Michigan Occasional Papers in Women's Studies* 13, Women's Studies, University of Michigan

Wise, Sue (1990), 'From butch god to teddy bear? some thoughts on my relationship with Elvis Presley' in (ed.), Liz Stanley, *Feminist Praxis: Research, Theory and Epistemology in Feminist Sociology*, Routledge, London, pp. 134-44

Wise, Sue and Stanley, Liz (1987), *Georgie Porgie: sexual harassment in everyday life*, Pandora Press, London

Wittig, Monique (1980), 'The straight mind', *Feminist Issues*, 1:1 pp. 103-11

Wittig, Monique (1981), 'One is not born a woman', *Feminist Issues*, 1:2 pp. 47-54

Wittig, Monique (1982), 'The category of sex', *Feminist Issues*, 2 pp. 63-8

Wittig, Monique (1983), 'The point of view: universal or particular?', *Feminist Issues*, 3 pp. 63-70

Wittig, Monique (1985), 'The mark of gender', *Feminist Issues*, 5 pp. 3-12

Wolff, Janet (1990), *Feminine Sentences*, Polity Press, Cambridge

Women's Studies International Forum (1987), 10:1 Special issue on 'Personal Chronicles: Women's Autobiographical Writings' edited by Dale Spender

Wood, Michael and Zurcher, Louis (1988), *The Development of a Postmodern Self*, Greenwood Press, New York

Woolf, Leonard (1960), *Sowing*, The Hogarth Press, London

Woolf, Leonard (1961), *Growing*, The Hogarth Press, London

Woolf, Leonard (1964), *Beginning Again*, The Hogarth Press, London

Woolf, Leonard (1967), *Downhill All The Way*, The Hogarth Press, London

Woolf, Leonard (1969), *The Journey Not the Arrival Matters*, The Hogarth Press, London

Woolf, Virginia (1925/1979), 'Olive Schreiner: review of *The Letters of Olive Schreiner* edited by S. Cronwright-Schreiner', in (ed.), Michele Barrett, *Virginia Woolf: Women and Writing*, The Women's Press, London, pp. 180-3

Woolf, Virginia (1928), *Orlando, A Biography*, Hogarth Press, London

Woolf, Virginia (1929), *A Room of One's Own*, Granada, London

Woolf, Virginia (1931), 'Introductory letter' in (ed.), Margaret Llewelyn-Davies, *Life As We Have Known It*, Virago Press, London, pp. xvii-xxxxi

Woolf, Virginia (1933), *Flush: A Biography*, Penguin, Harmondsworth

Woolf, Virginia (1938), *Three Guineas*, Penguin, Harmondsworth

Woolf, Virginia (1940), *Roger Fry: A Biography*, Penguin, Harmondsworth

Woolf, Virginia (1941), *Between The Acts*, Hogarth Press, London

Woolf, Virginia (1978a), *Moments of Being* (edited by Jeanne Schulkind), Granada, London

Woolf, Virginia (1978b), 'A sketch of the past', in *Moments of Being* (edited by Jeanne Schulkind), Granada, London, pp. 71-159

Woolf, Virginia (1985), 'The journal of Mistress Joan Martyn', in The Complete Shorter Fiction of Virginia Woolf (edited by Susan Dick), The Hogarth Press, London, pp. 33-62

Worton, Michael and Still, Judith (eds) (1990), Intertextuality: theories and practice, Manchester University Press, Manchester

Young, Michael (1983), 'Our name is women: we are bought with limesticks and limepots: an analysis of the autobiographical narrative of a Kalauna woman', Man (ns), 18 pp. 478-501

Zimmerman, Bonnie (1984), 'The politics of transliteration: lesbian personal narratives', Signs 9, pp. 663-82

Name index

Subject index